Happiness and Benevolence

Happiness and Benevolence

Robert Spaemann

Afterword by Arthur Madigan, SJ
Translation by Jeremiah Alberg, SJ

T&T Clark
Edinburgh

Originally published in German under the title *Glück und Wohlwollen* by Klett-Cotta © J. G. Cotta'sche Buchhandlung Nachfolger GmbH, Stuttgart 1989

Arthur Madigan's "Robert Spaemann's *Philosophische Essays*" was originally published in the *Review of Metaphysics* 51, no. 1 (September 1997), pp. 105–32, and is reprinted here with the permission of the publisher.

Published in the United States by
University of Notre Dame Press
Notre Dame, Indiana 46556

This edition published under licence from
University of Notre Dame Press by
T&T Clark Ltd
59 George Street
Edinburgh EH2 2LQ
Scotland

www.tandtclark.co.uk

First published 2000

ISBN 0 567 08740 9

British Library Cataloguing-in-Publication Data
A catalogue record for this book is available from
the British Library

Manufactured in the United States of America

Contents

Foreword

MY HOPE is that these thoughts on ethics contain nothing fundamentally new. In seeking answers to questions about the right kind of life, only the false could be really new. Still, given that the actual conditions of life and the concepts available for our self-understanding change, even that which humans have always known has to be rethought from time to time. The challenge which ethical reflection presents remains fundamentally unchanged since the fifth century B.C. This gives us grounds for speaking of an anthropological constant, at least a constant in all developed cultures.

We are presented with a double challenge. First, our various and particular drives do not, of their own, integrate themselves into a life which turns out well. Human beings have to "lead" their lives, and this has to be learned. The immediate satisfaction of desires does not stand in a pre-established harmony with "happiness." Ancient ethics focused on this theme: *eudaimonia*, that is, how to lead one's own life so that it turns out well. Everyone wants his life to turn out well, and yet it is not clear to most people in what this well-lived life consists. Ancient ethics taught the art of living.

The second challenge stems from the lack of a pre-established harmony between individuals' interests in the turning out well of their own lives and the interests of others. "One person's loss is another's gain." In culturally developed, complex societies, parasitic behavior remains largely unpunished and therefore often "pays off." Hence, we are seldom in a position to cooperate with the welfare of others or with the *bonum commune*, unless we set aside our own interests. This is the focus of modern ethics. For Kant, just as for an utilitarian or an ethician of the discourse theory, individual happiness is subordinated to a higher standard, which first determines the "worthiness of happiness."

The difficulty for any eudaimonistic ethics consists is the grounding of a principled interest in the welfare of others. In addition to this it must make intelligible the notion of an accountability not only *to* one's own self but *for* one's own self. On the other hand any ethics which universalizes what "ought" to be done, faces the difficulty of explaining why anyone would have a real interest of the kind that brings an individual to will what he sees would be good if everyone else would also will it.

In the last few years a certain rehabilitation of the eudaimonistic morality of prudence has begun. But faced with the logic of universality, this rehabilitation has not progressed beyond a kind of stalemate. There are two reactions to this stalemate. One is resignation. Such resignation lets the issue remain undecided, with two completely independent sources of ethical orientation which cannot be reduced to each other or any more basic principle. This implies a renunciation of philosophical ethics. Two signposts which point in different directions are as good as none at all, as long as we cannot find a third one by which their difference could be interpreted. This third signpost would be the philosophic one.

The other reaction attempts to relate the two approaches to each other by some order of priority, and in this way to integrate one of the approaches into the other. Ancient ethics clearly thought of the fulfilling of duties toward others as an integral part of *eudaimonia*. Kant argued in the opposite direction. For him, as for utilitarian ethics, the concern for one's own prosperity becomes a conditional duty, a commandment of the categorical imperative or a part of optimizing the world. Kant saw it as an ethical duty to nurture one's hope for the highest good, the convergence of morality and happiness, not because such hope is consoling, but because it promotes moral behavior. Neither attempt at integration truly overcomes the dualism between eudaimonism and universalism; rather they merely reproduce it on a higher level.

The reflections in this book are searching for some principle more fundamental than this dualism, a principle which could make sense of the dualism itself. For now it remains an open question whether such a more fundamental principle, even if discovered, can be adequately proven. Perhaps our principle can only be pointed to, not articulated in terms of more fundamental principles. The question, Why be moral?, would then be incapable of a reasoned answer, since the question itself is no longer moral. The question does not adhere to reason, but asks beyond it, into the emptiness beyond it. One cannot demand to hear reasons why one should listen to reasons.

The eudaimonistic answer always leads to merely hypothetical rules of prudence, which make the unconditionedness of morality disappear. Diderot already confronted the demand for universalism with the sighs of the *homme troublé*, who is not in the position to separate himself from himself and his own wish for happiness. Rules and commands, like conceptions of happiness, are never primary; they presume perceptions. Perceptions, in turn, presume someone capable of perceiving. *"Agere sequitur esse"* ("Action follows being") as Thomas Aquinas puts it and also, *"Qualis unusquis- que est talis finis videtur ei"* ("What appears to someone as a desirable goal depends on what kind of person one is.") Fichte formulated this insight in quite the same way. The perception which makes the human human is the perception of being. Emmanuel Lévinas understands `being' in a modern sense as objectivization. Therefore, the revelation of others comes for him from somewhere "beyond being."

In its classical as well as its everyday meaning, being means first and foremost being a self, the self as a being already beyond all objectivization. Since its paradigm is human *being*, it is not then to be defined in *reference* to the human, that is, to human subjectivity. There is no ethics without metaphysics, but ethics no more precedes ontology, in the sense of first philosophy, than the latter does the former. Ontology and ethics – the one as much as the other – are constituted *uno actu* through the intuition of being as being a self. The second part of this book, under the title "Benevolence," proceeds from this intuition, which presumes the separation of practical from theoretical philosophy. The antinomies implicit in the thought of happiness only resolve themselves only for the person who has awoken from slumber.

January 1989

Translator's Preface

For Prof. Robert Spaemann, "ethics" is the teaching about how one's life can turn out well. To formulate ethics in this way already gives a strong indication of how he will proceed. One could characterize this book as an attempt to reconstruct the ancient notion of *eudaimonia*, often translated "blessedness," but which Spaemann translates as "a life which turns out well," in light of the Kantian critique that deeds done out of the hope of reward lose something of their moral purity. One does the right thing because it is right. One cannot obtain happiness, but one can live in such a way that one is worthy of happiness.

According to Spaemann, human life can be conceived of as a whole. In fact, it must be so conceived, and this whole can be said to turn out either well or badly, to succeed or to fail. Failing at life as a whole is a sobering thought, and sobering thoughts help to rouse one.

"Have I awakened to the reality of the other?" This was the question that kept recurring to me as I first read *Happiness and Benevolence.* It recurs to me still. Has the other become real to me, or does this one remain remote, a mere extension of myself? And yet it remains in the nature of this awakening that one cannot directly will it. The condition of slumber renders the person incapable of making this act of the will. One has to be awakened. Perhaps this book can serve as an instrument in one's awakening. Perhaps it can help one to become aware that one stands in need of awakening. That itself is no small matter.

Spaemann writes in an "essay" style. This form corresponds to his conception of what philosophy in general and ethics in particular are. If ethics is the teaching about the life which turns out well, people who have an interest in their life turning out well should be able to read and understand the book. This is not to say that it is an "easy read." Spaemann's erudition is vast, and he wears it lightly. This creates problems and opportunities for the translator. Spaemann is not playing with the language in the way that some post-modern writers or even Heidegger are. Thus, there is no need for creative solutions for untranslatable word play. On the other hand, I hope that the readability of his German is somewhat preserved in the translation. It is a difficult task to have flowing English that also remains faithful to the German.

I am sure that specialists will want more exact references. I have only been able to track a few of them down. There is only one footnote in the original, and it is marked in the translation as coming from the author. All other footnotes are from the translator.

I wish to thank a number of people for their kindness and support in connection with the publication of this translation. Rev. Richard Schenk, O.P., showed me how poor my first attempt at translation was, and what it would take to make it better. It is mainly due to his efforts that this manuscript is being published by the University of Notre Dame Press. Rev. Arthur Madigan, S.J., used an earlier version of this translation in a course and so was able to give me many concrete suggestions for improvements. He graciously agreed to have his outstanding article on Spaemann's *Philosophical Essays* serve as the afterword to this book. In his kindly tenacious way, Rev. Paul McNellis, S.J., encouraged me to see this work through to its end. For that I am very grateful. Prof. Ralph McInerny and Mr. Jeffrey Gainey at the University of Notre Dame Press have been extremely good at shepherding this project through to completion. Finally a word of thanks to Prof. Spaemann himself. At a time of great discouragement in my own life, he was benevolent toward me. It has made a great difference in my life. If this translation is viewed as a small token of my gratitude, then I shall be very happy.

Jeremiah L.Alberg, S.J.
Tokyo, Sophia University

Happiness and Benevolence

While awake,
we have one common world.
But dreamers turn each to their own.
Heraclitus

PART I

Chapter 1

Ethics as Teaching How Life Can Turn Out Well

AS WITH ALL REFLECTION, practical philosophy is concerned with what is right and wrong. We meet right and wrong in a variety of ways: in all that is beautiful or ugly, meaningful or absurd, expedient or inexpedient, in all that is healthy or sick, profitable or unprofitable, and finally in all that is good or evil. Right and wrong are present in scientific as well as in non-scientific talk about reality, facts, laws of nature, or numerical proportions as what is true or false, since this talk consists in propositions which are either true or false. It is also clear that human actions can be right or wrong. In general we use the word, "actions," when it concerns an action which can be judged from the viewpoint of right or wrong.

I

Actions are not simply right or wrong but can be so in various ways and these ways form a clear hierarchy. In many cases the rightness or wrongness of an action can be traced back to the truth or falsity of the underlying assumptions about the reality involved. There is a certain philosophical tradition which analyses all rightness or wrongness in this way. We call actions which follow from errors "mistakes." Mistakes correspond to the errors from which they proceed. We could be in error, for example, about the predictable laws of nature: The tailor of Ulm jumped from the cathedral steeple because of this kind of error.[1] We can also err as to whether some fact, which is of significance for attaining a goal, holds or not: Someone could go to work on an electrical wire, mistakenly assuming that the current was turned off. We can also make mistakes due to insufficient knowledge of conventional ways of acting. The novice at chess might leave his rook unprotected because he does not know that it may be taken by the pawn standing diagonal to it. This kind

---

1   In 1811 A. Berblingen, known now as the "tailor of Ulm," attempted unsuccessfully to fly across the Danube by attaching wings to his arms and jumping off the bastion. He survived the attempt. The belief that he jumped from the cathedral tower appears to have entered the local folklore.

of ignorance could lead us to break the rules of etiquette in a foreign country. A Christian man might appear in a synagogue bare-headed or a Jewish man in a Christian church with his hat on. The errors which underlie all these mistakes are of a theoretical kind. They are false assumptions about reality or about laws of nature or about facts, and here the existence of certain conventions belongs to the notion of "facts." Since the facts are unknown to someone, they make a mistake.

Nevertheless the wrongness of an action is not the same as the error which underlies it. This wrongness, the mistake, consists in the fact that agents do not reach the goal of their action. The agent's purpose is not realized or it causes something that was never intended. Certainly there is a difference between the agent who simply makes a false conjecture about reality and acts with consciousness of the risk involved should this conjecture prove false, and the agent who believes he knows what, in fact, he doesn't. Only the latter case is designated by the word "error." An error is "counterfeit knowledge" in the same sense as "counterfeit money," that is, paper that looks like, but is not, money. When action is defined as the intentional bringing about of something, then that action which rests upon error appears to be "false" in just this sense. It looks like an action and was also intended as an action, but it turns out badly in being an action. What is brought about is precisely what was not intended. The error appears to destroy the character of the action as an action.

Reflection on this insight can lead us deeper. It is the insight, upon which is based the so-called "intellectualism" of Platonic philosophy and the tradition following it up to Spinoza. According to this tradition, all bad action is based upon error, so that no one freely acts wrongly, and accordingly, every wrong action has the character of a "mistake." Right action and real action would be one and the same. With Fichte we could thus formulate the moral imperative simply as the demand: "Act!" The presumption of this line of thinking is that there exists something like a final intention of acting, a last for-the-sake-of-which, and that this for-the-sake-of-which our actions take place is not itself the result of a choice, but rather that it defines "by nature" our being-for-something. This means, too, that we can be mistaken about our knowledge of this for-the-sake-of-which and about the means of its attainment, so that we strive after something "false." But this falseness does not consist in the fact that the action does not measure up to some standard higher than the acting itself and extrinsic to it: How could standards of measure which are not immanent to our efforts take on meaning for the judging of these efforts? The falseness consists simply in this: What we take to be the ultimate for which we strive is not, in the end, our ultimate desire. And with this, we fall into contradiction with ourselves. We want what we do not want.

In the course of the following reflections it will become clear what elements of this classical view mark a discovery which ought not to be forfeited. Correct action has in fact something to do with insight, and wrong action, with blindness. And yet apparently, insight and blindness must be of another type than that which we call "knowledge" and "error." In judging an action we do distinguish that wrongness which we consider to be a "mistake" from other forms of errancy, such as aberration, being blameworthy, criminal activity, or maliciousness. We regard it as a frivolity or as a deliberate paradox when an evil act is called a "mistake." "Mistake" points only to the lack of personal intention, not the wrongness of the intention itself. The type of errors and ignorance which lead us to make mistakes does indeed appear to reduce the wrongness of such actions. Plato himself was the first to draw attention to this paradox, making it clear that the "intellectualism" sketched out above in no way adequately characterizes even his own theory. Plato has a character in the dialogue *Hippias Minor* maintain that a doctor who knowingly and intentionally makes someone sick is a better doctor than the one who commits a professional error and injures his patients out of ignorance. Granting this for the moment, Socrates asks in response whether one must not then also say that the intentional liar, the one who does in fact know the truth, is better than the one who lies involuntarily? Only knowledge puts one in a position to choose between true and false discourse. The result of this part of the dialogue is expressed so: "Then it is a matter for the good man to do wrong intentionally, and for the bad man to do so unintentionally . . ." (376B) In the end Socrates admits that he cannot content himself with a conclusion so counter to intuition, but that he simply does not know where the mistake might lie.

We are inclined to quickly jump to his aid by explaining the ambiguity of the word "better." In one case it obviously means the same as "more capable," "superior," while in the other case it denotes "more upstanding," "more ethical." Of course, the Platonic Socrates does not need such help. It is the very intent of this dialogue to help us to see this double meaning. We miss the point of the Platonic dialogue, if we understand it from the start as pure equivocation. The Greek language of that time had available two different words for good, one with the meaning of profitable, favorable, desirable; the other with the meaning of morally good. The first word was the *agathón*, the "good"; the second, the *kalón*, the "beautiful." The Greeks assumed that the good need not always be beautiful, and the beautiful need not always be good, that is, the advantageous is not always noble, and the noble is not always advantageous. Plato intends to show that the beautiful is in itself "good" and not only secondarily so for some other external reasons. But this is to say that the beautiful lies in our true interest and even defines what true interest is. In the end the word "good" is equivocal for Plato only so long as this true and original interest has not been understood well. It is the task of philosophy to bring about this understanding. Philosophy demonstrates that crime is in fact a mistake, but not that it was a mistake apart from being a crime and not that in reality it was "only a mistake." It shows much more the reverse: A crime is in fact a mistake and even the worst mistake precisely for its being a crime.

When we stop to consider the usual meaning of the word "mistake," the equivocation of "bad" appears merely to have shifted itself to this word, since there seem to be mistakes which it is better to make voluntarily than involuntarily, and other mistakes where the reverse is true. Aristotle took up the question of the *Hippias Minor* in the 6th book of the *Nicomachean Ethics*. For the first time it was clarified through a terminological and objective differentiation: "In matters of art whoever makes mistakes willingly is to be preferred, but where it is a question of practical wisdom, as in the virtues, it is the reverse" (*Nicomachean Ethics* 1140b20). Why? Thomas Aquinas provides the answer in the *Summa Theologica* (*S. th.* I a II ae qu 21) along quite the same lines as Aristotle. He too distinguishes between "technical" and "moral" viewpoints, between technical and moral "mistakes," when he writes: "Reason is related in one way in the area of what is technical and in another to what is moral."

By how are the two viewpoints distinguished here? They are not distinguished from one another as sections of some larger reality, nor are they distinguished by some extrinsic standard of measure. If they were, the question could be posed: Why is precedence always to be given to the moral viewpoint rather than to the technical? The interrelationship of the two aspects corresponds much more to the relationship of the whole to the parts. The "moral viewpoint" judges the action as good or bad in view of life as a whole, whereas the "technical viewpoint" looks to the attainment of particular aims. That our life turns out well as a whole is a goal which we, as consciously living creatures, necessarily find already given in ourselves. But a particular aim is a freely chosen and "thought-out" (*excogitatus*) aim: the production of automobiles, the manufacture of a bomb, the cure of the sick. All of these are possible aims, about whose achievement the words "better" or "worse" could be applied meaningfully. But in each case it is only a matter of a relative better or worse.

We are dealing then with three levels of meaning for these words and also for the concept "mistake": 1. the "objective," socio-culturally pre-formed goal of action – the *finis operis*; 2. the subjective goal of the agent – the *finis operantis*; and 3. the objective-subjective goal, the life which turns out well.

Concerning the first level of meaning: An "objective" goal of action is, for example, the production of a car or a bomb. A good car and a good bomb are those which optimally fulfill that aim or purpose, which their respective use normally associates with them. When they fulfill the purpose badly or not at all, we speak of "mistakes."

Concerning the second level of meaning: The one who commits such an "objective" mistake does so either intentionally or unintentionally. When he does so unintentionally, then he also commits a subjective mistake, since he also misses the subjective goal of his own action. He understands his "art" poorly and is in this regard worse than the one who intentionally makes a mistake. The one who intentionally does poorly reaches his subjective goal precisely in missing the objective goal. He would make a subjective mistake if his product happened to turn out mistake-free or if the one whom he wished to deceive by the lie were to be enlightened about the truth, as is in fact often the case.

Concerning the third level of meaning: We have here available a level of meaning for "good" and "bad," or "turning out well" and "being mistaken," which allows us to judge once again the intention of those who do something intentionally well or badly, rightly or wrongly. This intention can itself be either good or bad. The good technician, who intentionally makes a bomb badly, can be better therefore in this third sense. The good medical doctor, who intentionally makes someone sick, is in this sense worse, precisely as a "doctor"; for our concept of a doctor, in distinction to that of the medical technician, implies the idea of an intent to heal in addition to basic medical technique. This third level of meaning is that which Thomas Aquinas intended in the text mentioned above, when he distinguished the mistake which someone makes *inquantum artifex* – as an artisan, from the one which someone commits *inquantum homo* – as a human. Each case has to do with failing one's goal. The mistake which makes a technician a bad technician does not consist in the production of a bad product, but in the production of a product which is better or worse than intended. The wrongness lies in the disproportion of the action to its aim, i.e., in its defectiveness as action. But what is the "mistake of the human," or, as Aristotle puts it, a "deficiency of wisdom"? This mistake also consists in defectiveness, in failing to reach its goal. Indeed, as Thomas Aquinas says, in failing "the common goal of the whole of human life," by which the word "common" does not primarily mean "common to most people," but rather that which integrates all the goals of any human into a single whole. This goal is that "of humans, insofar as they are human and insofar as they are moral." In distinction to particular goals it is neither "planned" nor "thought out"; rather it is always already given as that for which our lives are lived and as such constitutive of our existence: *eudaimonia*. This goal cannot be intentionally failed. Every intention must have its own goal. Some other goal must constitute the intention behind failing any immediate goal, and this purpose lies at the root of every intentional failing of a goal, of every intentional mistake. The goal, which I intentionally fail, is precisely not *my* primary goal and purpose. Plato's thesis, that no one intentionally does the bad, addresses first of all the purely formal fact that no one can intentionally act in contradiction to the fundamental structure of intentionality without giving up the purposeful, i.e., "action" character of this action. It is impossible, so runs this line of thought, not to want the goal of a life which turns out well. There is no motive which could move us to that, since, if something should move us to sacrifice all other goals, then precisely this something else would form an essential component of that which we view as a life which turns out well.

II

Thus the truth of what classical philosophy calls "eudaimonism" would appear to be merely a logical truth, that is, a tautology and a purely formal thesis without any content. "Eudaimonism" is not the name of any particular content that-for-which life is lived, but rather it presents a certain form of reflection, out of which that for-the-sake-of-which life is lived first comes to be. Accordingly, the critique of eudaimonism can only be a critique of this form of reflection. A content-oriented critique can only be applied to the different contents with which the concept eudaimonism is filled, for example, "pleasure" or "virtue." Admittedly, there is almost no translation of *eudaimonia*, itself a term of mythical origins, which does not already imply an interpretation filled by some definite content. The traditional translation of "beatitude" suggests identifying eudaimonism with a state of subjective euphoria. The translation suggested here, "a life which turns out well,"[2] on the other hand, could mislead one to the view that "life" is the objective product of the attempt to optimize life in utilitaristic terms; thus, turning out well would be actually inseparable from the conscious perception of turning out well. No one word, only the conceptual development of the thought which it seeks to name, can exclude misunderstandings.

The thought that life can succeed or fail, that no one can want the failure

---

2   The original German is *"Gelingen des Lebens."*

of his or her life, and that there are nevertheless conditions of success which are not arbitrary, this thought implies three more conclusions which are in no way trivial: First of all, it implies that life itself can be something like a whole, or, at least, that it is our concern to grasp it as such a whole. It implies, secondly, that what is amiss in a moral sense, that is, what is amiss in regard to the sense of a "general goal of the whole human life," rests upon a lack of insight into the conditions of its turning out well. Whoever has grasped these as necessary conditions of what is desired cannot but help willing them too. Ultimate happiness, a life which turns out well, cannot have a price which is too high. It has no price, since the adequate relation between all those things we strive for and their "prices" is itself an integral component of the life which turns out well. Finally, the third implication would appear to demand that, in a moral sense, bad deeds are "false deeds," and therefore not real deeds at all, since we do not do by means of them that which we want to do. There would also be that which is bad, but the basis of all practical badness would be in reality only a theoretical wrongness: mistakeness, lack of insight or some extrinsic control over oneself, compulsion, lack of self-determination. That particular kind of being practically amiss or bad, which we call "evil," would simply not exist. Without ruling out this possibility from the start, one must be clear about the burden of proof which one takes upon oneself, when one denies the specific qualities of a *practical* good and a *practical* bad, i.e., evil. If this denial is correct, then fundamental human reactions like admiration, praise, gratitude, contempt, anger, indignation, reproach, and accusation all are founded entirely upon error. In point of fact, the very lack of such reactions is regarded normally as an indication of callousness or contempt for humankind and, in a word, as a serious deficiency.

Such reactions are not usually directed toward the deeds of others in as far as their deeds contribute to their own lives turning out well or poorly, but rather insofar as their actions hurt the lives of third parties. Even when this is not necessarily the case with admiration and contempt, or praise and blame, it does hold true for gratitude and indignation. These reactions appear to apply standards to the evaluation of actions, which differ from those applied to the ones involving only the *eudaimonia* of the agent. According to the viewpoint that we have developed so far, these standards could only appear relevant only to agents themselves, if it could be shown that, for example, their ignoring them would keep their own lives from turning out well and that ignorance of this kind would mean being blind to an insight essential for *eudaimonia* itself.

One of the most important questions of ethics concerns the meaning of this "lack of insight," this blindness, which affects the whole of life and the conditions of its turning out well. "The gloomy people, who have lost the good of knowledge," is Dante's name for the *massa damnata* who populate hell (*Divina Commedia*, Inferno, 3rd Canto). In a certain sense Aristotle had only repeated the Platonic conception when he wrote: "Every bad man is ignorant of what he ought to do and what he ought to leave undone, and it is always by reason of an error of this kind that humans become unjust and in general bad. . . (*Nic. Eth.* 1110b28–30). Nonetheless, he goes on to distinguish the "error of this kind" from other types of errors, including those which we named in the beginning: errors that refer to laws of nature, to facts, and to conventional rules. Here it is a *blameworthy* error. But if some error is at the root of every case of guilt, how then can this error be blameworthy? The guilt, which is at the root of this error, would have itself to be based on a further error, and so on. The insight or blindness which is at the root of life's turning out well or badly is obviously not to be defined by a theory of adequation in the sense of a correspondence or lack of correspondence to reality. It cannot be so defined precisely because the insight, with which we are concerned here, is an element of reality itself. The issue at stake here, life itself, is reflexive. Life can turn out well only as conscious of itself. And knowledge of the conditions for life's turning out well must know itself to be the most important condition for this to come about. This means, however: the condition can only be known when it is already fulfilled; and vice versa: when it is fulfilled, it has already come to be known. Every stabilization in the structure of drives, which first makes possible something like an insight into the conditions of a life's turning out well, cannot itself be caused by the insight it will make possible. It is a divine or a human gift. For example it could be the result of training, which in the beginning is imposed from without – accordingly, we speak of "education" or "rearing" – at whose end stands that ability to "lead" one's own life, which, since ancient times, has been called "virtue." According to the teaching of the ancients, only a consciously led life can be viewed as turning out well.

III

Aristotle was the first to give a consistent presentation of those dispositions for action which are constitutive of a life which can turn out well. He sought to describe "rational practice." He coined a new technical term for this new presentation – "ethics." The word is formed from the Greek word *ethos*, which indicates not only a habitual place of residence but also the structure of habits and mores, which carries and guides our acting and, in turn, is reproduced and modified through our acting. Aristotle names this discipline the "philosophy of human affairs" in distinction to theoretical philosophy (*Nic. Eth.* 1181b15).

At the same time he names his presentation of rational practice a "political investigation" (1094b11). Why? The life which can turn out well is not exclusively an affair of individual acting, individual standards, and dispositions to act. At least this is Aristotle's view, and here he is in agreement with common sense. Among other things the turning out well of life depends upon the circumstances of good fortune, which cannot be the object of science due to their fortuitousness. Health is one such circumstance, as is freedom from poverty, so also the possibility of self-determination. The life of a slave, whose own personal orientation toward action does not seem to matter, cannot turn out well according to Aristotle. Beyond the above, in order to turn out well, a life depends upon certain structures of communal life, upon a certain constitution of public institutions, which represent the structure of human possibilities to act and give orientation to action. If the way we are raised forms our dispositions to action, then clearly the way in which a child is reared is not a matter of indifference for life's turning out well. Similarly important is the kind of mores, customs, and laws, which underlie such rearing and which in turn are passed on by it. Acting rationally would not be possible without such institutions. Still, it would be completely impossible, were acting rationally to be understood only as a function of existing institutions because then it would no longer be acting in the real meaning of the word; at best, it would be passivity. Conscious living would only be a part of a greater whole and not itself a whole. If life is in some way a whole which can be judged under the viewpoint of turning out well, then individuals must be able to understand their own institutional prerequisites as conditions for their lives turning out well. They must be able to come to an understanding of these presuppositions with their contemporaries. This, in turn, is only possible in a "polis," in a community of free citizens. Therefore Aristotle can say that humans, as rational beings, only come to the life suited to them, i.e., only come to the fulfillment of their "nature," in such a polis. The famous statement of Aristotle, that the human is a political being by nature, does not mean that we live in a social unit like ants and bees, but rather that we are beings which can only come to the fulfillment of our nature in a polis-styled manner of living together. Only such a life together counts – at least for the majority of humans – as a life which is turning out well. The polis is precisely "a community of households and generations with the goal of a self-sufficient life" (*Pol.* 1280b30–35). In this way political science for Aristotle stands next to ethics as the study of the appropriateness or inappropriateness of political institutions in regard to the conditions for life's turning out well. It is the study of their naturalness or unnaturalness.

It is striking that the polis is not defined as a community of individual humans, but of "households" and "generations." Mediating, as it were, between ethics and political science, we have here a third element of a life which turns out well: the "household" and "generation," the economic "business" and the family, entities outliving the lifetime of any individual.

It is not the task of these introductory reflections to discuss in detail the mediating function of these entities, without which there could be, in fact, no free societies. To understand them only as "socializing agents" of the "society" would mean to misunderstand them in their own sovereignty and right and thereby to contribute to that deformation of social living which can be given the name "totalitarianism." For Aristotle the teaching of the household as an economic unity, *oikonomia*, forms the third of those disciplines which in the peripatetic tradition are grouped together under the title "practical philosophy."

For reasons which can be discussed later, political science and economics emancipated themselves in late antiquity and then again in modern times. They disassociated themselves from the context of the teaching on the good life. This separation led to a far-reaching transformation of our understanding of what is ethical. This transformation finds its logically consistent expression in antiquity with the Stoics and in modernity with Kant. Action as moral no longer knows itself to be woven into the circumstances of mores and carried by these. It cannot understand itself any longer as a reproduction and modification of these circumstances or define itself in terms of a responsibility for these. From this view of ethics, political and economic circumstances are "products of nature" and therefore something external to ethical concern. Acting is condemned to being without consequence in reality and cast back upon itself. Ethics becomes an "ethics of conviction." The only good in a good action is the good will of the agent. Agents no longer find their concrete orientation in the circumstances of given mores – friendship, family, professional collegiality, national or religious community – but in imagined and ideal legislation. Agreeing with this idealized law constitutes the morality of an individual's maxim of action.

This process becomes visible in late antiquity. It would seem that a differentiation of ethical motives emerges only under such conditions. Completely in opposition to the demand of the New Testament that the right hand should not know what the left hand is doing, Aristotle sees those persons as noble who are concerned with honor and recognition by their peers rather than with money or pleasure. But Aristotle is already being anachronistically archaic. Plato, in order to work out the purity of moral motivation, had already suggested the idea of the crucified one, who is completely just but appears to be completely unjust. Can one say that the life of this man has turned out well? In order to be able to say this, Plato must extend the perspective of ethics beyond the boundary of death in a manner quite analogous to Kant, when he speaks of "the highest good." But, with that, the turning out well of life, the *eudaimonia*, ceases to be the criterion for distinguishing between good and bad. The criterion for this distinction has to be known in other ways, in order then to link life's turning out well, so to speak "after the fact," to the conditions of goodness. Does such an ethics remain at its core a study of how to have one's life turn out well? Since Kant, every ethic which orients itself in terms of this concept is suspected of having missed from the start the specifically moral. For Kant eudaimonistic ethics is only a bare instrumental theory, which teaches how to reach specific goals, but does not teach which goal at which price it is justifiable to desire.

Such a theory reduces all moral guilt in matter of fact to mistakes committed in error. Obviously though, this is not what we understand by guilt. And what reason would we ever have for thanking others, when everything that they have done was merely a means for them to satisfy their own desires for happiness? Every eudaimonistic ethics is then, so runs the other objection, essentially egotistical, while the specifically moral phenomena are to be sought precisely where someone acts from a viewpoint which is not self-interested. The effectiveness of an unselfish, disinterested viewpoint, of a disinterested motivation, shows itself most impressively wherever action motivated in this sense goes against the very own interests of the agent. True, Leibniz had defined love as "joy in the happiness of others" and ethical action as the satisfaction of such altruistic tendencies. But a Kantian objection can, of course, be made against this, in that what is moral will be made dependent on the chance presence of a certain altruistic tendency or that there is something like a duty to cultivate such a tendency in oneself. If such a duty exists, then it cannot have its basis in this same altruistic tendency, nor can the desire to possess this tendency be interpreted as a result of the tendency itself. As Kant says, the desire must stem from practical reason and not from the desire of the individual for happiness. This anti-eudaimonistic argument remains basically unchanged even when, as in several new moral theories, the discursive pursuit of a common understanding about our acting replaces Kant's practical reason; that is to say, when it replaces conscience. The willingness to reach a common understanding is urged upon us not as a means of attaining our own greater happiness, but it is demanded of each rational being as a condition for the justified pursuit of one's own claims to happiness.

To view the acknowledgment of the claims to happiness by others as a mere means to satisfy one's own claims, would be to misunderstand altogether what the word "acknowledgment" means.

As to the first Kantian objection, it is an objection against transforming ethics into a kind of psychical therapy or technology for inducing states of happiness. In this objection, however, the Kantian school has already reduced the classical eudaimonistic concept to the concept of pleasure; here eudaimonism means simply hedonism. The expression, "life's turning out well," avoids this misunderstanding. It also avoids the misunderstanding that life's turning out well has to do with any one particular goal of action, which we could just as well *not* want. So we might even reject what is generally called happiness for the sake of some other seemingly more important goal or for the sake of another person. By way of contrast, the concept of a "life turning out well" has a strictly formal character. It expresses only a certain way of viewing life as a whole, of finding it as wholly somehow "right." Precisely for this reason, however, the concept of a life turning out well does not suggest an instrumental understanding of ethics. To be sure, the turning our well of life is not a particular goal, in relation to which other contents of volition are degraded to mere means. It is much more the determinate, reflectively obtained, "conceptual essence,"[3] which allows all that is desirable in all its multiplicity to grow together,[4] into a desirable whole.

At this point, however, the second objection arises, which claims that this reflexive whole is precisely not that with which we are concerned in moral action. Reflection on life's turning out well is, as the objection goes, essentially egotistical and thereby unsuited to seeing the moral standpoint in its unconditional character. This objection cannot be adequately discussed at this point in our argument. The concept of "a life turning out well" needs to be clarified beforehand. At this stage we can only provisionally justify the renewed choice of a eudaimonistic starting point for ethics. This choice is dictated by the fact that the type of ethics which detaches itself from the question of life's turning out well and rigorously separates this from all

---

3   Perhaps the best English translation for what Spaemann is saying would be the word coined by G. M. Hopkins: "inscape." W. H. Gardiner explains this term in the following way: "Hopkins is mainly fascinated by those aspects of a thing or *group* of things, which constitute its individual and 'especial' unity of being, its 'individually-distinctive beauty,' or (if 'beauty' is not involved) the very essence of its nature. For this unified pattern of essential attributes (often made up of various sense-data) he coined the word 'inscape'"; cf. *The Poems of Gerard Manley Hopkins*, ed. W. H. Gardner and N. H. MacKenzie, (Oxford, 1970), p. xx.

4   To concretize (*concrescere, concretum*) in its etymological meaning.

moral concerns, has, since Nietzsche, forfeited its indubitable plausibility. Kant himself was certain that morality's point of view would not stand a chance in real life, if, in the end, it did not converge with the turning out well of life. He used the concept of this convergence to think about the "highest good"; still he thought of this convergence from the moral point of view; that is, he thought of ultimate happiness as the reward for being worthy of happiness and this in turn as morality. Morality, however, should remain capable of being defined independently of any eudaimonistic components. In his *Letters on Esthetic Education* Schiller would distinguish explicitly the moral evaluation of a human from the "full anthropological" evaluation. Schopenhauer radically detached the moral point of view from every eudaimonistic one. Schopenhauer mocked even Kant, who taught an ethics of disinterestedness, only to hold out his hand for the reward at the end. But Schopenhauer was also the one who drew out the consequences of such separated, "pure" morality: He admitted its hostility to life and affirmed it. Right living meant for Schopenhauer overcoming the very will to live. Nietzsche adopted this understanding of morality, but turned it against morality itself. Nietzsche tried to purify the thought of a life turning out well from all elements which were traditionally regarded as ethical. This was primarily the thought of universalization and the postulate of "justice." Nietzsche's thesis was that the traditional rational ethics of either a Platonic or Stoic or Christian character were at the very least detrimental to life's turning out well. For Nietzsche, however, this does not speak against life, as it does for Schopenhauer, but against morality.

This is not the place to go into the historical and intrinsic reasons for this renewed separation of the *kalón* and the *agathón*, whose synthesis constituted the Platonic foundation of philosophical ethics. In the Kantian tradition it appeared as if just this separation would allow the essence of what is moral to shine forth in all its purity. But a rationalistic ethics, purified of all reference to the reality of life, comes to be a mere postulate, open to every ideology-critique from without. The hidden interest is uncovered right behind the apparently pure rationality. Not even Kant himself was able to clarify the "Sitz im Leben" of the ethical. After futile attempts to derive the categorical imperative, he finally came to acknowledge conscience as an underivable fact, a "fact of reason," an erratic block in the midst of the otherwise structured course of our life.

We do not wish at this point to determine prematurely the question whether a unification of these divergent viewpoints, i.e., the intersubjective justification of action and a life which can turn out well, is possible without one side doing violence to the other. It is enough to see that the "autonomy" of a philosophical ethics which would seek to constitute itself independently of the concept of eudaimonism is only an apparent autonomy. It will be unavoidably overtaken by the concept of eudaimonism, but in a destructive way. It will appear as an ideology, which misunderstands itself and which threatens or is inimical to life itself. This interpretation destroys the moral dimension because it defines the moral, which has been detached from life, by referring to aspects of life which are premoral and nonmoral, that is to say, in reference to life understood in a naturalistic sense. The nonmoral view of what is moral was the remarkable postulate of Nietzsche. In such attempts at reductionism, it is always supposed that it all has to do with life's turning out well and that we know in what this consists. And yet every biologism, even that of Nietzsche, is quite far from knowing it. It has only the vaguest of ideas of it, and when these ideas are defined more closely, they are easily seen to be false. Neither for the purpose of apology nor for the purpose of uncovering some supposedly sordid truth does the moral dimension allow itself to be constructed functionally out of a concept of life or life's interests, unless this moral dimension was already present in the thought from the beginning. Any such reconstruction constructs something other than what is meant as moral, since it has to put aside precisely that characteristic unconditionedness which is essential to the moral order.

Without an understanding of that which we actually hold to be a life which turns out well, we will not be able to come to a common understanding of the meaning which justifiable action has in the context of our lives, nor will it become clear what could be instances of such justification. We will never understand what meaning common discourse with others about justification can have in the life of an individual. Duties are only one part of our lives, and an attentiveness to duty is only one aspect of our actions and omissions. The meaning of this aspect cannot be explained without our seeing it in reference to life as a whole under the comprehensive aspect of its turning out well.

Whether this meaning can be deduced in any strict sense, whether it is in fact identical with life's turning out well, or whether, on the contrary, it stands in an irremedial tension to such turning out well, these questions must remain open for the moment. To anticipate the answer which emerges in the end: The Socratic question: "How should one live?" has, as the more comprehensive question, a priority over those others: "What is my duty?" and "What may I or what should I do?"

Chapter 2

Eudaimonism

I

"ALL HUMANS WANT TO BE HAPPY." This thesis expresses the common conviction upon which are based all ancient teachings about the right way to live, no matter how different they otherwise may be. All humans want their lives to turn out well. A second thesis goes beyond the first and states that everything else which humans will is willed for the sake of this goal, their ultimate end. A third thesis which is, in a narrower sense "eudaimonistic," says that the rightness and wrongness of human action is judged in light of this ultimate end, i.e., whether or not an action is inclined to be conducive to this goal. All three of these theses have been disputed by philosophers in the modern period. Against the first thesis it is objected–primarily by Max Scheler–that neither one's own happiness nor the immanent moral value of one's own action could be a meaningful motive, since both merely follow and are based upon actions whose direct intention is something other than one's own happiness or morality. Against the second thesis it is arguable, and has in fact been argued, that it assumes an internal coherence in human willing which cannot be proven, at least not empirically. It is really necessary to assume that all volition has some ultimate common goal? And even if the answer is yes, could it not be otherwise defined? Could we not see this final goal as self-preservation, in line with the functionalistic viewpoint of biology? Or else, along with Nietzsche, see it merely as a directionless "release of strength." As for the third thesis, it seems to miss the specific nature of ethical motivation, whose ultimate end is something other than the turning out well of one's own life, something other than one's own happiness. Don't we admire most those actions in which an agent disregards the turning out well of his own life for the benefit of another, disregards his own "self-fulfillment"?

What is the phenomenological basis for the idea that our volition heads toward some ultimate goal which encompasses all our determinate goals of action? Is it that rather frequent experience of getting something which we wanted, only to find that we have not, in fact, obtained that which we *really* wanted. Apparently there was something else we wanted in and with that which we wanted. This feeling can appear in many different guises. The simplest case is that in which we choose to do something as a means to an end, but then it becomes apparent that it was an ill-suited means. We would never have willed it, if we had known that it wouldn't lead us to our end. We made a mistake – in the normal sense of the word.

We can also come to relativize a goal, which had seemed for a time so important, simply because we had neglected to consider the goal in its relativity. Only subsequently do we become aware that this seemingly unconditioned aim was in reality only a means whose worth is measured by how far it leads us to our goal. Thus, a revolutionary can put off raising questions about the form the government will take after the revolution. Bertolt Brecht is correct in his observation that whoever has to escape from a burning house cannot stop to ask whether it is raining outside; but the metaphor is also misleading in many cases. The situation described is so bad that it cannot get any worse; any change is an improvement. In such cases one can dispense oneself from thinking about prospective alternatives during the struggle for change. But most of the time it is not this way, and often our situation could better be characterized by the warning: Don't jump out of the frying pan into the fire!

Another way in which a goal is relativized comes about when we consider that something is in itself worth working for, and then work hard toward it and finally attain it, only to realize that the price was too high. The goal was only meaningful as a partial goal. It would be too much to pay for the joy of reaching the summit of a mountain, if we would suffer a fall during the descent and be left paralyzed. Apparently the goal upon which we had partially concentrated was only conditionally willed, i.e., as a part of a greater whole, namely, life, into which it fits proportionately. Clearly it would be an over-interpretation, if we tried to infer from this simple observation a positive goal like "the turning out well of life." It is enough to say that we are not usually prepared to pay for any one goal with our overall capacity to pursue goals, in other words, with our future freedom to act. Thus, most all of our willing seems to be accompanied less by the ultimate goal of happiness than by the limits imposed by the conditions for preserving our freedom to pursue goals at all. Of course, there are goals for which people consciously risk their lives and *a fortiori* their further freedom to act, and they do this in such a way that the sacrifice of their life is not understood as a failure to turn out well.

But let us stay with the phenomenon of frustration that sometimes comes about after the attainment of a goal pursued for its own sake. It can happen that a goal reveals its true essence only when it is attained. It becomes clear that in striving after it we had been searching for something other than that which we actually found. We recognize this phenomenon in its pathological form known as neurotic compulsion. The agent keeps pursuing the same goal and yet simultaneously experiences this fixation as an affliction. Neurotics can be liberated from their affliction by becoming aware that they are in fact seeking something else and that their action is a symbolic compensation. But even in more normal life it happens that what we strive after no longer appears to us as worthwhile once it is attained. There are people who possess the unfortunate trait of not being able to enjoy what they already possess or have attained; people for whom happiness consists only in "progress from passion to passion" (Thomas Hobbes). They lack the freedom from themselves necessary for an authentic experience of objective value. The only thing that they are capable of experiencing is momentary subjective satisfaction. And for this they constantly need new "material," which they do not see or value in its own being. Even without this particular defect of the blindness to value, all of us experience the way things and situations grow stale which, as long as we were striving after them, had seemed to us the quintessence of happiness and a life which turns out well. We could say that they did not "keep their promise." This turn of phrase presumes that the things which we strive to perceive or enjoy or possess can somehow promise something other than their "true selves." If this were not so, how could anyone claim that they did not actually find what they sought, even though they attained exactly what earlier thought they were seeking? What is this "other" that things seem to promise? It is the fundamental experience which underlies Plato's teaching on the "Good itself"; people and things which awaken our desire can promise something other, something greater, than themselves, something, however, which they themselves in principle cannot contain. This experience underlies Augustine's famous saying: "Our hearts are restless, until they rest in you, Lord!" However this "greater" goal is ultimately to be defined, we observe the phenomenon that the goals of our actions are relativized by the more comprehensive Why and Whither and What-for of these actions, even when this ultimate goal is understood as merely "unhindered progress from passion to passion." The ancients named this horizon which encompasses all our concrete individual aims *eudaimonia*. We speak here of "life's turning out well." Were there no such horizon, then the individual goals of our actions would be completely incommensurable with one another. We could not weigh one goal against the other in any way. We could not set them in relation to one another. Our goals would have, so to speak, no existential exchange rate, on the basis of which we could rationally sacrifice one goal for the other, and yet this is what we do all the time. Goals can be compared to and weighed against each other because we understand them as means to further goals. In the concept of a life which turns out well, we construct a comprehensive goal, which enables us to maintain our freedom to act rationally in the face of various goals.

However, before this horizon can be more closely determined, a few misunderstandings, which accompanied the concept of *eudaimonia* from its inception in ancient times, must be cleared up. The axis around which these misunderstandings turn is an ambiguity in the concept of "goal," *telos*. Aristotle distinguished between that for which we strive and that on whose account we strive for something else (*De Anima* II, 4). There are certain goals which point beyond themselves to goals of longer term for whose sake the former are willed as means. Even when we set our eyes on an ultimate goal, a difference remains between this which we strive for and that "for-the-sake-of-which" we wish to attain the end. When we wish that our lives turn out well, we are speaking of an ultimate aim. For what, or for the sake of what, do we wish to attain this aim? To answer each seeks it "for the sake of him or herself" is not self-evident. In fact, this answer is the subject of a logical paradox, since "my life" does not signify a factum, which would allow it to be placed vis-à-vis myself in some relationship which would be anything other than a self-relationship. My life is my being; I am it. To wish for a life which turns out well means to wish for the turning out well of that which I am. Is there some other motive that can be discerned out of these circumstances? One can classify philosophies according to whether they affirm this question – they are philosophies inspired by Plato – or deny it. We will speak more of this later.

When the Greeks speak of *eudaimonia* as a goal, they suggested two further misunderstandings. Goals structure our volition. They make action possible by making a selection out of the endlessly complicated effects which we produce in the external world. A physical event takes on the quality of being an action when an event or a few events out of all the complex chain of consequences is thematized by an agent as a goal or is expressly desired for itself. All the other consequences are reckoned as means, costs, or side-effects. The fact is that we simply ignore the greater part of the consequences, in that they do not enter into the definition of the action. This is true primarily for consequences in the microscopic dimension, which is not real for us unless it works its way back into the area that we can experience – as in the case an infection caused by bacteria or a virus. The consequences which we experience without desiring them directly the so-called side-effects. When these begin to affect our lives negatively, then we speak of costs. The rational agent considers the costs in light of the gains brought about by the goal of the action. We distinguish anything which we directly will and purposefully bring about from such side-effects or costs, only because these wished for consequences are the direct conditions for realizing goal which we seek. One could say we put up with them, that we must will the means in order to attain the end. Still, there is a distinction in principle between tolerating an undesired side-effect and putting up with the fact that one must will a means in order to reach a goal because the means must in reality be willed. The willing of the means constitutes itself a proper action. This willing of the means can itself become detached from its goal. Hegel was the first to notice the fact that every culture rests upon this detachment of the means from the original aims of action (*Wissenschaft der Logik*, III. 2. Abschnitt, 3. Kapitel).

II

The question now becomes: Can the turning out well of life outlined above be a goal of an action? The answer seems to be no. For clearly the selective function which is constitutive of the goal is missing. The turning out well of one's life is not one effect of an action among others, one which could be relegated to the level of a side-effect or a cost in relation to others. It does indeed appear as if we must somehow "pay" for life's turning out well. But we have already seen that that is mistaken. Costs are considered in relation to the goal of the action. But against what can life's turning out well be weighed? It is only possible to weigh goals and costs, to compare them by a more comprehensive standard which we call a life which turns out well. With what then is this standard commensurable? Any price we pay for this goal is itself a part of our life, which we then characterize as well or as poorly lived. The positive balance of a business which is the result of comparing the credits and debits cannot account for costs which are not explicitly financial. Nevertheless, if we choose such a positive end – that is, profit-making – as a goal, then this is because we do not include as factors in the balance all the activities which go into reaching this goal. The business person is always something more that just a business person. Success in business is *one* goal among others. Making a profit can never become financially "costly," since then it would cease to be a gain. But it can become costly in other ways, so that attaining the result "does not pay," since the person pays for the financial success with happiness. Life's turning out well, in contrast, does not have any "external costs," so that one would be able to say, "my life did turn out well, but it was not worth it." Only a misunderstanding or even a reversal of the relationship between *eudaimonia* and profit could allow for a statement like that. Indeed such a reversal underlies the joke in which the rich father says to his son, who thinks that he can only be happy with his penniless Sally: "Happiness! – How much of that do you own?"

Nevertheless, it appears that there is something resembling external costs to be paid for life's turning out well. Only these costs are those which *others* have to bear in the form of a lessening of *their* life. In a certain sense this is the problem which serves as the starting point for most efforts at a philosophical ethics. Philosophical ethics can be defined as the attempt to internalize all of the external costs and so to work out the concept of *eudaimonia* which no longer has a price, since it is the essence of life's turning out well. Of course, such a goal is unthinkable as a goal of action (that is the point of these considerations), since it lacks the selective character which is constitutive of actions. There is no such thing as an action, which would be defined only through the intention of life turning out well without any other special particular intention. But there are actions which hinder life's turning out well insofar as they promote some particular desired goal. The omission of such actions can only result from their being a hindrance. Let's look at this significant asymmetry.

Another reason why life's turning out well cannot stand in the relationship of ends and means with other goals is that this "goal" does not allow any exclusion of "side-effects," nor does it reduce the other goals of action to mere means. The ancients' talk of *eudaimonia* as a final goal encouraged such an instrumentalization of the particular contents of the good life on the conceptual level. Augustine settled this in a way rich with consequences by his terminological distinction between *uti* and *frui* and his thesis that all finite objects of the will could only be means to be used. This applies especially to the hedonistic variation on ancient eudaimonism, and that not by accident. The only form of well-being which can be directly intended and not mediated through the experience of weighing various values is bodily pleasure. The instrumentalization of all objects of desire to the status of mere means for subjective well-being brings about the homogenization of their content by which they become commensurable, which means that a consideration between them as furthering of a rational lifestyle becomes possible. This type of rationality is represented in Jeremy Bentham's hedonistic calculus. Its contradiction lies in that fact that the particular objects of the will forfeit their specific qualities through their being instrumentalized. The objects reveal their qualities only when we subject ourselves directly to their demands. Although Aristotle also used the eudaimonistic language of 'end' and 'means,' he saw that the objects of the will as contents of the good life do not stand in a means-end relation with the good life itself but rather they are related to one another like parts to a whole. In the end-means relationship the end is definable independent of the means and determines as such the search for the means. However, what a life which turns out well is, cannot be known independent of the contents which make up this life. The contents are not reducible to the function of means when they are prioritized in terms of such a whole and so do not become in principle interchangeable. Individual life-moves do not stand in a relation to the life which turns out well like the brush stroke of the artist stands to a picture; rather they are comparable to the relationship between a part of the picture and the whole. In this relationship the whole does not one-sidedly determine the parts; rather there is a mutual determination. The parts of a symphony are not primarily interchangeable "means" for reaching a predetermined goal. Other parts, other measures would give a different symphony. This means, however, that we cannot evaluate the success of a symphony by whether a predetermined goal was reached by the chosen means. We can evaluate it only by the criteria which emerge from a deepening mutual relationship of the whole and the parts of this work of art. This also means that the criteria cannot be exact. It is not a matter of set parameters but of the relationship between mutually dependent variables. We call life's turning out well a goal, in the same sense as we speak of the finished piece of art being the "goal" of the ordering of the parts. In reference to this relationship Kant spoke of a "purposefulness without purpose."

The comparison with a piece of art must be further adapted if is to be used to illuminate life's turning out well. An art work is the result of a *poiesis*, a "making," and that in turn is embedded in the life of the artist. This making demands time, energy, concentration, and effort, and yet these external factors do not become a part of the work itself nor do they form the viewpoints from which it is judged.[1]

---

1   It is characteristic of certain contemporary artistic productions that the circumstances of their production are held to be essential for an understanding of them. For example, in order to understand the *Golden Hare* by Joseph Beuys it is essential to know that it came into being through the recasting of an emperor's crown which was expressly made for this purpose by a goldsmith. This was an attempt to overcome the difference between art and life. However, the attempt was in vain. First, the accomplishment of artistic purpose, in contrast to that of life, is connected with the judgment of the beholders and when they believe that the work came to be in the manner in which it is explained to them; it does not matter whether the information is true or false. Second, the artist did not, fortunately, get hold of the real emperor's crown from the Viennese court but allegedly commissioned a goldsmith to produce a crown that was to be destroyed. This series of events was designed exclusively to serve his artistic purpose. Third, because the artist melted the crown immediately after its production and recast it as a hare, the work of the gold-

Life's turning out well reveals itself to be of a different order from the turning out well of a work of art in that, not only do the realized goals count in life, but also the actions, through which the goals are realized, are themselves part and parcel of its turning out well or ill. This turning out well is not the result of a *praxis*, of "doing" – a distinction that was first made terminologically clear by Aristotle. It is possible for us to reach an important goal and nevertheless afterwards to regret the time which we had spent on its realization. It can happen that we have the feeling that somehow we have missed "living," whatever we might mean by that. The opposite can also occur: We spend a great amount of time to attain some goal, fail to attain it, and yet we do not regard the time spent as lost. Perhaps we enjoyed ourselves, or we unexpectedly reached, not what we thought we wanted, but something else that was equally desirable. Or perhaps we have developed through the experience some skills which will be useful in other ways. Life's turning out well is not simple a function of the attainment of goals; rather it gives actions themselves a meaning, which they do not possess through the immediate objective of the agent, that is, through his or her direct intention.

III

There is an area of life in which the immediate relation between action and goal is always reversed, an area where not only the doing has priority, but where the making itself is only a subordinated moment of *praxis*, of doing: the game. The participants in the Olympics – at least in ancient times – certainly competed to win. But the actual goal of the games was really not victory, as it would be in the case of actual war, but rather that the games take place. In this case the saying is true: Being there is everything. Anyone who loses at parlor games and therefore finds it was not worthwhile to have spent the evening that way does not understand what a game is. This person has confused a game with the "gravity of life." But we may find a clue to what life's turning out well means from the fact that we are able to understand life as a whole by an analogy to a game. The Stoics had this view when they taught that one ought to view one's own life as an actor views playing a role. What interests us at this point is the reversal of the immediate relationship between action and goal. In this immediate relationship the goal which con-

---

smith was instrumentalized by him in an absurd manner. With the intention of making art the same as life, Beuys succeeded in making a part of the life of another man completely subordinate to his art, and not in the sense of *serving* his art, which would have had its own dignity, but in the sense of an instrumentalization which destroys the individual worth of the means.

stitutes the action is the ground of the action. It is the reverse in drama. Here, the cobbler does not perform the action of making shoes in order to make a shoe; rather he makes a shoe in order to show forth the action of making shoes. The immediate goal is something other than the one that the act itself leads to. And yet, this new purpose does not stand in the same relation to the action as the original immediate goal. The immediate goal of the doing lies beyond the action of doing. Shoes are real shoes only when the shoemaking is at an end. But precisely in this way does the orientation toward the goal form a constitutive moment of the action itself. This orientation cannot be made explicit without the goal also being made explicit. On the other hand, the presentation of the action as the goal consists in showing the action as itself. The showing does not take the place of the immediate goal, since this goal persists. It is as if the whole consisting of action and goal is bracketed and pointed to precisely as this whole. It is worth mentioning that the becoming visible of the action is not a goal which can displace the goal of shoemaking, since then the action exhibited would no longer be the action of shoemaking. The action is still constituted by its immediate goal, but that goal is no longer its ground. The ground is rather that it should be seen. In order that it be seen, it must be shown, and in order that it be shown it must occur.

It is important that the *tertium comparationis* of this analogy between life and drama not be missed. It consists in the fact that every action, directed to life's turning out well as a whole and judged from this viewpoint, is freed from an unmediated fixation on its goal. The action can then be considered together with its goal as a part of the turning out well of something else, in the one case the drama, in the other case life. With this the meaning of an action becomes located in the action itself, in its occurrence. The occurrence becomes more important than the immediate goal. This metamorphosis takes place on a much more radical level in life than in theater. In theater the particular goal of action is taken up in other larger goals, such as displaying the action, and this is done in such a way that the goal "develops" through the latter. Displaying something is accomplished by the manufacturing of appearances, e.g., the appearance of making shoes. Under certain circumstances the appearance can be produced well without the action actually being performed. The performance does not add anything. In the case, however, where action finds its orientation by contributing to life's turning out well, then everything depends upon the actual occurrence of the action, upon the presence of the elements which define it as that particular action, upon the action being taken seriously. I knew a child who used to play cowboys and Indians in the woods with other children. Naturally, it was part of this game not to go on the wide paths in the woods but to creep through the underbrush. One day the child made a discovery that ended this kind of make believe. He said to himself: "Real Indians, if they had paths, would have used them instead of crawling through the underbrush." The child could no longer manage to make an unconscious separation between play and reality. In this moment the game came to an end. Make-believe or convention is a part of play. The meaning of actions which are directed to the whole of life's turning out well is to let such actions be just what they are and not to "un-realize" their *intentio recta* through a *intentio obliqua*, as is done in the performing of drama. Rather, this kind of direction gives to the actions a new, higher dimension, in which the *intentio recta* is relativized without losing its reality. It is no longer a matter of attaining a goal which is constituted by the act *at all costs*, but rather it is a matter of right action. These actions should actually occur and not just appear to be. This is because life's turning out well has to do with an absolute audience, one who is not fooled by appearances. Actions can be truly shown only when they are "authentic." Seneca comments about this absolute audience in the following: "There lives in us a holy spirit as observer and as watchman of our good and bad deeds" (ep. 41).

How does this relate to the viewpoint of life turning out well? Does this viewpoint ultimately remain without consequences, since the direct intentions of our actions, the immediacy of our interests in our goals, continue to hold good over against it? Indeed, they do hold good, but they are also bracketed, so to say; they lose their blind absoluteness. Rational agents are not simply the objects of drives like an animal. Insofar as they give their "attention" to other things, they remain true to themselves; their actions take place within the medium of knowledge of themselves as agents. Only insofar as they pursue their goals can they at the same time can be concerned to do well, what they would do anyway, and also to omit what they cannot do well under any circumstances. Further, a kingdom of action-relevant interests would be revealed to this agent, interests which would remain completely hidden to someone who did not live in the horizon of reason.

But what is this horizon of reason? We have got to know it as the horizon which presents life as a whole under the viewpoint of its turning out well. What does that mean in terms of content? Are there any criteria which allow someone to distinguish life's turning out well from its turning out badly? Is it not true that we can determine whether our life or that of another has turned out well or not only after the fact, so that it is impossible to orient ourselves or our actions from this? But is this later determination anything other than the expression that we are satisfied in the moment with the determination to have lived in such a way and not some other? Can someone hold the life of another to have turned out well when that person held it to have failed? When we put the question in this way, the problematic of the translation of *eudaimonia* with "a life which turns out well" becomes clearer. In the translation life appears as an objective problem to solve, in which case it can easily occur that someone correctly solves a problem, although he mistakenly believes that his solution is false. The other translation of *eudaimonia*, "blessedness," suggests the opposite, that the appraisal of a life has only to do with the subjective perspective of the individual. Whoever feels happy seems to be so. But is that true? Would we be prepared to trade places with that person? What is *eudaimonia*?

Chapter 3

Hedonism

I

A HISTORICAL DISCUSSION of the question of life's happiness must precede a systematic one, since the question does not naturally – that is, always and of itself – arise. It is true that some kind of orientation toward a wholeness of meaning always belongs to the *conditio humana*. A being who is not instinctively bound to an environment definitively given through its own organization has to ask "Why" in order to act. However, the answer is not necessarily oriented toward the turning out well of the life of the one who poses the question. The answer can be dictated by vital needs, which immediately obtrude themselves. For the one who thirsts, an arrow pointing in the direction to water is sufficient reason to head there. The question of life's happiness becomes a point of view that is relevant to action only when the worry for immediate survival does not take up all one's energy. If this coercion on account of need is experienced as coming, not from nature, but as mediated through society, then the revolt against this coercion can become even more important as mere survival. "To fear a wretched life more than death" (Bertold Brecht) has been held from time immemorial as a higher habit of being. And yet, most often when slavery is seen as a system oriented, not toward the turning out well of the individual, but only toward their usefulness for this system, which itself sets the limit conditions, then the revolt against it is the result of a certain loosening of these conditions. It is this loosening which first allows the rebel to reflect and to no longer see himself through the eyes of the master. The happiness of one's own life remains unthematic as long as traditional, religious and social horizons retain their unquestionable validity so that the habits, through which these horizons are interiorized, have the character of being second nature. Only when their coercive force is loosened can our "first nature" assert itself against the second. And when this happens in a reflective manner, questions about the conditions for a happy life emerge, especially insofar as these conditions may or may not be fulfilled through our own action.

This was the situation which characterized the origin of philosophical thinking in Athens in the fifth century B.C. Beginning then and continuing until today the central theme of discourse was the question concerning the right kind of life. At first it had the form of a question concerning the grounds for the binding force of that which was established, of the *nomos*. Such a grounding became necessary when the established norms, i.e., the customs and laws, no longer functioned as a second nature in which the mere consciousness of the command kills the one who violates it under certain circumstances. We call norms of this type "taboos." Taboos do not need and are not susceptible to justification. The ethnologist can attempt from outside to find functional grounds for certain taboos. However, to those for whom the taboos are taboos, these grounds are not the reason for their validity. Rather, the functional grounding loosens the validity of the taboos and makes room for their equivalents on a functional level. The absolutist representatives of the graciousness of God in the seventeenth and eighteenth centuries understood full well why they so decisively rejected the functionalistic theory of its foremost apologist Thomas Hobbes. The maintaining of a taboo, which is rooted in the primordial past, can be a form of maintaining humanness against functional rationality. Under the pressure of functional rationality such maintenance will feel the necessity of being grounded in some way. Antigone's holding fast to the primordial duty of piety toward her dead brother by resisting Kreon's prohibition, which was grounded in the functionality of domination, becomes here a manifestation of the good life. Antigone linked her identity with the old *nomos*: "Not to hate, but to love am I here." This is not meant in the same way as the disarming, but at the same time subhuman, apology: "That's just who I am," which would refer to a pure *factum brutum*. Rather it is intended teleologically, as an indication of a condition of the life which turns out well. Antigone is "there for something," namely to love. Her life, whether short or long, can turn out well only when it realizes this project, which it itself is. This project comes under the primordial *nomos* which commands her to help her brother find rest in the underworld. Antigone did not burden everyone with the task of fulfilling this law by placing their life in danger of death. She even kept her weaker sister Ismene from it. Not everyone is in the position "to choose the better part." Still, Sophocles does not allow any doubt as to which part is the better. Better for whom? It was by means of this question that the Sophists reflected upon the unmediated validity of the moral life. Within it certain ways of acting were considered outstanding. They were termed "beautiful." "Beautiful" was used by the Greeks as a one-place predicate. It was neutral in regards to any one perspective of interest. The sophistic exposé asked about these interests. It questioned whose interests were served in the application of certain standards of beauty, for whom were they good, and this implies that good is always an equivocal predicate. Here "good" means "good for. . . ." From this viewpoint the "beautiful" way in which Antigone acted would be, at best, good for Polyneikes, her brother, since she obtained rest for his soul. But it appears that it was bad for Antigone herself, since she paid for this with her own life. But the entire spectrum of ancient thinking agrees that no one can have a reason to act badly for oneself. In the argument between the philosophers and the Sophists, it was a question of which of these standards is the standard of good and bad, that is, what should be seen as "a true advantage," "true usefulness," what should be viewed as *eudaimonia,* as blessedness, as the happiness of life.

The answer of the Sophists is a more radical form of common sense. They viewed the good as divisible. What was good for the one was not necessarily good for the other. It did not consist in partaking of a *koinon*, a shared content of the type that the sharing of the one does not impede the other. It consisted rather in an essentially particular appropriation of a private good which could very much cost the other. From this point of view the interest which the individual was able to have in acting "beautifully" meant that the goal of the agent became understandable only in terms of objective values, which are essentially open to everyone, and so, this interest could not be made any more understandable. The interest could be understood only as an interest in compensation, which the individual receives in the form of recognition, social position, honor, or money, that is, more goods which are divisible and are of the type which imply that the partaking of the one means a lesser share for the others. To be sure, the principle of honor in this way of thinking was ambivalent. To the degree that honor, especially posthumous fame, does not bring some other advantage to the individual, there is already contained within it a moment of disinterested appreciation of the beautiful itself. This is the reason that Aristotle holds that the one who acts for the sake of honor rather than for the sake of material gain or pleasure is the more noble. The same order of precedence is found in Augustine and in the Christian tradition, even though here, as with Plato, it is only a relative priority. Compared to the one who acts on account of the "good itself" or from love of God and neighbor, the motivation of honor resembles seeking one's own advantage, since honor is a kind of good that some individual enjoys to the exclusion of another, that is, to the exclusion of the *koinon*. Honor posits a distinction. And in order to acquire honor it is enough, as Plato says, to have he appearance of virtues rather than their reality. Common sense acknowledges such "beauty." In principle it admires unselfish action, but cannot really understand it and therefore in reality half-tends to deprecate it. Sophistry developed the art of such unmasking. In its radical form it unmasks not only the person who appears unselfish, but also the very idea of a beauty which is not defined by individual utility, the idea of the moral, the idea of a possible legitimacy of demands made on the individual. There always stand behind such demands, so it is claimed, the interests and wishes of other individuals. When these others, be it through personal superiority or through their number, are powerful enough to make the fulfillment of their desires the condition of the fulfillment of the desires of someone else, then this can be a motive for fulfillment of these demands, that is, for obedience. From this viewpoint the educator has the most power when he can succeed in making the pupil internalize the demands that are placed upon him so that the pupil himself makes these demands. Given that the educator succeeds, then could not one say that the production of something "integral," something "beautiful" has come about? For it appears that when B, for whatever reason, wants what A wants, all antagonism is done away with. The slave, who is not aware of his slavery, appears to be as free as his master.

Ancient thought, of course, never accepted this answer, the answer of totalitarian cynicism. It began from the insight that in our volition and striving we can also miss our "true interests." The Greeks developed a concept which allowed for true interests to be distinguished from false ones, and to measure each valid *nomos* by these true interests: the concept of the "natural." The natural was for them the ultimate measure, beyond which one could not question. And this measure determined in what a happy life consisted. But what is the natural? Can one say that the primordial grounded divine law, to which Antigone appealed, is natural? The Sophist answered this question in the negative and gave instead an answer which must remain the beginning of ethical theory. We call it the hedonistic answer. It says that there is a for-the-sake-of-which that determines naturally the striving of all living things and gives them their inner unity. A for-the-sake-of-which, which needs no justification, but carries its own self-evidence with it, which proves it to be the ultimate: pleasure. Every living being strives by nature to feel good. Certainly this is not conscious in all living things. In order to distill the essential moment out of the material which moves and drives us, reflection is required. Only when we reflect upon our *physis*, which is defined by obtaining pleasure, will we come to ourselves. Our action will gain an unsurpassable consistency, and we will avoid the frustration which always arises as long as we are fixated on matters like owning, honor, material consumption, power, and so on, not yet having discovered that these things are never goals in their own right, but are available means for the single goal of pleasure. The one who feels good is the one whose life is turning out well, since this one not only has what he or she believes to be desirable, but has what he or she actually desires. No one will say that he feels really good, but that feeling good did not contain what it promised; that he is nevertheless discontent. Discontent means precisely: not to feel good. Thus far the truth of hedonism appears to be a trivial truth, similar to skepticism, and thus on similar grounds refuted as the reflection of skepticism, which adds to each thought which I think the further thought that I am the who thinks this thought. The Kantian insight that "I think" must be able to accompany all our representations is the result only of the process of skeptical reflection positively expressed. According to Hegel, true philosophy is "fully accomplished skepticism." In a similar manner the philosophical thought of *eudaimonia*, the happy life, is secured only in going through the hedonistic reflection. In order for something to become a motive for us, we have to take an interest in it; what otherwise may always be an in-itself must be able to appear to us as something "good for us." However, just as skepticism overcomes itself by bringing the standpoint of doubting into doubt, so does hedonism overcome itself in that the hedonistic reflection looks at itself and questions whether we really feel our best when we are concerned with nothing besides feeling good. The answer to this question is no.

II

There is a dialectic of hedonism, just as there is a dialectic of skepticism. It is a three-fold dialectic.

1. The first contradiction is not immanent in the hedonistic standpoint itself, but emerges when this standpoint is theoretically formulated as a general claim with general validity, specifically when it is formulated as the claim that humans do what they do on account of their own well-being, or even that they act rationally only when they do what they do on account of this goal. The contradiction arises when one asks whether the formulation of the hedonistic thesis is itself only a means of increasing the well-being of the one who utters it. Indeed, the thesis leads to contradiction even when it is intended as a theoretical expression about the true nature of our intentions, just as when it is intended as a recommendation for the one coherent and satisfying life, that is, as a recommendation on the art of living.

In the first case the thesis implies the impossibility of a genuine orientation toward the truth of statements. Statements and system of statements, theories, become no more than means to augment the well-being of the one who utters them. Their "correctness" or "wrongness" consists, not in their truth or falsity, but in their suitability for bringing their author or propagator approval, material gain or something else which is for him a source of pleasure. If, as a matter of fact, someone gains pleasure from true knowledge, that can only be by chance. This means that the cause of pleasure is, in principle, interchangeable, even if it happens – which we could never know – that it in fact is not for a certain person. One could object that it has nothing to do with the intention of the holder of a theory, that one can test this thesis for its truth without knowing about this intention, that the truth can come through an intention which is indifferent to the truth. That is surely correct. But in the case that the theory of hedonism is true, its truth cannot be tested. Whether it is true or false for someone depends on whether it is convenient for that person to hold it as true or false. The hedonist could say in reply, "Yes, that's enough. We do not need a theory for anything more than being aware of having our needs met." But with that, hedonism's claim to being a theory is surrendered. It now says no more about the condition of the one who holds this view than that he or she feels good about it. Nothing more can be said about the possibility of other intentions of other people.

It is similar for those who, not wanting to state anything about the real motivation of all people, still recommend hedonism as an art of living. We must assume that they propagate this teaching because it meets their needs. Why does it meet their needs? Perhaps on account of their altruistic tendency and on account of the satisfaction derived from the fact that others receive continuous enjoyment like themselves. Their ultimate goal, however – according to his own teaching – is not the enjoyment that others have, but their own, for which – again by chance – the enjoyment of others represents a suitable means. But how are we to know this? Maybe this doctrine is only a means of making themselves interesting to others. Maybe it is even an expression of *ressentiment*: They themselves, incapable of excitement, love, fascination, devotion, and not in the position to experience joy, which comes from sources such as these, begrudge others this joy, and wish to reduce everyone to the same meager enjoyment of their own position. Hedonists, who wishes to defend themselves against such an interpretation by seeing it as a form of discrimination, still have to allow that they themselves do not recognize any obligation which does not have its roots in the striving after pleasure. If they regard something as a means for the enhancement of their pleasure, then that justifies it. In principle we can know only that it ought to be expedient to themselves, when they grant us their counsel. Whether part of this expediency includes the fact that the advice is also expedient for us, evades in principle our judgment. That could only be the case by chance. Their assurances that this is so, serve, according to their theory, only their own well-being.

That hedonism cannot be formulated in universal terms without contradiction does not of itself, of course, say it is not a genuine art of living. It may be that the argument which has been brought forward with such energy since the time of Nietzsche is correct, whereby universalism is exposed as an illusion, and whereby "correct" does not mean "theoretically true," but "effectively destructive." Even granted all that, the dialectic of hedonism does not effect just the theory. It is immanent in the hedonistic art of life itself, and this in a double sense. To see in subjective well-being the ultimate goal which tells us whether an action can or should be allowed means to reflectively cancel the intentionality, the orientation of our psychical condition, its constitutive self-transcendence. By nature human beings are precisely beings who do not understand themselves naturally, but beings to whom something matters, something which they cannot understand as a function of their own condition of comfort or discomfort. It is only in reflection that humans can complete this functional return – the *curvatio in seipsum* (Augustine) – which cancels the self-transcendence and conceives itself as "only natural."

Hedonism's immanent dialectic emerges from the fact that what is described as a condition of pleasure cannot in the end be described as a mere state of the subject. On the one hand, the condition of pleasure, which is its only measure of a life which turns out well, can only be described by a hedonist as being both a momentary state and a subjective state. On the other hand, this state possesses according to its immanent structure a double transcendence in the one sense of a temporal "retention" and "protention" and in the second sense of an orientation toward something which in no way can be described as a state of the subject.

2. Let us examine the temporal dimension. The most important result of Plato's dialogue *Protagoras* is the insight that life itself is not a state of pleasure, even when it is understood as a whole consisting of states of pleasure. And the question concerning the conditions of an optimal pleasure-balance of life ought not be answered from a hedonistic viewpoint, but rather must be answered from a truth-functional standpoint, since the answer to a question which is true rather than the one which is most pleasant is the one that will insure us a most pleasant life. But what is the most pleasant life? Only momentary states are pleasant. The momentary state of the prospect of future pleasant states can be pleasant, as can the remembrance of past pleasant states, but so can the remembrance of past unpleasant states, corresponding to the old joke: "Why did you hit your head against the wall? Because it felt so good when I stopped." On the other hand, the remembrance of past unpleasant states, just as with pleasant ones, can itself be unpleasant: "I had it once, which was so exquisite; the human agony is that one never forgets." It is an art – and it belongs to the art of living of Epicurus, the most sublime and

most reflective of the hedonists – to make the remembrance of past joy into a source of present comfort in situations of suffering. And this art belongs to the epicurean way of life just as much as excluding the vectorial character of our sensitivity, that is, defusing fear and hope according to the possibility which belongs to each. Because both fear and hope are intentional states, which means that they essentially refer to something other than themselves, even when this other consists only in states of the same subject. It is enlightening to look at the example of fear since it is a state of discomfort. But first, is not hope a feeling of well-being and, therefore, according to the maximize-pleasure view, a state that should be wished for? The same degree of hunger can be experienced by one as torture, and by another as "the best spice" depending on the present prospects of each, i.e., the prospect of starvation or the prospect of a well-prepared meal, and this is valid even should the prospect prove itself illusory. Nonetheless, there are two types of illusory hope: Either someone dies suddenly before the hope is fulfilled or the person experiences the "disappointment" of the hope not being fulfilled. In the first case, the hedonist would have to characterize the situation of hope as desirable, and in the second case as undesirable. The disappointment then causes something noteworthy which is also difficult to connect with the hedonistic meaning of a pleasurable state: Disappointment makes the preceding pleasant state of hope come to nothing as it were. The disappointed person does not say: "At least I had the joy of anticipation"; rather, the failure to attain the object of anticipation so turns the emotional character of this state into its opposite that it no longer appears as a positive element in the balance of pleasure of life. In fact there are always overtones of this aspect of hope in our dealings with others. The human, inherently teleologically, is always in the middle of a project and, therefore, always in anticipation. We see this clearly, when we remember pleasant hours of friendly dealing with a person, only to learn later that his friendship was only a sham and during that time he had already acted in a malevolent way toward us. This knowledge retroactively poisons the memory of the joyful experience. Life does not consist in a series of states lacking transcendence whose emotional value allows itself to be fixed from some neutral watch tower and as such summed up. Rather, it is a continuous process of integration of the past and future in a present which is constantly renewing itself, and it is this present which decides the meaningfulness of the past and future.

Now this insight was not hidden from Epicurus. On the contrary, he was the first who formulated it and oriented his life according to it. Nonetheless, he also misinterpreted it as a kind of solipsism of the present moment. For him, remembrance of the past and expectation of the future as moments in present experience were not states which contributed to the truth, but states which contributed to pleasure and as such were to be correspondingly manipulated. Even the metaphysics of Epicurus is worked out from the standpoint of insuring humans undisturbed enjoyment of the present without transcendence by freeing them from fear and hope. The transcendence of present pleasure is appearance, and this appearance will be destroyed by the wise. In this way Epicurus is the father of a reflective naturalism. It is not an accident that his theory of a teleology of *physis*, which is inverted in that it is capable only of heading for its own state of satisfaction, was verified by observing animals and infants, beings for whom that which is encountered is not yet distinguished from its own experience of encountering. Nonetheless, animals and infants are at the mercy of their encounters, while hedonistic wisdom has taught people to direct these encounters according to the principles of maximizing pleasure and minimizing pain.

Hedonistic reflection attempts to revoke the self-transcendence of a time-bound being who brings forth itself. Only the conscious present has reality. But a vector-like character, a directional sense belongs to the phenomena of lived present. The present is not a static moment for which the past and future are symmetrical "ecstasies." We can, on the one hand, think of the present as "constant now," through which the stream of events flows, which therefore has a continuously changing content. On the other hand, we can understand the present as defined through its content and therefore passing away with it, that is, becoming "past." In the final analysis the present is not raised above time or its origin; rather, it is itself a dimension of time and defined by a sense of direction. It was the future of the past and will be the past of the future. It constantly integrates anew the whole of that which has gone by into the "past," but through the coming of the next moment it itself becomes an element of bygone time, which will be integrated into a new present. This is the view of common sense. We experience ourselves in everyday consciousness swimming in "the stream of time." And it makes a huge difference to the way we feel in the present whether time is heading toward or away from our well-being. The emotional value of a moment of life does not add up to a "sum of happiness" without some consideration of the direction in which it is heading, just as we do not judge the moral quality of a life without reckoning whether a person developed into a better or worse person. In distinction to Bentham, Epicurus saw clearly that the turning out well of life in its hedonistic meaning cannot come down to a neutral calculus, from which the states of a life are added up. Epicurus' solution consisted in his art of raising the present moment to an "constant now" and in depriving it, considered as the integration of all time dimensions, of time. It is enough to so master memory and anticipation that they are only moments of a plea-sure-function in a present experience without any transcendence.

It is noteworthy how close the hedonistic understanding of time comes to the mystical. Time is insignificant in mystical experience. In its radical tran-scendence of all finite states the subject enters into the space of a *nunc stans*, in the face of which all temporality becomes an unreal appearance. In this experience the finite subject transcends his finiteness in such a way that the question about the turning out well of one's life disappears because the expe-rience allows it to become unimportant. To be absolutely closed up in the finitude of momentary self-enjoyment stands in a paradoxical analogy to the absolute transcendence of mystical experience and to the maxim of the way to be oriented in this experience: "One of the most important rules of the spiritual life is to place oneself in the present moment without looking out from it" (Fénelon, *Oeuvres complètes*, VIII, 511). But the hedonistic ap-proach ends up in contradiction by being closed up in the present moment. The *nunc stans* of the mystic is such that it encompasses the whole of life and time. However, the *nunc stans* of hedonism, the pleasure of the moment, can be cut off from any thought of an earlier or a later moment only at the price of unconsciousness. Unconsciousness would not be compatible with any feel-ing of well-being with which Epicurus was concerned. Certainly, the ecstasy of passion knows no earlier or later. However, this not-knowing is for hu-mans a not-wanting-to-know, a conscious and intentional forgetting. It al-ways contains an element of self-deception. Epicurists do not get outside themselves, since then they would give up the guarantee of a positive bal-ance of pleasure and expose themselves to all the dangers of disappointment. Their calculus heads in an opposite, an ascetical, direction. The lower the ho-rizon of expectation, the more likely its fulfillment; the fewer the needs, the easier their being met. Painless contentment is finally the only thing that counts. Ultimately, even being free of pain can be renounced. Remembrance of earlier joys is enlisted as a help. Holding firm to the thought of *eudaimonia* becomes a compensation for the thing itself. The Christian mar-tyrs – for example, Lawrence on the grill – found consolation in the intensity of the hope for the real happiness of the approaching unity with God. Wise epicurists should be able to endure the same. For them, though, the past and future are merely symmetrical dimensions of the present. They find consola-tion in the remembrance of bygone joys, that is, in mere thoughts, in the ab-straction of pleasure which reduces itself to the functionality of its pure concept without transcendence. And so Epicurus bequeaths to us words worth thinking about: "The wise person will be happy even when he is tor-tured. Nevertheless he will also moan and groan," and "When the wise man is roasted in the steer of Phalaris, he will call out: it is pleasurable and does not concern me" (Fragment 601). A hedonism that is consistently thought through cancels itself out.

3. This self-canceling becomes even more evident when it concerns not the "vectorial" present of time-bound being, but the self-transcendence of humans toward that which is not themselves, toward other things and people, toward reality. Every deep human joy has an intentional content, as Max Scheler has made convincingly clear. Modern psychology has understood feelings as mere subjective states, which are caused by outer influences, but without these "causes" entering in a qualitative way into the definition of the determined joys. In the seventeenth century it was only the great Arnauld who said that the objects of joy conduct themselves toward the joy not as *causa efficiens*, but as *causa formalis*. They are not the "causes," they are the "content," of joy (Dissertation sur le prétendu bonheur des plaisirs des sens, *Oeuvres* X, 62). The ancients knew this well. As an example of a pleasure which is only the pleasure itself, and is only a feeling caused from without and not transcendental joy from outside, Socrates named the enjoyment of that which itches and scratches the itch. Only pure physical pleasure of an undifferentiated kind – not even experiences of taste – are non-intentional, having only causes and no contents.

Our language distinguishes elementary and higher forms of well-being and indisposition. For the one it distinguishes "pleasure," "enjoyment," "contentment," "joy," and "happiness," and for the other "discomfort," "dissatisfaction," "pain," "discontent," "worry," "sadness," and "despair." The higher forms of well-being can be suffocated by very intensive corporal pain and temporarily made impossible. When they are, however, in some way present, then according to their nature they are dominating and determining in a decisive way the overall condition of our being. The enjoyment of a countryside, of music, of the presence of the beloved, the joy of one's own existence or the joy of God's existence can be made to disappear by serious physical discomfort. The joy itself does not as a rule make physical discomfort disappear. When, however, the two co-exist, then it is always the more spiritual, the intentional feeling, that is, the joy which sets the tone and positively disposes our being. Corporal pleasure and superficial enjoyment, on the other hand, can go very well with a deep disgust with life. There is, incidentally, a peculiar feeling which neither has an intentional content in its precise meaning, nor can it be described as plain local discomfort – the feeling of boredom. Here feeling makes the absence of a content which engages and challenges the person to self-transcendence noticeable as discomfort. A fulfilled intentionality is inseparable from human happiness.

Epicurus noticed a fact which was extremely disadvantageous for his theory. As a man of the ancient world, he could not think of any life which really turned out well without the joy of friendship. He knew that one of the deepest, most indispensable, most reliable conditions of one's well-being consists in having friends. And he also knew that one cannot have good friends unless one is oneself a good friend. True friendship cannot prosper when the one views the other only as a means of one's own enjoyment and is prepared at anytime to let the other fall, when the costs of the friendship become higher than the profit, that is, the enjoyment which we derive from it. The full enjoyment of friendship only comes to the one who is not fixated on the enjoyment. And Epicurus draws out the consequences without reservation. The saying that giving is more blessed than receiving, which we know from the Gospel, is found also in Epicurus. One could understand it in such a way that one must, in order to enjoy life, engage oneself to a certain degree, but always in such a way that the costs-benefits balance. Epicurus goes farther: "Under certain circumstances the wise one will also die for the friend." For, only under this condition is the friendship authentic. And only when it is authentic do we have from it what one can have from friendship, its full "enjoyment." The wise one chooses, according to Epicurus, the way of living which holds the greatest enjoyment. The dialectic of hedonism, its self-negation, cannot be more clearly articulated. The saying, "The one who keeps his life will lose it" is valid for every *selfish system.* With regards to practical philosophy one could use a variation of the famous words of Jacobi about the thing-in-itself of Kant's philosophy: One does not enter into practical philosophy without reflection on one's own happiness, and with this reflection one goes no farther.

Chapter 4
Self-Preservation

I

THE RESULT of our reflections thus far can be summarized in the following way: We cannot define life's turning out well as a whole made up of subjective pleasures which are extensively and intensively maximized. That would mean constructing something like an objectively conceived whole out of atomic subjective states. Still, the concept of a happy life is, in fact, thought of as something both subjective and objective. Apparently though it is inappropriately conceived of as something objectively stringed together from a series of subjective states. This is so because, either the integration of the many states of life occurs in some yet further atomistic state, which fits into the series, and then the "whole of life" is only a thought or a feeling of the whole of life and this feeling is itself only one individual moment of life. Or we are thinking about the moments being brought into a whole by an external observer, but then these moments of life remain completely indifferent to their integration. Life is a whole only for the observer and not for itself. The old Greek proverb says: "Count no man happy before he is dead." This is spoken from the standpoint of the observer. One must have the life as a whole before one's eyes in order to be able to judge it. But only those who survive its passing, that is, only others, have it before their eyes as a whole. Hedonism represents the other extreme. For the consistent hedonist there are only enjoyable moments without before or after. Life cannot turn out well; only monad-like units of experience can be happy or unhappy. A thought experiment can make clear that this hedonistic "reductionism" is not the fulfillment which we really want. Imagine someone lying unconscious on an operating table with wires inserted into the brain. Through these wires a mild electrical current is applied which induces a state of mild euphoria. We are assured that the state of euphoria will last until someone turns off the machine and thereby terminates the life of the patient. This example can clarify two things. First, when it comes to this kind of life, length has no importance. The state of subjective well-being would not be influenced, positively or negatively, by length. The patient would know nothing about the end which approaches, and so it does not exist. In each moment the patient is as euphoric as in all the others. Epicurus was completely consistent when he wrote that death did not exist because he meant that "as long as I live, I am not dead, and when I am dead, there is no me anymore," that is, no more person for whom death would be a reality. Death has no reality, only the thought of it. Since the imaginary patient does not have this thought, there is no death for him but then there is also nothing like a wholeness to life. What becomes especially clear in this thought experiment is primarily the following: Although this patient feels subjectively perfectly well, none of us would want to change places with him. We would rather have our average lives, with their mixture of comfort and discomfort, lives then which have to do with reality, with the satisfaction of real needs, with the realization of real goals, with the meeting of real people, above all with the experience of reality, be this friendly or resistant. If we – following a suggestion by Hare – were to call "happy" the state of those with whom we would be prepared to change places, then apparently this euphoric patient is not happy. It seems that the unity of life which we presume by the concept of "the turning out well of life" is not adequately comprehended, if we describe it as a consequence of a subjective state of pleasure, of well-being, or of contentment. There is no turning out well of life if the price is the loss of reality. And what reality is cannot be defined from an inner perspective which withdraws itself from all reality. The purely inner perspective, which cannot mediate itself with its own outer view, is the opposite of what it itself experiences. We have already made this clear by the example of an anticipation which we later only reluctantly remember, when the anticipation has proved itself illusionary. It is precisely insofar as a state is something purely subjective that it is something purely objective when viewed from the outside – that is, something which we do not understand, but can explain only causally, something which we cannot jointly experience with the one who has it, even though we can manipulate it psychologically or chemically. The intentional experience, the experience of reality, the fulfillment of life of another cannot be "made," but mere subjective non-intentional pleasure states can be produced technically or chemically in others. We – the observers – experience the ones who find themselves in such a state as mere objects of external determinations and observations, without their being able to mediate their views, which they offer from without, with their inner view; and without being able to integrate this inner view into their "view of their selves."

This already hints at the fact that the happiness of life has to have something to do with an overcoming of the distinction between inner and outer, between being-for-one's-self and being-in-one's-self. One way of overcoming this distinction is naturalism, but it remains within the framework of hedonism, which we already sketched out above, in that it interprets all tendencies in human life as non-intentional states. Naturalism though does interpret these states as "objective" and from the outside. It interprets subjective states of desire, of pain or of well-being, as functions of an objective context of preservation. Although naturalism can never penetrate to the interior of experience, it can interpret this interior in its invincible subjectivity as that which is unessential, as that which has its truth only in its objective-functional meaning which we give it. Even though we experience hunger as discomfort, we do not congratulate those with chronic loss of appetite on account of their lack of need; rather, we worry about them. Why? We interpret hunger – as well as the enjoyment of eating – as a subjective signal of an objective need, the need for self-preservation. In the same way, we know that the sexual urge and the pleasure from its being satisfied function for preserving the species. Pleasure and pain can, in fact, be separated to a certain extent from their objective "natural" functions. Pain continues even when its function has long been fulfilled and no possibility of saving the life exists. The sexual urge also continues. On top of these there are artificial needs, like drug addiction, which destroy life. The pleasure and pain of a natural being can be used as a means to make this being docile to the purposes of another who is in a position to enforce his wishes with the help of rewards and punishments or threats and promises. One of the central teachings of ancient philosophy on the proper life is the teaching concerning the conscious and practiced connection of a desire for pleasure with its natural function in the service of the "beneficial." The primary point of Plato's critique of sophistry and rhetoric is that these arts concern themselves with fostering a proficiency at producing pleasure without producing the "good," that is, without the benefits of which pleasure is naturally a subjective form of appearance.

But then what does "beneficial" mean, if it does not mean "pleasurable"? The immediate answer is: Beneficial is that which promotes preservation. The horizon within which our goals of action relativize themselves and through which they become commensurable with each other determines itself from the viewpoint of preservation. Of course, Plato himself did not reduce the good to that which is expedient to the preservation of life, and Aristotle explicitly distinguished between that which is expedient to living and that which is expedient to living well. At a critical juncture in the dialogue *Gorgias* 512d)? Indeed, almost all of Plato's examples for the beneficial boil down to showing it as that which preserves. However, it is that which preserves, primarily because it is good, and not good because it preserves. The strict functionalizing of pleasure and pain in the service of self-preservation was much more the thought of the great philosophical school which for centuries competed with Epicureanism, the Stoics. It was solely from the principle of self-preservation that the Stoics acquired the content of their idea of a life directed by nature. That which preserves is good and that which destroys or is parasitic is bad.

II

In the same way that Epicurus pursued hedonism until it canceled itself out, so the Stoics pursued the principle of self-preservation. Accordingly we wish to look at this principle first, not in its radical version, but in the form it is usually presented, the naturalistic form. It is, of course, a question whether it is meaningful or not to draw a connection between the principle in this form and the thinking on a life which turns out well. This would mean that it would not be subjective states which make a life into one that turns out well. Rather, it is the self-assertion of life which becomes identical with its turning out well, and states of well-being or unease are only reflections of successful or unsuccessful self-assertion. Accordingly, the concept of self-assertion does not actually give meaning to the concept of a happy life; it replaces it. This apparent equivalence is suggestive of something. Looked at from the viewpoint of its preservation, rather than from a hedonistic standpoint, life can become for us something like a whole. This viewpoint once again allows for the derivation of striving for pleasure from a unified principle. Self-assertion has a similar theoretical advantage over hedonism in that it can formulate the unified principle as purpose, in relation to which "correct" actions appear as rational means, so that their correctness can be deductively ascertained. Doesn't this thinking correspond to our intuition? We try to avoid pain. But we also realize that pain functions as a biological signal. What it indicates is some danger to self-preservation. As a rule we struggle against pain precisely by interpreting it in terms of its function: We try to get rid of the impairments of our organism to the capacity to live, i.e., the cause of the pain. No one thinks about taking a drug that would permanently re-move their capacity to experience pain. We realize that we would not survive long in that state. So it does not appear that being free of pain, as Epicurus contended, is goal of life; rather, the goal is that state in which the signal of pain is not necessary, that is, the state of being healthy. Artificially induced painlessness is sought after in only two cases: first, when we cannot figure out the causes of the pain, then, although we assume self-preservation to be the purpose of the pain, we correct nature which is not successful in shutting off the signal at the moment that it loses its function. Second, in cases in which we provide possibilities for medical treatment which are not provided for in the state of nature and are so painful that we have to temporarily turn off the pain center. But here we are dealing with measures to save the organism. We turn the signal off because we understand its message or because we know it anyway.

The logical consequence of a hedonism so understood as we have explained it above is the assignment of the role of the central principle of action, which endows unity, to self-preservation. When we disregard the intentional structure of our feelings and understand our striving merely as striving after subjective pleasure states, then the question of its "objective" function inevitably arises. In this way self-preservation can be conceived only as that which already is. The reduction of all intentionality, of all going out of the self, to states of the organism is that which defines the naturalistic option. An interpretation that allows that a natural being could be concerned with something other than itself, and that, accordingly, an action could have in the last analysis some other function besides stabilizing the subject of this action – the organism or the population – would burst the basic methodological approach which is dictated by the naturalistic option.

Following this option entails the dropping a distinction which Aristotle had introduced into philosophy and which corresponds to a distinction which we make constantly in daily life. Aristotle distinguishes for all higher forms of life between the tendency to live and a tendency to live well. In line with Plato he writes that nations came into being out of the need to survive, but that they continue to exist for the sake of living well (*Politics* 1252b). Practical philosophy – political philosophy and ethics – does not deal with the mechanisms of development and preservation, but rather with that which constitutes the content of the well-lived life. But the well-lived life consists in a manifold *praxis*, whose inner unity is not derivable from some principle or from some ultimate end. Aristotle does indeed speak of an ultimate end, namely *eudaimonia*, happiness of life, but this happiness – as we have already seen – is not related to the particular conditions of actions and states like an end to the means. As a unity of rational self-realization it is inseparable from the actualization of particular potentialities which are grounded in our nature. The whole of this life constantly strives after preserving itself, but its inner form cannot be defined as a function of its self-preservation; the well-lived life cannot be reduced to bare living. Modern philosophy begins with what I have, in another place, called "the inversion of teleology." The distinction between living and living well gets flattened out. The content of the well-lived life becomes nothing other than the functions of self-preservation. The former is derived and presented as identical with such functions. Thomas Hobbes taught that there could be no such thing as a "highest good." There is only infinite progression "from desire to desire." Of course, nothing like a unity in human life comes from that. Instead this unity originated for Hobbes only in the fear of death. And so from this fear of death also comes "natural law" and the laws of ethics. They are nothing other than the commandments of self-preservation. Peaceableness is the highest of these commandments. The second is the unconditional submission to the conditions of preservation, especially under the power of the state which holds violent death in check by monopolizing the power. Once a state exists, then ethics ultimately exhausts itself in obedience to the state laws.

Aimless progress from desire to desire, perpetual expansion of options without one standard being set by reality itself, by the idea of a life which turns out well, would be for the Aristotelian tradition the conceptual contrary to the well-lived life and would not appear as its fulfillment. The standard, as something interiorly grasped, posits boundaries and thereby allows for the first time anything like meaning. The Greek word *telos* has the double meaning: boundary and goal. With the presuppositions of the anti-teleological option, it falls apart into subjective goal and objective boundaries. Simply because the subjective goal, obtaining pleasure, can be grasped biologically as a function of self-preservation does not mean that the individual subject of the drives in his pleasure-seeking has to make this "goal" his own. A consistent naturalistic view should no longer define self-preservation as a *telos*. Nietzsche was the first who ferreted out of the modern anti-teleology a teleological remainder: "Be careful of superfluous teleological principles, the drive for self-preservation is one such" (*Jenseits von Gut und Böse,* SW XV, 20). And then Freud explicitly distinguished submission to the conditions of preservation as "reality principle" from the "pleasure principle." According to him the original natural make-up of humans is a diffuse form of pleasure seeking, the libido. Children quickly run into a resistant reality, which does not comply with this seeking. They must conform themselves to this reality, submitting to its conditions in order to survive, in order to be able to at least partially satisfy their libido. Reality is not thought of here as the sole element in which the needs and strivings of a rational being are satisfied. It is understood as boundaries which we accept on the possibilities for our satisfaction. One could say that a human is a handicapped hedonist and narcissist. Human culture originates only in this handicap, and so is inimical to happiness.

The tension between pleasure and self-preservation is a product of the decay of a teleological view of *eudaimonia*, in which the concepts of goal and boundary mean the same thing. The dualism between the pleasure principle and the reality principle results of course only from the inner perspective of subjectivity. The unity of libido and the instinct of self-preservation is thought of on this level as a unity of compromise, a compromise, which is to be accomplished by the subject. Aristotle consistently thought of this unity as thoroughly "metaphysical." Far from reducing all intentionality to mental states and then suggesting that all mental states are a function of self-preservation, he interpreted the instinct for self-preservation of all finite beings intentionally, that is, insofar as the being's respective nature allowed, as a striving after "participation" in the lasting being, that is, in the divine (*De anima* II, 4). The monism of modern science reverses this relationship. The idea of the divine itself is nothing other than a fiction which helps the self-preservation of the human species. Present-day systems theory and the theory of evolution of the present day have worked out this new monism to its ultimate consequence. The systems theory understands all power systems as functions of self-maintenance in a environment from which the system differentiates itself. The inner differentiation of the functions of the system is also an achievement of adaptation in the service of system maintenance. Organisms are such systems, but psychic structures or social constellations can be interpreted in a systems theory fashion. Interpreting the human in terms of a systems theory has, however, the same implications as interpreting the human in terms of the function of preservation. Biological evolutionary theory has worked from the beginning with such a schema. It no longer proceeds from something like a drive for preservation as its ultimate given. This drive – as well as the drive for self-preservation and species preservation – is understood as the result of random mutations and selections. From those things which happen to come to be, a few, namely those who are most fit, prevail. Therefore, complex forms, the preservation-function structures, develop something like characteristics of a system, and then they are, in fact, more stable than other complex forms. The co-existence of three pebbles, a lily of the valley, and a beer bottle one by the other is not in this sense a system, so long as no specific structures emerge which are suitable for stabilizing precisely this arrangement. If in the course of evolution certain schemes of action have been developed, if moral ideas or religion have been developed, evidently this is because of the functional advantage for communal preservation offered to those who possess such schemes and ideas. That which gives to the living a scientifically replicable identity and also gives our action something like an inner unity which penetrates the diversity of our desires is the preservation-function of the partial structures and the individual actions directed toward more complex structures.

This is not the place to ask to what extent the theory of evolution is capable of explaining the way of being of the basic types of living creatures as a function of survival strategy and to what extent it is capable of reconstructing that which we understand as knowledge. The question to be discussed is whether any inversion of teleology, especially the system-functionalism which is oriented by the basic idea of self-preservation, is capable of interpreting adequately the thought of a happy life which orients action.

To ask this question is to answer it. Naturalism is as little able to answer questions of orientation in its system-theoretical form as it is in any other form. A being which is capable of reflection is either through no fault of its own – "by nature" – compelled to certain ways of behavior, or it is capable of determining itself according to reasons. If the latter is ever the case, naturalism cannot give this being such reasons. The fact that certain ways of acting have consequences for the preservation of the self or of the species, says something for these ways of acting only if we want preservation. Naturalism concretizes in a theoretical manner the drive for preservation of the self and of the species as a contingent product of evolution. We could reflect upon it and free ourselves from it. And indeed, in those areas where we do not feel ourselves up to that, we could, far from seeing it as an ethical norm, complain about our being chained to it as dependency on a drive. We could curse the being along with the drive toward its preservation. The preservation drive of others, which they have in common with all living beings, is of itself no reason to preserve their being. There is no reason to take these naturalistic and subjective interests as one's own, when naturalism functionally reduces all experience of meaning, which overcomes contingency, to the preservation of contingent forms of life whose being is better than their not-being only for themselves. Since this interest is only a function of the existence of a living system, it cannot ground this existence for a reflective being. When every value is only a function of preservation, then the value character of appreciating disappears along with the subject of value appreciation. It is an arbitrary affair whether the continued existence of humanity and of the other living things on earth play a role or not in the motivation of action. To this extent naturalism and existential nihilism imply each other.

III

Stoicism, which first used the functions of preservation as material principles for the constructing of ethics, was aware of the non-naturalistic character of such an ethics. In fact, there is no such thing as a drive for preservation as an observable fact. That hunger, thirst, and sexual urges are functions of either self-preservation or preservation of the species is an interpretation of observations. The capacity for such interpretations first opens the choice between the acceptance of these functions or their conscious elimination. It is precisely the obscurity of the functions, their latency, which guarantees their fulfillment independent of human willing. To overcome this latency means to place their function at our disposal. When the Stoics taught to take on the functions of preservation in freedom, they did so because then the Logos, the meaning of the whole world, cooperates with this functionality. For a rational being, a being who itself partakes in the Logos, the single meaningful choice is to adapt itself to the Logos. Such a being is no longer caught up in drives. It is not "caught up" in life; rather, it affirms in freedom each world-law by which the nature of the living being is constituted through a specific preservation function.

There is then no such thing as an abstract preservation of being. Preservation is always preservation in a determined identity. This identity is the result of a biographical or historical process. The Stoics spoke of the *oikeiosis* as the process in which the human successively appropriated the world, first by appropriating one's own body, then by appropriating the surroundings which "belong" to us. Preservation means the preservation of that which essentially belongs to us, that which makes up our identity. What, however, makes up the identity of a rational being? The answer from the Stoics is: the universe. The human *oikeiosis* has no natural boundaries. As a thinking being, the human thinks the whole. The preservation of a being who thinks the whole and identifies itself with the whole is always guaranteed, since the whole does not perish. The individual perishes, but the order of the whole maintains itself in the individual's destruction. This does not mean that the rational person, the "wise," has no interest in self-preservation as a natural individual. On the contrary, it is only as a part of the order of the whole that the individual acts "correctly" when it does what by nature is conducive to his preservation. But as a rational being the individual does this with the distance of actors in a drama who give a consummate performance in their role. They fight for their lives; they die. But the for-the-sake-of-which is the same in both cases: the play in which they have their role. This identification with the whole is called wisdom. No life can turn out well except that of the wise. Whether there has ever actually been a wise person is not for the Stoic to decide. What the Stoic knows is this: If there has never been a wise person, then there has never been a human life which turned out well. The identification with the divine whole means the expansion of the *oikeiosis*, of the appropriation, of the making-oneself-familiar, beyond all boundaries, since reason is by its nature universal. This universal *oikeiosis* has a two-fold form in its practice. For action it means that agents make their own the teleological meaning-intention of nature. For this they have to have freed themselves from the immediateness of the natural drives, the passions. They conduct themselves toward their own nature and to the situations presented to them by fate like good actors toward their roles. In order to perform them well, they must identify themselves with the goal, but they should not confuse this with the immediateness of life. And that means that they experience the frustrations and the defeats which their role specifies, not actually as defeats, but rather that they affirm them as a part of the play in which they perform. Thus wrote Seneca in his letter to Lucullus: "For the good person there is no unhappiness outside of the fact that he considers much that exists in the world to be his unhappiness" (ep. 96). The good person's struggle for justice is exactly so specified by the circumstances of the play as is the acceptance of defeat in the struggle. What the wise attains is perfect self-sufficiency, successful self-assertion. Perfectly successful self-assertion is that of a rational being when nothing more can clash against his will and nothing can go against the will of the one who has willingly accepted in principle everything which occurs. No one has more consistently thought through this position than Spinoza. "The striving for self-preservation is the essence of things" – so goes the central axiom of this ethics (Cf. *Ethica* III, Prop. VII). And the end of this ethics is the *amor Dei intellectualis*, the identification which thinks with the whole of reality, which means with that which purely and simply preserves itself.

In this way the conception of the turning out well of life, understood as successful self-assertion, ends in a position in which individuals offer up their finiteness, in order to unconditionally identify themselves with that which occurs regardless. The Stoics even taught suicide as the final escape for those for whom a rational, and therefore self-sufficient, life is not possible due to internal or external reasons. Voluntarily making one's exit from the stage, when one can no longer contribute to the success of the play, is the ultimate form of self-expression. Just like Epicurus, who started from the thesis that the only thing that matters is physical pleasure, and yet ended up with the conclusion that all striving is to be restricted to striving after freedom from spiritual discomfort and that the sacrifice of one's life for one's friends is to be viewed as a form of life which turns out well; so the Stoics began with the thesis that self-preservation is the primary concern of all natural beings and ended by teaching the disinterested fulfillment of our duties and the identification with that which cannot be changed as the highest form of a life which turns out well, indeed, as its only form. We have here an analogous dialectic, an analogous self-reversal of the self-preservation ethics, as with Epicurus and the self-reversal of hedonism. The fact that modern naturalistic ethics does not end up in such a dialectical reversal is due only to its lack of consciousness. It has methodologically pretended that it is possible to understand the question concerning the happiness of life and even concerning proper action. Over against this the stoical teaching on life has become the most deeply influential ethic of the European tradition. Striving after pleasure and striving after self-preservation were not for Epicurus or for the Stoics simple naturalistic data, as they were for the French materialists of the eighteenth and for the evolutionary biologists of the twentieth century; rather, they were aspects for reflection through which life is grasped as a whole which can turn out well or badly. In both cases the turning out well is linked with the fact that humans must gain some distance from themselves, that we come to ourselves in an indirect relationship. *Apathia* and *ataraxia*, indifference and imperturbableness, are concepts with which these schools of thought define this indirect relationship.

Chapter 5

The Aristotelian Compromise

I

PLEASURE AND SELF-PRESERVATION are concepts derived from reflection, the results of a *intentio obliqua*, which take the place of the *intentio recta* of living our lives. They formalize the thoughts concerning a life which turns out well and abstract from the contents which give us joy and make our living worthwhile. Examples of other such concepts are health, freedom, and peace. They do not characterize so much the positive contents of a life, as reflect the absence of certain kinds of impairments. The concept of pleasure is capable of indicating a certain "experience," but the experience is valid only for purely physical states of pleasure. Every higher kind of joy is intentional, a joy "in something." It is determined by its content, and it is only through abstraction from this content that it is thematized.

Of course, the possibility of this kind of abstraction is essential to human beings. To be able to reflectively distance oneself from every determined finite content and to be able to relate to the whole of the "good" is constitutive of human freedom. But this is just one side of freedom. There is a lack of freedom when someone so loses himself in a certain endeavor that it becomes an absolute. This is exactly what takes place when the endeavor becomes divorced from all other considerations, and the agent is prepared to pay any price for it. "There is nothing in the world for which I would be prepared to pay any price"; this sentence from *Cancer Ward* by Alexander Solzhenitsyn expresses an essential condition for the life which turns out well. Later we will have to discuss the fact that there are certain prices which are always immoral to pay, certain means which cannot be justified by any end, since these prices and means are in principle incompatible with the life which turns out well. Here we speak of finite contents, which humans cannot unconditionally want without finding themselves involved in an existential lie. The lie consists either in the ideological equation of such contents with the transcendental idea of a life which turns out well or in the passion which feigns an instinctual "could-not-do-otherwise." Kant suggested once imagining that a guillotine is set up on the spot where the sought-after satisfaction of a passion is to take place and that this guillotine awaits the one who feigns that he "could-not-do-otherwise." The fiction would be immediately be exposed as a lie.

But the incapacity for passion, for unbroken *intentio recta*, also makes for unfreedom. It is the unfreedom born of the fact that the force of any reflection lies in its abstracting from the contents of the good life and letting them exist in the deadened form of mere means for a good end, an end which always remains external to the content. In thought the life which turns out well appears to become a utopia somewhere between self-dissipation and self-preservation. Eichendorff presents these two ways of foundering in his poem *Two Companions*: a withdrawal into the comfortable middle-class world which does not allow itself to be moved and "peers out on the fields comfortably from its homey parlor," or the sinking into the "colored sounding mouth" by the one who allow himself to be grasped by the Sirens. There appears to be no escape from these alternatives of earthly failure, for the poem ends: "And when I see these two reckless companions, the tears well up in my eyes – Oh God, tenderly lead us to yourself."

The conception of *eudaimonia* which ends in contradiction has been captured in the words of Pascal: *"Le bonheur est ni dans nous ni hors de nous, il est en Dieu, et hors et dans nous"* (*Pensée*, ed. Brunschvicg, nr. 465.). [Happiness is neither in us or outside of us, it is in God, both outside and in us.] To so radically render the tension in the antinomy of the problem of happiness under the conditions of factual reality is inseparable from the conception of its solution in a life beyond the boundary of death; that is, it is inseparable from religion. There are three alternatives: the renunciation of anything like the thought of a life which turns out well; the replacement of hope in the afterlife with a historical utopia of real change, which should make such turning out well possible; or the reduction of the demand for happiness and the overcoming of the antinomy through compromise.

This last alternative is the way of Aristotle. In this he consciously disassociates himself from Plato. In the idea of the good Plato had thought of an unconditioned and the sharing in this could alone be called the life which turns out well.

In this sharing, however, humans are not lords of themselves. It is a type of ecstasy, a kind of Eros. Not in the sense of an irrational submersion, a going out of oneself, as in poetic intuition; rather, it is an ecstasy of reason itself, which touches in the Good that which is not itself, since the ultimate that-for-the-sake-of-which of all reality is not reason itself but is that which reason can grasp as its ground and highest possibility. The turning out well of life means allowing oneself to be grasped by this highest possibility, this allowing-oneself-to-be-grasped is called philosophy.

Besides philosophy a life can only turn out relatively well. This comes about when humans bring forth in their lives objective good through their own particular doings, that is, through their arts. They will be able to do this only when they live under the leadership of philosophers. In a poorly, and that means unphilosophically, organized society the life of the majority cannot turn out well. "There is no proper life in falsehood" (Adorno). The turning out well of the philosophical life, and it alone, is independent of social and political conditions, since a conscious sharing in the Good is also independent of them.

II

Aristotle did not want to give up the Platonic thought on philosophical happiness. Still against Plato he objected that "the Good," "the One," and "the Absolute" do not comprise criteria by which the turning out well of a specifically human life could orient itself. Aristotle rejected the conception of the turning out well of life which consisted in humans allowing themselves to be grasped by something which they were not, namely, the absolute, and in this realize their highest possibility. Accordingly in the *Nicomachean Ethics* he outlines a hermeneutic of turning-out-well, which orients itself on normality, on the *conditio humana* and partakes of its ambiguity. This is apparent in his handling of the question concerning what role the "pleasure" of subjective well-being plays in *eudaimonia*. The question is: Is happiness the same as the experience of happiness, or is happiness an "objective" turning out well which, in fact, is only assessable from the outside? This question is related to the further question: Is happiness a state or an activity? And when an activity: Is it the attainment of a goal after which one has striven, or is it the correct action itself regardless of whether the goal is attained or not? But then how will the correctness of the action be judged, if not by whether that which is wished for is attained or not? And finally: Can one say of something other than the whole of life that it has turned out well? When yes, then it could only be judged objectively, which, however, does not accord well with our intuitive understanding of the turning out well of life. Aristotle's answer to these paradoxes consisted in distinguishing – the only ancient philosopher to do so – two types of *eudaimonia*. The one is human in the proper sense of the word; it stays within the realm of middle-class normality and is based on compromise. The other is radical in the sense of the Platonic ecstasy of reason, and it would be perfect if it were to leave behind the *conditio humana* and were never to be overtaken by it again. It can be called absolute and perfect insofar as it is a rational partaking in the absolute and the perfect. But this partaking remains itself conditioned and imperfect as a mere part of the whole of life.

In Aristotle's understanding human nature is characterized by a deep ambiguity. This is grounded in the double role that reason plays in human life. On the one hand, reason is the organ for the mastering of life, the organ which orients and structures our praxis. On the other hand, reason is the disclosure of a dimension of truth, of goodness, of holiness, and of the absolute, that is, the disclosure of a dimension which would disappear, if one understood reason as having merely a practical function in the service of the preservation of the species. This disclosure of such a dimension of the absolute, of the divine, by reason causes Aristotle to say that reason is not actually a part of the human soul, but comes "from the outside in" (*De gen. anim.* 736b).

Normal, in its proper meaning, human happiness, is the leading of a life which turns out well. In this kind of life reason does not serve merely as a means to goals, which themselves are not subject to reasonable judgment. On the contrary, for Aristotle, the turning out well of life is possible only when that life is oriented by reason. But what does that mean? Whence does such a life takes its standard? How does it obtain that inner unity and wholeness which is inseparably connected with the idea of its turning out well? Aristotle's answer is comprehensible only when one considers that for him ethics is a part of political philosophy. The life of the individual is not in itself, as it was for Epicurus and the Stoics, a perfect whole; rather, it is a part of a whole, and the individual is a part of the polis. Only the polis is a self-sufficient whole, and only within a certain relationship to it can one speak of a life which is correct and turning out well. Only in this relationship are the initial contradictions of the idea of a life which turns out well brought to a – relative and precarious – reconciliation. This reconciliation concerns the contradiction between, on the one side, a judgment of a life made from a subjective perspective of experience and, on the other side, this same type of judgment made from the perspective of usefulness for others. Citizens of a free polis are living rightly when their lives are useful for their fellow citizens, for the preservation and welfare of the polis. But this usefulness is not that of slaves, whose activities are related to the well-being of others without, however, these slaves being a part of the whole to whose welfare they contribute. The life of a slave cannot turn out well. The virtue of citizens consists, on the other hand, in the disposition to act rationally. Reason means being open to the communal. Citizens of a free polis so identify themselves with it that this usefulness for the polis means at the same time their own contentment, because the welfare of the polis consists in nothing other than the welfare of its citizens, that is, in the turning out well of the lives of its citizens. For Aristotle the *eudaimonia* of the citizen is the reason why the polis exists. *Philia*, friendship, is the fundamental concept, which forms the core of the political philosophy of Aristotle. But it is characteristic of friendship that the subjective and objective perspectives of one's own life fuse with one another. Since a friend is a part of my life, the way that the friend sees me is itself a part of my own reality. And only in this fusion can lie that happiness which, as Pascal puts it, is "both in us and outside of us."

The polis then remains the presupposition of the solution to the problem posed by hedonism, since only the polis so honors "selfless" action, indeed the sacrifice of one's life, that the noble person is not cheated out of his happiness. What is granted to this person is "honor." Evil, ignoble persons will indeed ask: "What do I get out of honor?" They will not see in honor compensation for missed material gain or missed enjoyment and certainly not any compensation for losing one's life. But this is exactly why their lives cannot turn out well, since the subjective and objective perspectives of life remain antithetical. Honor is a kind of "indemnification" which will be experienced as indemnification only by those whose life has assumed the form of reasonableness that is called "virtuous." For the virtuous the thought of posthumous fame, even though they themselves can no longer enjoy it, gives satisfaction.

For Aristotle the integration of action into the context of the polis makes possible an assertion of self-sufficiency, in spite of the fact that agents relinquish themselves in the sense that the attainment of their goals no longer depends on them and since the long-term consequences of action utterly escape their grasp. Even this relinquishment is valid only if we isolate agents and think of them as placed in an unstructured flow of the world, in which their action entangles itself in an incomprehensible way. Citizens of the polis, as Aristotle thinks of them, are not in this situation. Their action flows into a closed system-context which it stabilizes and makes better. This system, which is comprehensible to the agents and can be wished for by them as such, since this, more than anything else, makes possible the interaction which at the same time reproduces it. This dependency on the whole does not impair the autarky, the self-sufficiency, because what Aristotle said about friendship is also valid for this dependency: "What we can bring about through our friends, we bring about, in a certain sense, through ourselves" (*Nic. Eth.* 1112b25).

Human action is intentional, and this intentionality appears to be destroyed through the self-thematizing of the action. On the other hand, this self-thematizing appears to be unavoidable, if we want in any way to thematize the turning out well of life. This contradiction resolves itself when the object of the intentionality so stands over against agents that they remain in themselves or return to themselves in self-transcendence. And this is exactly what happens in the polis.

The question whether it is the objectively considered wholeness of life that is to be called happy, that is, whether someone is to be called happy only after his death or whether present experience alone can be called happy, is considered in various ways by Aristotle. In these considerations he uncovers the paradoxes that are implicit in the question. The paradox that the only life to be praised as happy is the one of a dead person is actually made more acute by the fact that the fate of the friends and families after the death of the person is still a constituent part of the life which turns out well or poorly. It would – so says Aristotle – express a very unfriendly view if one were to separate someone's fate from the turning out well of his life. Can one say that a king's life turned out well if immediately after his death the policy which he instituted for his country leads to disaster? Or can one only say it, if the news of this can no longer reach him? No. Turning out well does not allow itself to be expressed in categories of an experience, which is indifferent to truth and illusion. Turning out well in its essence has to do with truth, with reality. But by this fact it appears to slip in principle from our disposition. For Aristotle this does not occur on account of the fact of a type of self-possession which he understands by the name of virtue. Virtuous persons are the ones whose lives are not the playthings of chance, but whose present condition places them in a position to anticipate their life-praxis as a whole. Their orientation does not vary according to circumstances, influences, and changing dispositions; rather, it guarantees an appropriate, free, response to the contingencies of life. It is reasonable. Although it is only reason that can ensure autonomy, it is virtue as a habitual disposition, based upon upbringing and practice, which allows those who possess it to rely on themselves as a reasonable agents and to answer properly for themselves to others. Accordingly, the present moment of experience does not become an atomistic state which then has to be integrated into the whole of life. Rather, this whole is much more present in each moment, since the reasonable orientation has become a medium wherein the pure now is already essentially transcended. According to Aristotle the one who acts out of such a habitualized orientation cannot be unhappy. His life cannot turn out badly because it does not subjectively fail and also because it can no longer regress to being a mere function of circumstances. Still, contrary to what the Stoics thought, if the circumstances are too untoward, then such a life cannot be happy. There remains then something to be wished for. The Stoics saw the *conditio humana* simply as the *adiaphora*, as those objectively given facts which materially determine the roles in the game of life but do not determine the players themselves, who can realize perfection in one role as well as in any other. Aristotle does not acknowledge such a distancing of humans from the role of their lives. The means by which he does obtain distance, the rational soul, is also the specifying principle of form which determines humans to be such-and-such as individual natural living beings, and so structures their life-world. Therefore, Aristotle hesitates to call happy the virtuous person who is plagued by misfortune. Certainly, his life can turn out well, but, Aristotle adds, "it cannot be blessed" (*Nic. Eth.* 1101a). In order to be blessed it requires the favor of fate, and we will count even the disposition of the person which inclines him to a greater or lesser blessedness among those contingent circumstances in which this favor shows itself.

Still, it is true that the habitual autonomy of the rational person, that is, virtue itself, insofar as it concerns the individual, is once again contingent. Virtue is acquired by regular, rational action. Virtue is potentiality. It is, however, an Aristotelian axiom that the actual always precedes the potential, so that the habit is acquired only by the action to which it then disposes. Virtue causes only the reliability and ease for such action, since it so conditions the pleasure-pain makeup of the person that it makes one happy to follow one's insight. But how then is such rational action possible before the acquisition of virtue? How is the acquisition of virtue itself possible? The answers runs: only through proper upbringing. This, in turn, according to Aristotle presumes the polis, presumes "good laws." And this does not mean just written laws but the whole order of common life which is realized in morals, customs, and laws. Such a common social practice, instituted over a longer period of time, is the condition for a normal, proper life, a condition which to a certain extent resolves the paradox, insofar as that is possible in the *conditio humana*. It is only the living cultural context which differentiates the multiplicity of human possibilities and allows the individual to grow into these. That is true even at the level of language, which is always historical and concrete, and which must already be spoken for the individual to realize the possibility of being a "speaking being," by growing into a world construed by language.

The happiness of the citizen is normal, human happiness. But it is the polis which founds and makes possible the normality. The standards of rationality are found in it. Interaction is only possible through it, since only in it does the symbolic dimension which grounds all understandings have reality. Which is to say, there are no private languages. Only in the context of the polis is there that normality which suppresses the opposition between self-interest and the common good, by making it generally profitable for the individual to act for the common interests and by sanctioning parasitic behavior. A saying like: "The one who lies once is not to be believed," is only valid in a context of life which is not anonymous. For the one who speaks daily with different people who do not know each other, this proverb has lost its meaning and its interest. The reduction of contingency by virtue, i.e., the habitualization of reasonableness, is made possible and strengthened by the reduction of contingency by normality which is guaranteed by the polis. The ethics of Aristotle is a hermeneutic of this normality and so it lies more in the tradition of the Sophists, the tradition of the "Avant-garde of the normal life" (Thomas Buchheim),[1] than in the tradition which leads from Plato to Epicurus and even to the Stoics for which only the philosophical life, by overcoming the paradoxes of normal living, deserves to be called of a happy life. Thus Aristotle consciously goes against Plato, but he is also conscious of the non-rescindable boundaries of this normality. He is further conscious of the fact that the antinomies contained therein are only suppressed and not settled. And even if he did not say it, nevertheless, he must have known that he already imagined in this normality a "style of life already become old" (Hegel). The small, familiar autonomous polis, which was founded upon the friendship of its citizens, belonged already in the time of Alexander the Great to an idealized past. And if it is true that Aristotle escaped the fate of Socrates by his flight from Athens with the remark that he wanted to protect the Athenians from so sinning again against philosophy, then is it also clear what separates him from Socrates. The problems which occur when the polis loses its power, which comes from its maintenance of normality or when that normality which it maintains is, as Plato was convinced, a false one in principle, these problems are not, according to Aristotle, compensated for by the philosophical life. Rather, according to him, philosophy is concerned with the contemplation of the perennial, and this species included for him the species of living things. Thus, the beneficial for each species could be determined by a study of the nature of the species. This is also valid for humans. Therefore, practical philosophy was entirely normative and not merely descriptive. But what human nature is cannot be discerned from the individual human. Dilthey's saying: "Only their history can show humans what they are" (*Ges. Werke*, VIII, 224) is the modern version of Aristotle's viewpoint that only the polis shows us what human nature is. However, "only the polis" means that not every kind of human society, not tyranny and not that political order which understands itself as a kind of household rather than a legally

---

1   Spaemann is referring here to *Die Sophistik als Avantgarde normalen Lebens*, by Thomas Buchheim (Hamburg: Felix Meiner, 1986).

constituted community of citizens will show us what it is. According to Aristotle's thought the latitude for legitimate constitutions, that is, for those which are compatible with human nature, is enormous. So also can the demand, to treat equals as equals, be fulfilled in a variety of ways, since the parameters of comparison can be diverse. They are not, however, arbitrary, and it is the task of philosophy to bring out this lack of arbitrariness. Still, what philosophy cannot do is present itself as a fully valid, of even better alternative to proper living in the polis. After all, knowing is not doing.

III

Plato had developed an emphatic concept of knowing, according to which knowing should have as its necessary consequences proper praxis. Anytime that the good, the beneficial, appears in a way which makes it impossible for knowers in their practical judgment to evade what is to be done in the here and now, is for him an instance of knowing. Aristotle saw that this appearance of the good does indeed point to principles of actions, but when it comes to "application," that is, to their translation into concrete norms of action, he also saw that these principles lose their compelling character. At that point concrete practical reason and judgment is necessary. At that point *doxa*, the correct conviction, takes the place of evident knowing, and a habitualized disposition is necessary in order to reliably follow this, as Plato too already knew. This disposition is won only by an upbringing within the confines of a moral order, since a weak, poorly raised person, or else someone fixated on a particular goal, can shirk the correct conviction.

To go still deeper: Reflecting on right and wrong remains distinct from doing even in philosophy. In theory, in making present in thought the perennial, humans step out of the natural life context. In this exiting they realize, according to Aristotle, their highest possibility. Wittgenstein wrote: Philosophy arises "when language goes on holiday" (*Philosophical Investigations* #38). For him this was an objection against philosophy. "Going on holiday" is supposed to mean: stepping out of the context for which language is made. For Aristotle this "going on holiday" is the highest form of being human. *Theoria* is a holiday. A holiday is not in the service of the everyday; it is not there simply to replenish energy in order to return refreshed to the everyday world; rather, it uses strength for the best. It does not serve *praxis;*, it is its ultimate and highest possibility. Insofar as reason steps out from the human life context on a holiday in order to make present "what is in truth" (Hegel), it is not human but divine. *Theoria* is self-sufficient, divine activity and thus *eudaimonia*, blessedness in its ultimate meaning. It was, by the way,

Wittgenstein himself who expressed this experience most radically in our century with the words: "The life of knowing is the life which is happy, in spite of the need of the world" (*Schriften* I, 176). The moment that we enter into philosophical contemplation, we enter into the context of a totality which is more comprehensive than that of the life of the individual, more comprehensive than even that of the polis and is removed from all contingency. The fulfillment, which occurs in this moment, is, therefore, the fulfillment of perfect self-sufficiency. Mystics from every historical period have related this as their experience. Spinoza has spoken of *amor Dei intellectualis* and Rousseau from an experience of *sentiment de l'existence*. And even if Aristotle did not view *theoria* as the solution to the problem of happiness and did not equate the turning out well of contemplation with the turning out well of life, that is because philosophical contemplation cannot constitute the whole of human life. "There is something in the soul," so writes Meister Eckhart, "of which it can be said that if the soul were to be it completely, the soul would be God" (*Predigen und Traktate*, ed. J. Quint, 221). Paraphrasing this one could say in Aristotelian fashion: "There is something in human life, of which it could be said that if life consisted only in this, life would be divine." Since life does not consist only in it, human life cannot be divine, it cannot absolutely and without restriction turn out well. Human life as human turns out well only to the degree that it keeps the contingencies of life within boundaries; to the degree that it maintains itself in its freedom in the face of these contingencies and institutionalizes those means which, at their best, are the "ultimate possible" for humans. Nevertheless, the dualistic conception as a whole has the character of compromise between "pure reason" and "practical reason," between reason and living. All the paradoxes of thought of human happiness rest upon this duality, and all visions of perfect happiness upon their resolution.

Chapter 6

The Antinomies of Happiness

I

FROM THE TIME philosophy began, seeing life as a whole, viewing it from the standpoint of its turning out perfectly well, was and continues to be constitutive. But the effort to think of reason's dream of perfect happiness in an adequate concept leads to antinomies similar to those resulting from the efforts of metaphysics to think of something like the whole of reality. Varro's 288 theories of the highest good were already an indication of the problem: The Christian answer was not to add a 289th to these but instead to bring about the Corpernican revolution of eudaimonism: That which we carry about in us as an image of perfect happiness cannot be adequately realized in principle under empirical conditions. It is a thought which transcends every experience. Nevertheless, we cannot stop thinking about it. It is always negatively present in the sense that it relativizes every satisfaction whose duration or content is limited and keeps humans, as distinct from animals, in a chronic state of unrest. Marxist thinkers have tried to see the absence of *eudaimonia* as a consequence of social relations, which are conditioned by shortages and make shortages perennial at the same time that they stand in the way of bringing about the identity of individual and species interests, which is the condition of perfect happiness for every rational being. But this conception errs not only in terms of the possibility of removing shortages from this earth; it not only overestimates the economic factor in the dualism between general and individual interests for a non-instinctual, reflective, and therefore constitutionally boundless being. Before all else, it misunderstands that the discrepancy between the dream of happiness and the possibilities of its realization is, of its very nature, anthropologically fundamental. Both the Aristotelian distinction between *eudaimonia* in itself and "human" *eudaimonia*, and the compromise-like character of the latter shows the ecstatic character of the anticipation of happiness: "No eye has seen, no ear has heard, and no human heart has penetrated, what God has prepared for those who love him" (1Cor. 2.9). At its best the social-critical argument could be so stated: Even this ecstasy is the expression of a reality which does not satisfy. A satisfying reality would reconcile humans with their finitude and not allow them to digress any more into dimensions which are essentially imaginary and lie beyond any possible *conditio humana.*

Of course, this argument must also condemn all art as a surrogate of real fulfillment. But the question is, what could real fulfillment still mean when robbed of its symbolic dimension and of the riches of images? A dream, which leads into a dimension which of its very essence transcended all possible fulfillment in this life, would deserve the full service of this life and even its sacrifice. This even holds for erotic delight, which does not reduce itself to the orgasm; it would not be what it is, if it were not the cause of a vision from whose essentially unrealizability springs all passion, which is inseparable from all great love – the vision of beatitude. And all happiness of love is an experience of this vision.

Before we ask about the reasons for the essentially transcendental character of the idea of an absolute turning out well, let's remind ourselves of the antinomistic conception which this idea unavoidably leads to if we understand it as an empirical concept.

To look at one's own individual life from the standpoint of its turning out well as a whole is characteristic of the experience of a being whose 'reality-space' is limitless. It does not belong therefore to an animal, for whom space is centered on itself, to have this experience. Traveling over the sea one is, day in, day out, optically in the center of a circle of water, which one looks out upon. On the map, however, a small flag is placed daily, which determines the position of the ship on the basis of parameters which are neutral concerning the ship's actual position. By means of our senses we experience ourselves as the center-point of the world. But every experience of knowing teaches us that, seen from other centers of perspective, we are on the edge of the horizon. For the animal the world is an environment. We, on the other hand, know – it is a reality for us – that we ourselves are the environment for other beings. This "eccentric position" (Helmuth Plessner) makes it possible for humans to imagine their lives as a whole. This view is essentially a view from the outside. In unmediated experience human life is always a "being out toward," always a "being ahead of oneself." And if it is not that, then it simply is no more. It becomes a whole then only in death. And the ancient saying, count no one happy before death, has the paradoxical consequences that this "beatification" can occur only from the perspective of others. To be able to know ourselves from the perspective of others, to see ourselves through the eyes of others, is also constitutive for our own being-in-the-world. "All generations will call me blessed" (Lk. 1.47).

But if the life of a person can be labeled only from the outside as turning out well, what then is the standard for this turning out well? In our judgment

concerning the turning out well of the life of others, it seems that we can neither disregard the way in which they experience their lives nor, in the other
direction, can we establish this experience as the only or even the decisive
criterion of life's turning out well. We would not honor someone as "happy"
whose life project turned out well after his death, if he, having lived and
worked for this one great project, died depressed thinking that he had failed,
anymore than we would honor someone in an unconscious state who was
kept for years in a mild euphoria without contact with reality. Who would
freely change places with that person? Apparently neither the subjective nor
the objective viewpoint can serve to define something akin to the turning out
well of life. The antinomy is grounded in the fact that human life becomes a
whole only when is seen after it is over and from the outside. Subjectivity,
being-for-itself, does not enter into the configuration, that is, into the
"in-itself," which the individual existence offers to the view of another. The
anticipation of *eudaimonia* is however the anticipation of a be-
ing-in-and-for-itself. But this being itself can appear in double form: theoretically, or objectively as thought, in the form of the in-itself, or
subjectively as lived in the form of the for-itself. Only in the second way do
we speak of *eudaimonia*, happiness, a life which turns out well. But how
could this be possible? It would have to be either the cancellation of finitude,
the metamorphosis of life into reason, for which the finite, organic life
would only be a kind of instrumental infrastructure, vulnerable to arbitrary
manipulation and reorganization. Or reason would reduce itself to the instrumental function of organic survival of individuals, without defining the being of this individual. In both cases there cannot be any talk of a specifically
human turning out well, since there cannot be any talk of a whole of this life.

II

The subjective perspective, the perspective of experience, cannot lead to
anything like a whole which turns out well. The objective perspective cannot
experience for itself the subjective perspective as happy in that it represents
something as a totality. The opposition between the two is only the subjective expression of the antinomical structure of finite knowledge, of the *fieri
aliud inquantum aliud*, of the "being-oneself-in-the-other." It is not by accident that the word in Hebrew for knowing also means the act of sexual union,
which underlies as a paradigm all our images of happiness. *Intelligere* was
interpreted by medieval thinkers as *intus legere*. But is there an understand-
ing-from-the-inside of the other? Surely, humans must be this tree in order to
understand it, instead of knowing the tree only *secundum modum*

cognoscentis, that is, incorporating it into our a priori schema of understanding. But if I were the tree, then I would no longer be me and so not understand at all what it means to be this tree, since the tree does not understand. Does that mean we can know adequately only ourselves? But the knowing of ourselves is not this type of conceiving. Our living and the self-reflection on this living introduces the dualism into our the leading of our own lives. They do not converge. The coming-to-convergence, the *adaequatio rei et intellectus* would be nothing other than the extinguishing of reflection. Extinguishing reflection, ecstasy, pure self-forgetting, immersion in the immediacy of living has always been synonymous with the dream of perfect bliss. But precisely this dream is irreconcilable with its realization. Certainly, in pure immediacy the dualism of living and being lived would be overcome. The pure being-with-oneself of living and the pure being-with-the-other of intentionality would be indistinguishable. The animal, because it is completely centered in itself, becomes merged without distance in the situations in which it lives. Distance from situations and distance from oneself have the same source. Still, immediacy can be experienced as happiness only in reflection. But reflection is what overcomes immediacy in that it reflects upon it. Ecstasy is perfect happiness only as remembered immediacy, that is, in retrospect. And so, this happiness exists only at all as "remembered." It only becomes something like happiness when it is no more. The perfect turning out well of life would be a fulfilled present, which could be anticipated only as future or remembered as past, and is, therefore, not that which constitutes its concept: present. The present is outside of time.

> You shepherd of the hills, so far from me with your sheep –
> What kind of happiness is that, which you seem to enjoy –
>   is it yours or mine?
> The peace, which I sense in your look, does it belong to me or to you?
> No, shepherd, neither to you nor to me.
> It belongs to happiness and to peace alone.
> You have it not, since you do not know that you have it.
> I too have it not, since I know that I do not have it.
> It is only it and falls upon us like the sun . . .[1]

Every antinomy comes out of the same structure of conscious life, of which we have already spoken in the chapter on hedonism. It comes from the fact that any integration of our life as a whole, which is somehow greater

---

1   Fernando Passao, *Albero Caeiro, Dichtungen, aus dem Portugiesischen übersetzt von G. R. Lind* (Zürich, 1986), S. 95.

than time, can be itself only an event within this whole. The whole becomes then a part of itself. We remember and we integrate that which we remember, in that we constantly determine its meaning anew from a plan for things to come. For its part this project is further determined by the remembered and unremembered past. We weave on a pattern; we give the individual actions and things which happen to us a meaning through constant structuring and changing the structure within the context of a "self-understanding." But we cannot see the whole of the basic pattern. The self-understanding itself is only a moment in the leading of our lives, a moment which, as a whole, will not itself be fully transparent. In each act of understanding a comprehensive sense is posited and anticipated, without canceling the understanding itself but of which the person understanding is not in control. That is, since the total sense itself is not authoritative, it can always want to understand the antinomy as an expression of absurdity and thereby do away with its understanding itself as an illusion. The inner image of *eudaimonia* has essentially the structure of memory and hope.

The antinomy of intentionality and reflexivity shows itself again and from a different side in the unresolvable opposition between autarky and fulfillment. The turning out well of life appears to be inseparable from autarky. Autarky demands self-assertion in the contingency of being. The Stoics had radicalized this thinking. The wise stoic is free from passions. This person is satisfied since he is indifferent to all goods which can either give fortune or take it away. Such self-assertion of freedom against even the gods tries to make life's turning out well independent of fortune, being happy, or having luck. But it thereby makes the turning out well also incompatible with beatitude, with fulfillment. Christianity had thematized the moment of fulfillment by an explicit turning away from the Stoics with the idea of beatitude, which presumes the relinquishment of autarky in the self-forgetting of *amor benevolentiae*. The stoical substitute for fulfillment, for "beatitude," is contentment. And in the end Epicurean hedonism also recommends this substitute.

Contentment appears to have the advantage that subjects who are content always remain within themselves. The libido pulls subjects out of themselves, entangles them in situations over which they are not masters. Thomas Hobbes taught that happiness in the sense of fulfillment is essentially connected with discontent: "Progress from desire to desire." Modern civilization is indebted primarily to the systematic creation of discontent for its type of progress. Even the "Tarry a little longer, thou art so fair" which is spoken to some moment of time, expresses a desire which reaches out to the future, the mad desire to stop time. Contentment, on the other hand, appears to be conclusive and a kind of ultimate end. As long as people who are content hang on to their contentment, every argument that they are missing the best remains irrelevant. It cannot touch them, since, in order to do so, they must already be discontent with their contentment. Contentment is the self-enclosure of subjectivity in its self.

However, this unshakeability is not compatible with the shock of love. The lover wants as little to trade places with the one who is content without love, as the latter does with the former. The difference between contentment and beatitude is grounded in the difference between reflection and immediacy which is constitutive for conscious life. Nothing is lacking the content person so long as the contentment lasts. As long as they are successful in remaining fully in the inner space of their autarky, and in excluding everything which befalls them and others as *adiaphoron* and in not comparing the fulfillment of their life with the one of some other, to this extent all objections remain mere objections from outside; they do not touch them. Nevertheless, strong bodily pain can destroy almost any contentment, since the needs of the organism are not purely interior. They are not at our free disposal.

Before all else, people who are and will remain content have to protect themselves from the penetration of the reality of the other, from the disturbances of love and pity, and also from the disturbance of great art. As compensation for happiness, contentment lives off the fact that the other has not become actual for it. Once this occurs, one cannot go back to contentment, one cannot even want it. Happiness as fulfillment pulls the subject onto an unending way, which, under conditions of finitude, is inseparable from the pain of insufficiency. Therefore, the antinomy of contentment and happiness is not to be overcome.

III

Ultimately the foundering of thought when it concerns life's turning out perfectly well has a deep connection with the contradiction contained in the thought of a total finite freedom. The realization and the self-maintenance of freedom also stand in an unavoidable tension. Each realization of freedom is at the same time a "using up" of freedom. Whoever wants to preserve all their freedom ought not to realize any of it. Rousseau once remarked he had often denied his tendency to help those who needed it, since there might develop through this an obligation, a kind of claim to further help, by which future spontaneity would be restricted. Rousseau refused then to follow his spontaneous tendency toward humanness in favor of the possibility of being able to follow it always in fuller spontaneity. He did not realize his freedom in order not to forfeit it. The tension between forfeiture and maintenance becomes politically virulent at the point where it concerns the institutional protection of civil freedoms. Each measure to protect freedom demands a restriction of its realization. The perfect system of insuring freedom would be then the doing away with all freedom. The reverse would be the unlimited realization of freedom, and this would just as quickly bring about its disappearance. The classical concept of *telos* means a measure, which comprehends at one and the same time the meaningful content of freedom and its conditions of preservation. Only where such a measure is consciously accepted in free self-determination does it cease being an external limitation to freedom. There must be, however, a reason for wanting the measure and not just an acceptance of it as compulsory. This reason can only be a reason if it emerges from some concept of turning out well, whose tempering to "a merely human sort of turning out well" in Aristotle was the starting point of our considerations, since this tempering already contains elements of resignation. Human nature does not appear here as the ultimate ground for thinking about the possibility of turning out well. Rather, it limits the vision of an absolute turning out well, without being clear what then should turn out well in such an absolute turning out well, if not human nature. Out of this vision of a turning out well, which is not restricted to the *conditio humana*, emerges the idea to recast human nature itself, to make it divine by means of "supernatural grace," or to let it become what it actually is only by means of a revolutionary reform or even to bring forth something better than humans by taking evolutionary events into our own hands through genetic engineering. The *telos* of human desires always points beyond the human.

It was Thomas Hobbes who completely denied a *telos* of human desires. According to him a final measure was set to the progress from desire to desire by the danger of death. Subjection to the conditions of preservation – concretized in the subjection to national sovereignty – conducts itself toward this desire like Freud's reality principle to the pleasure principle, which dictates from the outside, as it were, to the latter the subjection to its conditions of preservation. Given this, the human, according to Freud, is not made for happiness; culture is more the fruit of renunciation of the thought of *eudaimonia* than the medium of its realization.

The line of a scientific optimism, which came to its completion in Marx, is already traced out in Descartes. According to Descartes science is the name of increasing the happiness of all humans. It researches humans' organic and psychic conditions and provides the material means for the fulfillment of these conditions. As research it is, so to say, institutionalized discontent. People who dedicate themselves to science know that they do the ultimate and at the same time the only thing which it is possible to do for the systematic advancement of a maximum of human well-being. From this consciousness they create contentment for their own selves. The teaching of Descartes as regards individual existence is a stoical teaching on contentment. By projecting this fulfillment into a future, which we can then work to bring about, Descartes transforms the symbolic-representative relationship of earthly righteousness and eternal blessedness into a rational, instrumental relationship of present praxis and future happiness. Of course, even this future happiness cannot overcome the fundamental antinomies of the *conditio humana*, since that would mean that humans stop being human. Descartes was no more able than Marx to say in what the turning out well of life should consist, once essential activities are not longer directed toward the removal of obstacles. For Marx it seemed that beyond the "realm of necessity" only the hobby exists.

In its radical form the concept of *eudaimonia* is essentially ecstatic. Blessedness names that of which we have here only momentary presentiments, but what is unable to give form to our finite existence. "Human eudaimonia," however, the relative turning out well of life, rests upon a balance which depends on inner and outer factors, upon an integration of the multiplicity of our strivings, our doings, and our sufferings into a unstable unity. And this integration consists in an achievement which has to progress from moment to moment, always open to further future conditions of this whole and open also to an ultimate failure. Neither the content, which makes the life into a good life, nor the imperative, to which we subject ourselves by pursuing our goals, can be deduced from the concept of such a unity. This subjection can be itself part of a life which turns out well or of a life which turns out ill. The "full anthropological estimate" (Schiller) is not identical with the moral estimate. It seems that the latter cannot be derived from the former, since its character of being unconditioned is incommensurable with the conditionedness and plasticity of "human eudaimonia." And so dualism seems to be the last word. The wish for the turning out well of one's own life cannot be the origin of the idea of ethical responsibility. At most it is able to accept into itself the realization of this idea. But the self-evident quality of both these impulses of life appears to have a different origin in principle. If this appearance ultimately corresponded to reality, then something like a philosophical ethics would not even be possible. From time immemorial ethics' central concern always comes back to the unity of life, to friendship with oneself and to justified action. But an action can be justified only when the standard the justification is a single standard. When the choice between two standards is no longer open to justification, then all justification collapses upon itself, because when it is valid only on the basis of a notion, which in itself is arbitrary, then it never reaches itself as a concept. Even the demand for consistency and coherence in action with reference to some standard is arbitrary, if it cannot present that which it demands as a necessary condition of a good life.

The inner antinomy in the concept of *eudaimonia* underlies also, as we shall see, the apparently insurmountable dualism between *eudaimonia* and the duty of justice. Justice is, on the one hand, a part of life, and its demands can be judged according to whether they are appropriate for promoting the happiness of life or for impairing it. On the other hand, every effort toward the turning out well of one's own life can be measured by its conformity with justice, whose commands inexorably relativize the individual's pursuit of happiness. If there is no possibility of grasping the dualism and thereby overcoming it, then the mutual relativization of the self-evident quality of the other leads to ethical skepticism and thereby to the impossibility of "living rightly."

PART II

Chapter 7

Specifying the Moral

I

THE ARISTOTELIAN teaching concerning the life which turns out well has in many respects the character of a compromise. The highest form of *eudaimonia*, the theoretical realization of divinity, is not "human happiness"; rather, it is something which is projected into life "from the outside." This projection allows us to grasp life in its deepest meaning, but this grasping remains episodic. It does not transform the whole of life. On the other hand, human happiness, that is, the turning out well of life as a whole, retains the character of a precarious balance. What we can do is to make the best out of the circumstances. The life of "a good and reasonable person" (*Nic. Eth.* 1101a), who is in a good situation, can never be a total failure. Still no one can call anyone who meets the fate of Priam happy. It is not by accident that Aristotle chose the example of Priam. The contingency of individual life is, to a certain extent, absorbed into the totality of the polis. But this totality is not exempted from contingency. Troy was destroyed, Hector was killed, and Priam's battle was finally in vain. The turning out well of human life is so precarious because human beings – as distinct from animals – can anticipate in thought a turning out well whose conditions of realization cannot be fulfilled. We can make present in thought a totality which is not contingent and of which we ourselves are only a contingent part. Nevertheless, according to Aristotle, the identification with this totality is accomplished only in thought and as such is only an episode in the whole of our particular existence. We cannot define the turning out well of our life independent from the turning out well of our goals which extend out beyond our death, nor apart from the fate of those who we love. But this future lies in darkness.

It is surprising at first that Aristotle explicitly distinguishes human *eudaimonia* from simple *eudaimonia* (*Nic. Eth.* 1101a20). What can "simple turning out well" mean, if not that the life of a being which has such and such characteristics turns out well? Doesn't turning out well mean that a being is completely that which it is? What can it mean, then, when the Greeks say the gods are more blessed than humans? Apparently a universal standard of turning out well is presupposed, according to which the happiness of the one surpasses that of the other. This has something to do with the paradoxical situation that the thinking on a life which turns out well, which appears together with the very emergence of thought, has the character of "Utopia." It anticipates a kind of happiness which, at the same time, it acknowledges is unrealizable for mortal beings. By transcending its own finite horizons of interest, this being can relativize its mental interests without ceasing to be this finite being with finite interests. They can think of God without being God. Reason, which allows the thought of turning out well to come into existence, is also that which recognizes this thought as utopian.

For Aristotle the polis is the place which, as compensation for the "no place," the *utopia*, of absolute turning out well, allows for "happiness which is humanly possible." His ethics are a teaching about this turning out well. With the end of the autonomous polis, however, philosophy becomes the teaching of utopian, absolute happiness – be it, as with Epicurus, in a radical reduction to the finite, or be it, as with the Stoics, in the fiction of the wise person, who has overcome all individual interests and has, as medium of pure reason, identified himself with the world-logos. Christianity begins its confrontation with ancient teachings on life by uncovering the fictive character of this philosophical promise of happiness. Thus, Augustine writes in the Book 19 of *The City of God*: "Anyone, however, who thinks that they can find goods and evils in this life, and who transfers the highest good to the body or to the spirit or to both; in order to say it more clearly, in pleasure or in virtue or in both, in quiet or in virtue or in both, in pleasure and quiet or in virtue or in both, in the primary natural goods or in virtue or in both, all of these in astonishing blindness want to become blessed here on earth through themselves. The truth laughs at them . . ." (Chapter 4). Augustine asserts the claims of common sense against the tranquility of the Stoics or the apathy of the Epicureans. The metamorphosis of all the external and contingent goods and evils into *adiaphora* remains pure theory. "And what kind of friend would a person be, if they were indifferent about the betrayal or faithfulness of friends? And indifferent about the troubles of the city, the civil war, the injustice and distress which comes from it, about the scourge of humanity, war, unjust as well as just?" "Whoever tolerates these or thinks about them without a troubled soul, is, if they considers themselves happy, actually all the more miserable, since they have lost their human sensibility" (XIX,8). Augustine reasons further that the thinking which sees the natural striving of humans after happiness and the turning out well of life fulfilled in morality, in a life of virtue, does not recognize that virtues are born out of necessity. Looked upon as the capacity to assert the rational life against the pressure of the chaos of the passions and the external adversities, the virtues are "signs of their lack of blessedness" (XIX,4). Thomas Aquinas – without Augustine's emphasis, which is later renewed by Pascal – will take up this line of reasoning and develop it: The virtues, as modifications of the passions or external behavior, cannot be ultimate, "since the passions and external things can be subordinated to other things" (*Summa contra Gentiles* III, 34). Morality is itself not a goal, but a means to a life that turns out well. Thomas, like Augustine, insists upon the insuperableness of contingency, especially in the form of mortality. As distinct from animals, humans know about their deaths. Death looms in life as knowledge of the fragmentary character of our life. To want not to die is constitutive for all life. But humans know that they must die. Thomas characterizes the threat which destroys even the moral self-assertion of rational life, i.e., madness, "which is a possibility for everyone" as the most extreme, beyond even that of death (*S.c.G.* III, 48).

Resignation before the necessity of death and before the threat of the loss of moral self-determination is not that which we anticipate in the concept of blessedness. The existence of this anticipation in us as a *desiderium naturale* legitimates for Thomas the certainty of its fulfillment. "Then nature does nothing in vain" (ibid.). Since the fulfillment is not possible in this life, it must occur after this life. In this context Thomas refers to the first Book of the *Nicomachean Ethics*, and its distinction between "blessedness in itself" and "blessedness *modo humano*," whereby he interprets the *modus humanus* as a restriction which allows one in the *modus divinus* an intuition of God beyond the boundary of death, and "the need of these outstanding spirits" is reduced to their ignorance of this (ibid.). In the place of a pure turning out well of earthly life there is hope: "We becomes happy through hope. And so we do not have blessedness or holiness as something present, but we wait for it as something in the future and do so with patience" (*De civitate Dei* 19,4). "The philosophers," as Augustine writes, "want this blessedness, and since they do not see it, they do not believe in it and so seek to justify here a completely false happiness with the help of a virtue, which is more mendacious, the prouder it is" (ibid.).

II

With this morality and eudaimonism go their separate ways. The construction – first attempted by the Sophists – of an ethics as a teaching on the life which turns out well appears to break down both in its hedonistic form, i.e., the deduction of morals from a non-moral concept of turning out well, as well as in its stoical form, i.e., moralizing the concept of happiness. The connection between morality and happiness appears to become an indirect and external one. Kant later established it as a connection between blessedness and being worthy of being blessed, but in such a way that the criteria for achieving worthiness of happiness could not be derived from the thought of happiness. Rather, they were arrived at independently.

Talk of law, obedience, and reward is frequent in the Bible. The Psalms reflect over and over the experience that, contrary to what we should expect, earthly turning out well of life and uprightness do not go together; more often it goes badly for the good and goes well for the bad. At the same time the content of their constant entreaty is that this cannot and should not be the last word but that God must come to help the upright who suffer injustice. The *Works and Days* of Hesiod does not view it any differently. This coming to the aid of the downtrodden has three forms: The first is simply a changing of the earthly fate; the second is a strengthening of the heart, of inner peace and inner joy, the "light of thy face"; and the third is an eschatological compensation, comfort "in the bosom of Abraham." This is not anything different from *Works and Days* nor from Plato. What should Socrates say to the objection that it apparently does not come down to being good, but to appearing to be good? What good is the just person's justice, if he has to die on the cross? Does Socrates wish to hold even in this case that being happy and being good are identical? Socrates does adhere to it, but he must also bring into play the dimension which reaches beyond the border of death, the judgment of the dead, before which each one stands naked. The fate which will be allotted to each person corresponds exactly to the state of his soul. The state of his soul is a result of his actions. If, however, the correctness of these actions, their beauty, is something other than means to furthering the well-being of the agent, in what does it consist? There enters here a dualism of standards for judgment, which philosophy constantly tries to overcome and which nevertheless always succeeds in making itself visible. The dualism is already present in the two predicates which Greek makes available to describe human action, "good" and "beautiful," that is, "beneficial to the agent and "praiseworthy." The Sophists first attempted to reduce the beautiful to the good, and, so far as it was possible, to expose it as illusionary. Plato's intention goes in the opposite direction: The good for humans is ultimately only the beautiful. But it would then be a logical circle to derive the content of the beautiful from its advantageousness to the agent. This content must be arrived at independently of the advantageousness. If somehow the beautiful were to prove itself to be irrevocably unadvantageous, then its motivating power would be broken. On this Plato, Christianity, and Kant all agree. But they also agree that the advantageousness of the beautiful emerges out of its beauty and not the reverse, and that the unity of the beautiful and the good, which is sought in the concept of *eudaimonia*, is a postulate of reason or a promise, whose realization points beyond the boundary of death.

However, in Platonic or Christian understanding it is not the case that the relationship between morality and blessedness is purely instrumental or "reward-morality" in the sense that the individual is on his or her good behavior and follows the divine commands in order to be compensated for this by an eternal reward, without the content of these commands being in an essential relation with the "reward." But how can one think of such a relationship, if it has nothing to do with either the arbitrary connection of the well-being of others with one's own by means of a powerful sanction or with a direct instrumental relationship, that is, a simple means-end relation between doing good and well-being? We can reconstruct the Platonic answer in this way: Immortal souls appear before the judge of the dead "naked." Their fate is released from all contingencies of earthly existence and is only the function of their own being. When this being is formed by rational action, then is it a blessed being, self-sufficient like the blessed gods. In his dialogues Plato did not explicitly mediate the eschatology with the teaching about Eros and the "Good-itself." Christianity did that. And in so doing, it gave the most clarity and perfection to the connection of the Good and the Beautiful, of eudaimonism and a morality of unselfish love. The key to this was to think of the love of God as the fundamental motive of all morality, as *forma virtutum*. The merely theoretical position that a certain way of acting is beautiful, that it corresponds to certain moral intuitions, is not sufficient to make it the better policy, so long as it contradicts our own fundamental interests.

Kant expressed this clearly; his "feeling of respect" introduced a motive which is set over against the interests of the individual, which are thought of as consistently egotistical, and whose satisfaction is subordinated to certain conditions. But it does not transform the interests themselves. He explicitly separates the human will from the "holy will" and so raised the Lutheran teaching on the fundamental depravity of human nature by original sin to an anthropological determinant and, in so doing, to an object for philosophy. Love in a nature which is characterized by a *curvation ins seipsum* can be construed only as disguised egoism. Luther's *maledicta sit caritas* finds its philosophical echo here. Accordingly, the ultimate convergence of doing good and well-being, which Kant thought of as the concept of the highest good, can be thought of only "extrinsically," as an external coupling of morality out of "respect for the law" and the satisfaction of essentially egocentric tendencies. It is clear that under this presumption all morals would be corrupted, when they were supported by a motivation of reward. Instead they must remain completely independent of all reflection upon one's own blessedness. The inclusion of the latter in the "highest good" is therefore, according to Kant, not an essential component of morality itself, but a belief which is morally demanded for the support of morality.

III

Kant's specifying of the ethical, his detaching it conceptionally and in terms of motivation from a eudaimontistic context, stands in the Christian tradition. It is already visible in the dramatic conflict between Fénelon and Bossuet concerning the *amour pur*, concerning the essence of love of God – that is, in the last theological conflict which involved the Pope, the King, and all of educated Europe. The conflict was the consequence of modern ontology, which was no longer able to think of something like self-transcendence: Either humans are always and necessarily concerned with themselves, and then their love of God is a function of the human striving after happiness – this was Bossuet's thesis – or there is something like love of God for the sake of God. In that case purity of the motivation would coincide with the disappearance of eudaimontistic thinking – so taught Fénelon. (For Louis XIV he was "l'esprit le plus chimériqe de mon royaume" [the most visionary spirit of my kingdom].) With Kant the break is already complete; pulled down out of the heights of mystical theology, this break reproduces itself in moral philosophy. The constitutive unity and the solidarity of a life which turns out well with justified actions disappears with the consequences which have already been indicated in the first chapter. At one time the concept of love was thought of as a metamorphosis of self-interests, as the self-transcendence of a rational being, on account of which the reality of the other in its own teleology immediately became a motive of action. Leibniz expressed it so: *Delectatio in felicitate alterius*, "Joy in the happiness of others," and thereby hoped to leapfrog over Bossuet (e.g., *Brief an Magliabecchi* v. 3./13. June 1698. Dutens V, 126). The interests of reason are the interests of rational beings, only when these beings have found their way back to their original condition. Holiness is not their starting point, but the goal and result of their "conversion."

These interests of reason can be thought of only as actual self-transcendence, since they do not concern abstract generalities; rather – as love – they concern a God understood personally. Unity with the will of God is the Christian formula for morality, being one with God is the Christian formula for *eudaimonia*. That which motivates moral action – namely, love – is at the same time that whose fulfillment is thought of as blessedness.

Morality is not "disinterested" any more than blessedness is egotistical. The Christian thinking in terms of reward, which is so massively present in the New Testament, can be understood only in terms of God himself saying: "I myself will be your reward" (Gn. 15.1). Concerning the love which inspires all moral action, Paul said, it does not end, which means that it outlasts the stage of morality, which is only one of its forms of appearance.

The specifying of the moral as a form of love's appearance which is, so to speak, finite-categorically bound and structured, is made explicit by Thomas Aquinas in his answer to the question: "Must we always will what God wills?" (*S. th.* I,II, qu. 19, art. 10). Surprisingly the answer is: "No." And no, because we cannot always know what God wills, that is, precisely what it is that God wills to have occur. The complexity of the universe makes it impossible for us to direct our individual actions toward its optimization or to understand the moral as a function of such a willing to optimize. And that is what it means to want what God wants. We should, so continues Thomas, want instead "that which God wants us to want." We should follow the moral law, the law of "beauty," the conformity-to-being of human action. Its content is not derivable from a concept which stands secure, independent of its knowledge of its own blessedness, nor understandable as a function of a universal strategy of optimization. It is, on the one hand, determined through the specific responsibilities and loyalties of the agent and within these through "natural law," whose intuitive givenness must, on the other hand, be tested in rule-utilitarian reflection. Rule-utilitarian reflection forbids agents from conceiving themselves directly as subjects of universal responsibility, who would have the prerogative of not being constrained in the choice of their means but would deduce, nominalistically shall we say, the command out of the constantly unique situation. The moral law and its testing through rule-utilitarian reflection allows agents to conceive themselves as one among others and their actions also under their aspect as precedents. Nevertheless, it is characteristic of rule-utilitarian deliberation by Thomas – similar to that of Kant – that it does not originate from a universal utilitarianism, but serves to ascertain retrospectively the natural out of the results, that is, "that which God wills us to will," since it expresses the law of who we are.

If we were to proceed from the fact that the moral law – the "will of God which gives law" – is for God himself still a function of his "absolute will," which shows itself in history, then the discrepancy between the two would appear to be ultimately a result of the limitedness of the human insight into the "best," comparable to the "second-best way" of Socrates, who, on account of his inability to derive the constitution of the universal immediately out of the *nous* of Anaxagoras, turned to the ideas. Then, the betrayal of Judas would be justified, if Judas had recognized his function in the plan of salvation history – contrary to the words of Jesus: "The Son of Man has to be betrayed, but woe to the man by whom he is betrayed." The independence of the moral from all historical reflection is for the classical tradition even more deeply grounded. The impossibility of a universal ethic follows from the impossibility of a universal calculus of optimization, but this impossibility resides not just in obtuseness, but rather is it itself positively grounded. It has its ground in an understanding of reality in which each person is not only a part but also a representative of the whole and through this constituted as a whole. Accordingly, the legitimate treatment of persons precludes treating them in a merely instrumental way in reference to the whole of reality, rather it includes treating them as ends in themselves. The open disharmony which comes out of this double-status of each finite person was, of course, a consequence of original sin for the Christian tradition. In order for a world of sin, that is a world of disordered self-love, to reach the completion and perfection of the whole, the evil which occurs must be constantly converted into an instrument of the good, to a power "that would alone work evil, but engenders good."[1] In such a world the moral can no longer be grasped directly as a function of optimization. When Thomas writes that a judge has the duty to search for a criminal suspect, while the wife of the suspect the duty to help hide her husband, the antagonism therein has its grounds in the fact of the crime. Without this the securing of the *bonum civitatis* and of the *bonum familiae* would naturally converge.

The moral law is not primarily directed toward the bettering of an evil world; rather it already anticipates the good. For Kant the primary content of moral duty is not the bringing about of just legislation; rather it is every action which corresponds to such legislation, as if it were already in place. The ethical life is truth in the midst of falsehood, producing a healed world. How this can be united with responsibility in a broken world is a question which touches upon the relationship between morality and politics, which must be handled separately. Here I wish only to say, in order not to curtail the Christian determination of the ethical, that if our love for God could not posit a relationship thereby becoming *voluntas Dei absolute dicta*, that is, what God wills must be done, then ethical obedience to that which we are would ultimately be a kind of unfreedom. As ethical agents we would be mere "slaves who do not know what their master is about." Ethical action would merely be rational imitation of the action of animals guided by instinct, who follow their "nature" without questioning their place in the whole of reality.

---

1   J. W. Goethe, *Faust*, Pt. I, "Faust's Study" (ii), Penquin Classics, p. 75.

Thomas Aquinas, whom we have chosen as the interpreter of classical Christian ethics, asks the following question in reference to the judge and the wife of the suspect. Is the antagonism which emerges from their respective ethical duties absolute? Is it the last word? Or is there something that unites the two with each other? If the ethical motivation of both is grounded in the love of God, then each will at least acknowledge the duty of the other and will not want to divert him or her from it. Then the conflict of Kreon and Antigone would not take place. Still, the ultimate purity of motivation will show itself primarily in the fact that each of the two is prepared to calmly accept the outcome, even when it thwarts his or her own plans because what mattered to them was the beauty of the action which is pleasing to God and not the forcing of a certain outcome. Tranquility is the criterium of love of God. In this sense Martin Luther once wrote: "It is a certain sign of bad will, that it will not suffer being hindered" (*Ausgewählte Werke* ed. Borcherdt u. Merz. Bd. 1, S. 319).

The specifying of the moral from the eudaimonistic context on the one hand, and from the religious context on the other, is the result of an inner logic. It can only be understood, though, as an inner specifying process of a unified leading of one's life. When the unity itself is broken, then thinking about the possibility of the turning out well of one's individual life disappears, together with, on the one side, the real meaning of religious worship and, on the other, its ethical commitment. What remains is a social process which would be understandable only in naturalistic categories. The way ethical action sees itself would be seen as irrelevant to this interpretation and some other form of action would be looked for.

Chapter 8

Reason and Life

I

THE FACT that our intuition of blessedness is so constituted that it inevitably leads to an antinomy, that is, to the seeming impossibility of thinking about life turning out well without a contradiction, brings forth the question of the constitution of a being who cannot help but end up in this contradiction as soon as it begins to reflect. In the European tradition this constitution has often been formulated thus: Human beings are beings between animals and angels, or beings who belong simultaneously to the sensible and the intelligible world. Ultimately the classical definition of the human as *animal rationale* does not say anything different. In this definition reason could indeed be understood as *differentia specifica*, the distinctive character, which distinguishes the species, *homo sapiens,* from other living beings, much the way the elephant's trunk distinguishes it. In fact, however, this distinction is even more fundamental. It appears to ground a distinct genus, so that we place the human over against the animal in the same way that we place the animal over against the plant and, regardless of the biological proximity of humans to apes, place the apes together with earthworms as "animals" over against humans. This could be discounted as human "chauvinism," similar to the Greeks who labeled the rest of humanity "barbarians" or to the Jews who called the others "pagans." In any case, the distinctive mark – reason – stands in a peculiar opposition to the genus – living beings – within which it is supposed to distinguish humans. Reason and life behave in an antagonistic manner toward each other. Klages characterized the spirit as the adversary of the soul, and even Aristotle could not understand reason simply as a capacity of living beings called humans; rather he saw it as something which comes in "from the outside." Why? Because reason is the one human capacity which allows us, so to speak, to see ourselves with the eyes of others, that is, from outside of ourselves. Put more exactly, it allows us to know that there exists a view from the eyes of others, whose perspective is not that of the living being which we ourselves are. This is the condition of speech. Aristotle equated the rational being with the one capable of speech. Speech differs from all other forms of communicative behavior in that a speaker directs words to a hearer and the speaker anticipates in speech the hearing of the hearer. The speaker wants to be understood in a certain way. Speech cannot be a natural cry; instead it is a conventional sign system which is socially learned. Language learners experience not only that the other is a part of their environment, an intentional object, but that they themselves are at the same time part of the environment of the other. They make real the gaze of the other which is directed toward them. To live means being centered in oneself, in a organic center. A living thing is an interior, which shuts itself off from an exterior. It transforms that which is encountered in the environment and so bestows meaning upon it. And in that it gives a meaning to everything encountered in the space of its own self-preservation and self-realization, it "understands" the world. That which cannot be understood at all does not exist for the living being. For the rational being the direction reverses itself. *Fieri aliud inquantum aliud* is an old definition of its cognitive relationship to the world. "To become the other *as* the other" means to grasp it *as* not being understood, as something which in the first order does not *have* meaning in my world, but rather as something which is itself a subject for which there is meaning. Reason begins with the knowledge that something exists about which one knows nothing or which one does not understand. The words "being," "exist," and "there is" open up a horizon, whose extent is infinite and whose center is everywhere, and therefore precisely not there, where I myself am. To exist in this horizon stands in an irresolvable tension with the fact that the rational being is at the same time a living being, which goes forth, always standing in the middle point of its environment and which construes the world from the standpoint of its concern over its own ability to continue to exist.

The opposition between being animate and being rational, between organic life and reflection, is of the type that there is no continuous "development" from the one the other. Development is a category of the animate. The animate passes through states, which emerge one after the other in a series, which can be understood as a function of an undivided tendency, an immanent teleology, a going-out toward – toward, that is, the preservation and increase of one's being in adaptation to an environment, which is neutral toward this tendency. Modern anthropology has understood reason as a compensation for lack of being equipped with mechanism of system preservation. As a matter of fact, one can understand a number of the tasks which reason performs as ways of preserving both the individual and the species of a certain type of organism. Still, it is more difficult to make plausible how any condition of lack is to be thought of genetically, if it is not true that this condition was already "compensated" for by the provision of reason from the beginning. But we may leave this question of evolutionary theory unde-cided here. What is important in this context is anything that is left unac-counted for in this instrumental interpretation of reason, that is, in this interpretation of reason as a function of self-preservation. That which is "left unaccounted for," which does not allow itself to be so interpreted, consists in an opening up of a unconditioned dimension, that is, of a horizon which is, of its essence, not relative to the interests of an animate being or of a natural species, but rather allows all finite interests to be relativized in an essentially infinite horizon. Relativists, in spite of themselves, presuppose this struc-tural characteristic of reason, in that they claim non-relativity for their state-ment of the relativity of every theoretical or practical horizon. Relativity can be discovered only when it is not total, and so the perspective of its discov-erer remains only mistakenly in it. The words "being" and "good" open up such a horizon of unconditionedness: "Being" precisely insofar as it does not mean objectivity, being-for, but rather means being-a-self which grounds all objectivity. "Good" precisely insofar as it does not mean "good for," and thereby allows reflection to place the further question whether what is good for this one or for that one would then be good itself. The use of the word "good" as a one-place (*einstelliges*) predicate corresponds to the infinity of this reflection. This infinity cannot be got around by reflection; at most its legitimacy is disputable.

As we will later see, the words "being" and "good" are inseparably con-nected in this context. Only where a being is perceived as being without fur-ther reference, as being itself, does the use of the word "good" without any further reference obtain its meaning. The change to this non-functional use which has no further reference cannot be thought of as something which somehow "developed" out of a state of a finite living system which is under-stood functionally. It is a discontinuity. It jumps out of the circle of self-ref-erence and self-assertion. It is a *metanoia*, a conversion. I deliberately choose a term from the religious-ethical sphere of speech for this ontological jump here, since the ethical appeal "Convert!" calls for nothing other than some change to be explicitly realized, which, even though it constitutes the humanness of humans, still cannot be thought of as a result of a "develop-ment." Development occurs only in the context of a direction. A change in direction is not called a development, but rather a decision. Biblical myth speaks of such a decision at the beginning of the human journey toward be-coming human. The interpretation which Rousseau and those after him gave again and again to this myth misses the point, if we view the traditional re-construction of the myth as its authentic self-interpretation. Rousseau says that from the beginning human beings have been called out of the self-centeredness of natural living to a way of acting – more exactly to a refraining from this self-centeredness out of a super-individualistic, divine perspective. Humans refused the call. They were indeed awakened to reason through the call, but they then interpreted reason to be an instrument for their self-centeredness, which they should have given up. Thereby, the animalistic innocence of humans was lost. To be awakened by reason and to have once entered the horizon of the absolute means that the *curvatio in seipsum*, the remaining in the center point, can occur only in the form of hubris, that is, as "to wish to be like God." However, this "irrational reason" is, at the same time, unnatural nature, because the step which leads from animal to human nature – the step to humanity – is no longer a development. It does not constitute itself from itself; rather it has the character of a decision. When this decision occurs, a living being gives up its natural self-centeredness. But this step is not a self-creation; it is rather the explicit taking up of an eccentric position, in which we as humans by nature already find ourselves. The refusal of this step, which was characterized by Augustine as the "love of God to the point of despising oneself," falls short of what we in ourselves already are. It closes our eyes to the horizon in which we already find ourselves as rational beings. Thus, this refusal always has the character of an insincere lack of attention, of secretly looking away. So also the one who confesses to naturalism and asserts the self-assertion of individuals or populations as the invincible world-law wants to *say* something with this assertion and not just *express* this world-law. He has thereby already gone beyond naturalism in the form of the statement.

II

Up till this point, it appears as if the transcending of the dimensions of being alive is only a formal affair. But the dualism between living and reason emerges once more in the opposition between material and formal components, which we have already met with several times in our considerations. We saw that thinking about the life which turns out well, as well as the wholeness of life which it presupposes, are pure concepts of reflection of a characteristic formal nature. This form does not allow what the content of such life should be to be deduced from itself. The content is already given in the natural drive-structure of the animate being. Without this structure the thinking on *eudaimonia* remains empty. Of course, it does not conduct itself as though the content of a rational will exhaust itself in individual or general drive-satisfactions. From what we know about our own beginnings, it is clear that humans have culturally reworked many of the natural drives. The material content of the good life was never reducible to the demand for individual and race preservation or for physical comfort. When the antagonism between rational, merely formal, universality and mere organic living remains at this level, then it never becomes clear that this living has already transcended itself to the level of the universal consisting in rational and social life-forms, and that, vice-versa, reason is already present in such life-forms which are already so structured that they are rich in content. In every culture eating and drinking are not just an individualistic intake of nourishment, in which what the one eats, the other is deprived of. Rather they are forms of communal life, be it everyday or festive. And the reverse is also true: Rational generalization has never had the form of an equalization of natural interests. An equalization of these would be an impossibility. Only as the kind of interests which are already in their essence socially mediated, that is, already intellectual and therefore modifiable, can they even become objects of practical discourse toward equalization. We have already gone beyond naturalism long before such discourse takes place. Every real feast is such a transcendence. The feast feeds itself from vital energies. But the joy which comes from it is not the sum of the individual subjective states of happiness; rather it is, of its essence, a communal joy. And what one gains there is not taken from another. Feasts are not zero-sum games. They are "rational enjoyment." In any case, this is valid for feasts in which something is really being celebrated, and not for the collective "do-your-own-things" which are occasionally called "feasts."

III

Apparently the ambiguity of the concept of eudaimonia has to do with the ambiguity which is inherent in the usual form of conscious life. Intensive, unmediated vitality and consciousness, i.e., self-realization as drive-fulfillment on the one side, and self-realization as self-relativizing within the horizon of rational universality on the other side, stand in clear tension even when this tension, as we have seen, cannot be thought of as mutually exclusive, since fulfillment which does not know itself as such and can be judged successful only from the outside is not happiness. Indeed, we can think what life is only from the self-experience of conscious life. Modern biology does not do this. It tries to conceive of consciousness as a function of life, and then to reconstruct life as a systematic condition of inorganic matter. Such an "objective" concept of life is unavoidably reductionistic. Either we understand our way of experiencing our own selves as unreal and epiphenomenal or we understand animal and plant life by way of analogy with conscious life, that is, with our own. Talk of the unconscious is meaningful only as a limit concept of conscious life. I suddenly become conscious that I have been apparently hearing a sound or experiencing a slight pain for some time. What was the "hearing" of this sound or the "experiencing" of this pain before I was aware of it? It was surely something, since I did not begin to hear something or to have a slight headache only in the moment I began to pay attention. But what it means, "to hear" or "to have a pain," in this context can be understood only as such a limit-concept of "being consciousness of hearing or having a pain." Consciousness of these conditions is not the perception of objective "givens" which "in themselves" have nothing to do with be-coming conscious. Consciousness is life that has come to itself. Reason is however nothing other than fully aware consciousness – consciousness which knows itself and knows itself as a particular reality in an absolute horizon.

Then where does this ambiguity, this tension between reason and life and, as its consequence, the ambiguity of happiness come from? It appears that we must describe the ontological constitution which underlies this ambiguity thus: Life in its usual state is never fully aware. On the other hand, we still cannot say that reason slumbers or is only half-aware. If rationality, as we have seen, is not a product of development but rather a change in direction, then the horizon which reason opens cannot be opened gradually. Reason is essentially an anticipation of a completion. And as such, it is, as the Aristotelians say, *"semper in actu."* Life lags behind this anticipation of a completely aware reason. It cannot come to a pure consciousness of itself without causing that of which it is conscious to disappear. It cannot transform itself into a pure view of its own self. The saying, "the one who sees through everything, sees nothing," is applicable here. Subjectivity is the paradigm for any concept of substantiality, but a life perfectly raised to consciousness or a drive perfectly transformed into will would be an emptiness in which all content would disappear. Human, and therefore, finite reason is dependent upon receptivity. It cannot give itself itself to think. Receptivity presumes a causal, therefore precisely a non-conceptual, relationship to the other, and therefore a dimension of unconsciousness. The medieval teaching on the angels as well as Leibniz's *Monadology* recognized the impossibility of thinking of a pure consciousness, which does not know itself to be a living organism, as connected with receptivity.

Even so, a volition remains empty, and therefore would not be a volition, when its content is not given through the natural dynamic of drives. Kant's formal formulations of the categorical imperative obtain content only through the tacit presupposition that the will is to be understood as a rational form of drive, as a drive which comes to itself. The living being, which opens its eyes, does not transform itself into an eye.

Descartes had found something ultimate then in the *cogito*, something be-yond-which-one-cannot-go, which defies all doubts. But this ultimate does not have the character of a foundation. It does not allow anything to be con-structed upon it; it remains empty and without consequences. The idea of God, the idea of an absolute horizon, which alone allows the *sum* to be at-tached to the *cogito*, makes this *cogito* at the same moment to be a contingent and particular subject. In the horizon which is stretched out by the idea of the infinite, the subject appears only as a fact, which never merges into one with this horizon. It cannot return to its ground. The Cartesian *cogito*, by being fully aware, by being completely present to itself, is at the same time com-pletely empty, a now without memory and without future. And everything that it receives as content has a hypothetical character, whose reality can be ascertained only indirectly, that is, by means of a detour through the idea of the truthfulness of God. For Descartes the dialectic between an empty finite consciousness and the anticipation of an infinite consciousness presupposes that the concept of life is abandoned, since life is essentially not a *clara et distincta perceptio*. But life comes to itself in the *clara et distincta perceptio* of the "I." Finite reason is not a substance, but an event, the event of an or-ganic process becoming substantial. Since Descartes does not view the or-ganism as that to which the saying "I" refers, but rather as an object, in any case an empirical condition for the saying "I," he cannot distinguish the or-ganism from a machine. Life is either that which comes to itself in con-sciousness, or it is not life; rather it is a complex of material parts with the determined characteristics of a system, and is therefore identical with its simulation. We cannot form another analogous concept of life. Conscious life is the paradigm of this concept, and in conscious life the moment of un-conscious vitality is constitutive.

The fact that we cannot form any *clara et distincta perceptio* of blessed-ness is clear from what has been said. The concept of contentment, as a sub-stitute for blessedness, is clear and distinct. It is the practical counterpart of the *cogito*. But it becomes possible only by keeping the thought of its actual fulfillment at a distance. Real fulfillment, being blessed, can be thought of only as condition of the living. Just as we cannot think of an adequate con-cept of life without conscious life, so we cannot think of an adequate concept of happiness without conscious happiness. But the antagonism we were speaking of emerges in conscious happiness. It is unthinkable as self-sufficiency.

IV

The image for "rational happiness" is the feast, i.e., communal joy, and in fact joy *about* something, as in a celebration, as in a "good time." The vision of life as a feast is the vision of a merging of life and awareness into a common world, of which Heraclitus spoke. The half-awareness of our daily life is such that we can experience it as the opposition of reason and life, just as we often experience being half asleep as a struggle to wake up. Fully awake, we are again one with ourselves. Reason allows us to enter into a horizon which we can in no way emotionally fill, since it is set over against the centrality of life and relativizes our own selves into being one among others. The feeling caused by reason, Kantian "respect," is such that it "strikes down all egotism." To this degree it appears to be directly set over against the pursuit of happiness.

But the fulfillment of this pursuit occurs only through paradox, since human life is not animal life, which might someday become self-conscious. There is no self-contained vital form of the human, which could come to perfection in itself and then of itself be self-conscious as a rational being. From the start human nature is not a finite whole, which could be biologically perfected in itself and then be content in this perfection. The desires of the instinct-free being are endless. They do not come to a point of rest in their satisfaction; rather they want to desire further. Their chief enemy is boredom, the empty infinity of time. The "bad infinity" of the human drive structure makes known the good: Reason as *telos* and as an interior standard of the human *physis*. Plato shows in a definitive manner in his *Symposium* how Eros strives to go beyond all sensuous fulfillment and only uncovers its true essence as love for the "good itself."

For Plato the self-manifestation of the good is equivalent to awakening to reality, to the becoming real of the real for the one to whom it manifests itself. What does this mean? As long as living creatures are caught up in instinctual drives, as long as they remain "central," the world is not real to them. The other does not appear to them as himself or herself. The other appears only as a part of the environment, as an object of some drive. But then these living beings are also not yet real. They are for themselves too only an object of some drive. They are the bearer of only relative meaning, an "appearance," as Kant would say. They cling indeed to life, but this life, along with the clinging, can disappear when they experience more discomfort than pleasure. They do not know anything like an absolute meaningfulness of their own self and a saying such as: "What does it profit a person to gain whole world but thereby lose his soul," is unintelligible. An animal remains innocent in this centrality. It does not relativize itself or "dis-absolutize" itself since it does not have at its disposal the horizon of the absolute, the horizon of being. Humans can remain only in this centrality *male fide.*

There are two extreme forms in which this remaining in the center manifests itself. The one form is a kind of tyranny in which individuals refuse to acknowledge their equals as their equals, and instead reduce them to the status of objects. (In sadism there is added a "diabolical" moment, in which the reflective consciousness of turning a subject into an object is constitutive for perverse pleasure.) The other form is suicide, which according to Wittgenstein, is the immoral act pure and simple,[1] since in it people reduce themselves to the status of an object of drives. They ask whether they have had enough of themselves. They have become unsatisfactory as a drive object for themselves. They simply do not take into account themselves as a subject, for whom something has meaning. They are themselves not at all real. But they can only push aside the source of discontent, if they push aside the being for which something means pleasure or pain, that is, the reference point for meaning itself. By this they show that their centrality as the subject of drives is not the innocent centrality which is unavoidable in animals; rather is it that they know themselves as subjects and this knowledge turns against itself and makes them disappear like an object. This is the paradigmatic case of being half-awake, which I have called "insincere inattention."

There are, of course, suicides that are committed out of a consideration of others, for the sake of those to whom one does not wish to become a burden. Here the living creature has already gone out of itself and sees that it itself is a part of the world of the other and not just that the other is a part of their own world. Still, the other is now seen as being determined by their character, as a being with drives, for whom I can be only an object. In that I spare others the exacting demand with which my existence presents them, I do not respect them as rational, and that means moral beings, who are, for their part, capable of acknowledging being a self and only in this acknowledgment awaken to their being a self. We become really ourselves only in the face of the claim made by the irreducibly real. Kant, in his way, gave expression to this when he said that it is only under a moral demand that humans experience themselves, not as an appearance, but as a "thing in itself" which negates all causal determinism.

As we have already said, Kant could think of this claim only as a restriction of spontaneous vitality, as a restriction of the "will" *(Willkür)*. The opposition between reason and life seemed to him to be irresolvable, a "meta-

---

1   Wittgenstein, from "Tagebücher 1914–1916" in Vol. I of *Schriften*, p. 186.

morphosis" of life not possible. For Kant, therefore, freedom as a human reality is not experienced in any real sense. Only the "fact of reason" is experienced, the moral demand. The possibility of its fulfillment always retained the status of a postulate which is implied in the demand. For Kant the fulfillment of the moral command is therefore never to be thought of as a transformation of the human pursuit of happiness, by which this striving comes to itself for the first time in a real way. One thinks the thought of the highest good much more in terms of an external connection, which is guaranteed by God after the fact, between good behavior and prosperity without the goal of the pursuit of happiness being somehow qualitatively changed. It is merely restricted to harmonizing with the same pursuit of all others. The question about the turning out well of life never really appears with Kant. There is, on the one side, the moral intention and, on the other, states of subjective satisfaction. What allows life to become a whole is not experienced by us: the intelligible character, which comes into view in the moral development of the individual.

There is here an undisputable insight, namely that this whole does not reach a full-bodied reality for us in the usual conception of life. Our past and future states are less real than the present ones. The others are only concepts, thoughts, images, not life. Accordingly, they are not knowledge in Plato's terms; rather they are only opinion, *doxa*. When Plato teaches that no one acts against what they know to be better, then he understands knowledge here to mean: lively presence. In the *Laws* he defines the ultimate ignorance once as "the lack of congruence of pleasure and aversion with rational conviction" (*Laws*, 689b). Apparently knowledge is that experience of having lived through a concept so that that which is conceptualized is made present. Such a thing as "presence" exists only for conscious life. Through what could past and future bind themselves into a lively unity, if not through their reflexive relationship with the subject who is the being which grounds them? As mere "states" they sink into non-reality. We can, however, only discover ourselves as the time-encompassing ground of unity of these states, these experiences and these events in that we – moving out of the centrality of living – discover the reality of the other, insofar as the other is not merely a correlate of our intentional situations. This discovery cannot be purely theoretical. Theoretically we press ahead to objects. Being oneself becomes possible only in free affirmation, in an act of acceptance. This act, however, in which life transcends itself and in this self-transcendence comes to a whole which examines its various states, is only possible through the highest powers of life. This self-transcendence of life is the rational: In its most elementary form we speak of justice; in its highest, of love.

Chapter 9

Benevolence

I

DELECTATIO IN FELICITATE ALTERI US: This definition of love was viewed by Leibniz as his great discovery and as the solution to the problem of eudaimonism. He saw in it an answer to the question of how a primordial interest in the other could be integrated with a insuperable desire for one's own happiness. Kant, for his part, did not view this as a solution because the interest in the condition of the other, which duty dictates, was being made dependent upon a contingent feeling of sympathy. He would have accepted this formula as a definition of love, but then love was to him morally irrelevant. It is "pathological," that is, a passion, about which we can do nothing. It would seem then that it can no more be the ground of moral conviction than it could be the consequence, dictated by duty, of this conviction, since no one can be commanded to take joy in something. The Christian teaching, that love of God and love of neighbor is a grace which no one can give themselves, corresponds to this conception. This teaching also says that love is the normal state of a rational being and that the necessity of a special grace of conversion has its ground in the sinful deviation of the human person from the normal state. Of course, love is not understood here as the sentimental identification of someone with all the others, but as *amor benevolentiae*, as the benevolence of a rational being.

Benevolence presupposes two things. First, it presupposes the teleological structure of a living being for whom something matters, for whom something is good, conducive, or beneficial. For only then can one be benevolent to a being. But it also presumes that this being, whose well-being is at stake, will appear as itself. Aristotle distinguishes these two presuppositions as *finis quo* and *finis cuius gratia*, as "What for?" and "For whose sake?" This distinction appears to be without practical meaning when it concerns the interest of another. Could we perceive the other's interest, if we did not perceive the other's self? But perhaps we mistake his true interest and pursue our own interest in thinking that it must be his interest. In any case this is not true for one's own interests. The subject is hidden in immediate self-assertion. An animal would never picture itself as the goal of its instincts and desires. Practical reason distinguishes itself from instinct in that the goal of the agent is made explicit. "For whose sake" the agent acts emerges. However, one's own self appears only indirectly as this goal: as the other of the others. We discover that we seem to do that which we do, first and foremost, for the sake of ourselves.

In *Being and Time* Heidegger developed the thesis that the whole of human being-in-the-world is enclosed by a fundamental structure of care, on the strength of which our own selves and our own possibility of being become the things which matter. Only in this context do things take on significance. When Dasein awakes and discovers itself as the ground of all meaning, this discovery reveals that Dasein has no significance for itself, that it itself is not to be understood as being for the sake of some other goal. This discovery gets expressed as disorientation and dread. The importance of this expression we will leave untouched for the moment. One discovers beneath all of our purposes which have an "in-order-to-do-something" character, a goal which one can characterize as a "for-the-sake-of," and this discovery is accurately described in this analysis as awakening to "actuality." We could also say "awakening to reality," since everything in our world which has significance only shows itself in this its function, not as its own self, not in its own reality. Only the for-the-sake-of which goes beyond any involvement is the real pure and simple. It is a for-the-sake-of not just in the sense of a purpose to be realized but as that "final end" which is always presupposed as a reality in order that something can appear to us as worth striving for. When Kant call humans ends-in-themselves, or when, in the tradition of metaphysics, God is called the "final end," then "end" does not mean that which is to be realized, but that which is presupposed as a ground in every realization. The showing-itself of this ground is that which we call awakening to reality or "the becoming real of reality for me."

This becoming real of the real is that which was called in the previous chapter the awakening to reason. It is connected with that viewpoint which cannot be deduced from the perspective of instincts. We can best make this clear by the example of the so-called instinct of self-preservation. Talk of such an instinct has something problematic about it. Such talk is characteristic of the state of ambiguity which we have labeled the state of half-wakefulness between mere animation and conscious living. There is a self-preservation which is goal directed in the condition of unconscious, instinctual animation: the flight from pain, the flight from an enemy, or the seeking of nourishment. But it is only as rational beings that we interpret these instinctive impulses as functions of self-preservation, since it is only on this level that we can reflect on the self and its possible not-being. It is here that the dread of death begins. As soon as we construe this dread or the corresponding desires as "an instinct for self-preservation," we end up in ambiguity, since the self is not the goal of instincts. It is not a *finis quo*, but a *finis cuius gratia*, not a "for-which," but a "for-the-sake-of." This is revealed as soon as I ask for whose sake I wish my own preservation. Who is hurt, when I no longer exist? In the language of instincts this question cannot even be intelligently asked. The bumper sticker, "Think about your wife. Drive carefully." does not speak this language. It has already attained the rational standpoint, the standpoint of benevolence, and left the standpoint of instincts behind. The drive for self-preservation which would make the goal of the drive the one for-whose-sake the drive exists, ends by abrogating the self. It gives the self a certain "significance," but since this significance has this self, whose preservation is at stake, as its presupposition, this instinctual goal cannot stand before reason. The self-preservation instinct is not a "ground" for self-preservation for the one who is not chained to the instinct. Schopenhauer, who knew the self only as the goal of the instinct for self-preservation, had to see the self then as completely conditioned by this instinct. With the extinction of this instinct, the self sinks back into unreality. For Schopenhauer awakening to reason is the same as the disappearance of the self. The instinct cannot be the ground of its own free affirmation. Pain does indeed contain within itself sufficient grounds to warrant its avoidance. But whether this avoidance is to be sought in the removal of the external cause of the pain or in the overcoming of the self which feels it cannot be decided on the basis of the instinct. In the same way the fact that the other has instincts cannot be the basis for respecting the other's existence.

There is no compelling argument on the basis of instincts against murder, or put more precisely, against the painless murder of a sleeping human who has no dependents who would miss his or her existence. It seems no one would lose anything by this murder, given that the one who has lost his life is no longer himself, and therefore no longer the only one in relation to whom this life had value. The same holds also for exterminating the whole human race. If humanity is involved only with itself, if it has value that is relative to itself or to the self-preservation of each individual, then the standard of its worth, by which this existence possessed a meaning which made its destruction into a crime, disappears along with its existence.

Here then lies the limits of any ethics which would seek its foundation in a communication structure between finite subjects. It only reaches a hypothetical commitment. The existence of subjects who are in such a communication community is the presupposition of this commitment. Respect for the existence of John can be understood only as an obligation for those to whom either John matters or who would be impaired in their own feeling of security by the murder of John. An obligation to John to allow him to live when his existence has value only for himself does not hold, because his death removes the one for whom this death meant loss. This has the practical consequences for the killing of humans in situations where others no longer come into consideration. The killing of humans in this situation on the basis of this maxim no longer awakens for some any feeling of uncertainty. This touches, for example, all small children. They are at the disposal of those for whom they have no worth. This is the real reason why euthanasia and abortion are propounded almost only by people without religious convictions. Horkheimer and Adorno write that ultimately there is only a religious argument against murder.

Why "religious"? Because the argument is intelligible only when humans have become aware of a "holiness." The holy is the incommensurable, the functional which is not capable of being derived or grounded, the "good" in the sense of a one-place predicate. What is presupposed here is that a being has gone out of the centrality of mere living, in which everything which is encountered has meaning only in its function for a subject, who remains hidden as a self for whom nothing has meaning in itself. Only in this going out, only in this *metanoia* does the self become visible as the fundamental reality which grounds all "value." When Kant says that the human has no value, but rather a dignity, he meant by the word "dignity" something incommensurable, sublime, to be respected *unconditionally*. This autonomy, this non-relativity could be interpreted from the perspective of instinct-dependencies as that which, since it itself is without sense, first gets its meaning in its relation to others who are equally without meaning, which makes the whole context of meaning meaningless – the position of nihilism. Or the discovery of the radical autonomy of the finite subject can be interpreted as allowing this subject to appear in a splendor which is not its own. The impossibility of killing it, which is in no way a physical incapacity, derives from the insight that it is unconditioned, and unconditioned not in the way of its physical presence but in the way of the representation of an image. An image is something which *is* not itself what it shows. It is a physical object. An image is an image not through its physical existence but rather through that which it images. With the image of the unconditioned there are some differences. The image of the unconditioned is something precisely through the fact that it *is* in a emphatic sense, through its substantiality, which releases it from the process of becoming and makes its value incommensurable with its genesis. But this is not something which one happens upon as one would an object. Being is not capable of being an object. Being is substantiality, being a self, and this grounds all objectivity. The paradigmatic case of such substantiality is subjectivity. What Aristotle said about substance is valid for subjectivity: Everything else is predicated of it, but it is not predicated of anything else. It is not characteristic of a being; rather it simply *is*. And precisely in this simple being it is an image; it is the absolute in the manner of an image.

In what way, if any, can we experience the autonomous other, the holy? Doesn't experiencing something mean fitting it into a relational context? All experience is categorically structured and as such already a kind of relational structure. Still, religious practice knows a way of proceeding which makes present reality as absolute without relation to the subject and without the mediation of language: the act of worship. However the phenomenology of religion might more exactly analyze this act, it includes, at least in the Jewish, Christian, and Islamic understanding, the unconditional submission to the unconditioned ground of reality. And this means not just a reluctant submission, which would really not be a submission at all, since it would only be given as the price for something else, i.e., for something finite. Unconditional submission has the character of gratitude. And indeed the gratitude for that which *shows* itself in its pure otherness, for that which is called, in the language of the scriptural religions, "the glory of the Lord." *Gratias agimus tibi propter magnam gloriam tuam* ("We give you thanks because of your great glory") is one of the oldest Christian prayers.

In what does the showing itself of the totally Other, the absolute, consist? It consists in the being of each finite being, in which the thought of the autonomous being becomes absorbed in gratitude. The being which thinks this thought, that is, conscious life, obtains in this thought a certain autonomy, a certain "substantiality," by which it becomes the image of that which it honors, and recognizes in this very image in every other rational being. We call the deliberate attitude toward such a being "respect" or even "reverence." This attitude has before all else a negative character. It restricts how much a subject can grasp. It demands the pure "letting-be" of the other in its irreducible otherness. As self-respect it forbids one's own self from reducing itself to its appearance as an object of instincts. It demands that one's own self view itself as a representation of the unconditioned and therefore as definitively removed from one's own arbitrary disposition. Duties to one's own self are not of the kind from which one could dispense oneself.

II

The respect which is shown to the person – to the life which is regulated by the awakening of reason – is unconditional acceptance. The unconditional acceptance of a being, who has as a characteristic "being-out-for" something, that is, a being for whom something, usually its own self, matters, consists in the acceptance of this being-out-for. One cannot, however, accept a tendency without tending in the same direction, without being-out-toward the same. To be-out-for that which is beneficial to the other, that is, that which fulfills the other's being-out-for, is what we call benevolence. We could also speak of love. On account of the ambiguity of the concept of love, the philosophy of the Middle Ages and, following it, Leibniz distinguished between the *amor concupiscentiae* and the *amor benevolentiae*, between concupiscence and benevolence. The distinction does not coincide with the distinction between self-love and love of neighbor. Love of others can be *amor concupiscentiae*, insofar as I love the other as a part of my world, on account of the pleasure of his company or some other advantage, as Aristotle made clear. The other is loved in this function, and only so far as the other fulfills it. Otherwise, the other would be dropped. Conversely, not every form of self-love is egoism or *amor concupiscentiae*. "My life belongs to the King, not my honor," is an old saying which expresses the boundary of functionalization. And when the refusal to sacrifice the purity of one's own conscience for some "cause" is denounced as a sublime form of egoism, then it is not yet understood that nothing is sacred to the one whose own conscience is not sacred. Since the dimension of the unconditioned is hidden from him, so is reality as selfhood completely hidden. "Love your neighbor as yourself": This rule implies self-love in which the person realizes himself or herself. Love of neighbor can be the roundabout way through which one awakens to one's own self. The meaning of my life for someone else can become a motive for me to take myself seriously. In any case "altruism" is not an adequate translation of "benevolence" or "love," and neither is "selflessness."

To love the other "for his own sake" is that which Aristotle considered under the name "Friendship." The friend is the one who is loved for his own sake. Nonetheless this love would not be correctly described, if it were described as "selflessness." The friend, says Aristotle, is not loved on account of some characteristic, on account of which he or she is useful or convenient to me; rather for his own sake. The friend possesses human virtues which make the person lovable for his own sake. Association with him is a source of happiness for his friends, without one being able to say that the other is loved *on account of* this happiness. As distinct from enjoyment, happiness or joy cannot be willed directly. What Aristotle describes here is not expressible in the categories of instincts and the functionalism which derives from these instincts. Another means much more to me through that which he is, not for me, but in himself. What hides itself behind this paradox is what we have described as the awakening to reality. The ego caught up in instincts has not discovered the self or the other. It remains hidden from itself in the center of everything organic. In the act of awakening to reason, its own reality and that of the other become simultaneously visible. The showing-itself of the reality of the other has the same meaning as the complete realization of this reality as a teleological term, of the reality of a being-out-for. Only in this complete realization does the other become real for us, since, so long as they seem to us simply to be there, they are not for us what they "themselves" are. We can only know what it means to be a self through the fact that we live a self, and therefore have instincts but at the same time go out of our centrality and perceive ourselves as the other of the other, and the other as *alter ego*.

Such *amor amicitiae* is, according to Aristotle, only possible as the mutual benevolence of humans whose direction of will is comprehensible to each other, since they both have risen above mere instinct and have accepted the good as the general in their wills. So long as the two are fixated on possessing the same object, their wills remain antagonistic. If both want a decision which comes from an impartial viewpoint, then they want something in common and can be friends. There are limits to this transformation of particular interests into rational interest in just compensation. These limits occur when the particular interest is an interest in the real conditions of being oneself and where these appear to be incompatible with another's conditions of being himself or herself. There are situations of existential hostility, which cannot be resolved in a Socratic fashion. This is especially true when it does not concern *inimicus*, but rather *hostis*, that is, when the hostility is not something personal but something collective, i.e., political. To moralize this kind of conflict can have the paradoxical consequence that one party understands itself as moral, as the "peace party," and so discriminates against the other as the party against peace. When the battle is unavoidable, then being moral consists in treating the enemy as an enemy, that is, as someone whose perspective, given the present situation, I know cannot be brought into agreement with mine. When no considerations of justice or fairness can resolve the conflict, there still remains the renunciation of hate, the renunciation of reducing the other to the hostility, to the meaning that he as an enemy has for me. "Love your enemies" – this command commands us never to give up the perception of the reality of the other as a self even when I am in a relationship of hostility and struggle with him.

III

Contrary to the Kantian narrowing of ethics, it must be said that it is not the demand for impartiality which is the basis of all moral decisions, but rather that it is the perception of the reality of the other and even of one's own self. According to Kant, the demand for impartiality has no need of being further grounded. It appears to be the basis of every grounding. But why should we ground anything, if we are better off without grounds and justifications, relying on the natural relations of strength and if we see our advantage in not taking others into consideration? Here all grounding comes to an end, since the grounding of the grounding hangs in the air, if there is someone who does not want to ground their actions or hear of grounds. In Plato's *Gorgias*, Callicles grasps exactly this, when, having noticed that his strength lies precisely in not carrying on the discussion, he breaks the dialogue off. So a decision appears at the basis of every so-called final grounding after all. It is something else when the demand for impartiality, that is, justice, is grounded in the evidence of a perception, in the evidence of the reality of the other and of one's own reality as that of a subject and not primarily that of an object of instincts. This evidence is the real basis of all ethics. There is then no ethics without metaphysics. Solipsism cannot push forward to something like a moral obligation. And so long as I am at liberty to hold behaviorism as the real truth about all other beings who feel and think and to reject their feelings and thoughts as metaphysical hypotheses, just so long is there no object of moral obligation.

Does this mean then that moral obligations are only binding for those who accept certain metaphysical hypotheses which we are at liberty to accept or not accept?

It does indeed mean that each person would have the right to treat someone merely as an object, so long as they held a scientific theory according to which the person is merely an object. But wouldn't we categorically demand these people to so change their theory that it does not stand in the way of their perception of the other as a real, living, and rational being? But how shall this demand be grounded, if not by a truth claim, that is, through the statement that it *is* so? But this implies the demand to duplicate my judgment in the first person in their judgment in the third person, to say "he has pain" when I say "I have pain." This demand cannot be discursively grounded, since discourse itself depends upon the previous recognition of the discourse-subject.

This fundamental "metaphysical" evidence is not of such a kind that it would be impervious to any possibility of doubt. Nietzsche has shown how far doubt reaches. It is capable of calling into question the meaning of every linguistic utterance. Whoever concludes from this however that after Nietzsche metaphysics is no longer possible does not know what Nietzsche himself said. Then when one follows Nietzsche's logic, one must abandon every thought of meaning anything, including positing the denial of the possibility of metaphysics. Thus, the consequence from that which in Nietzsche ought to be called insight is something else. From the possibility of doubting everything, it does not follow that it would be good to do that. The necessity of positing the reality of the living is not a theoretical compulsion, but is itself a kind of moral evidence. Whoever loves a human, whoever has friends, cannot at the same time doubt the beloved's or the friend's existence. That person must hold the other's being alive as irreducible. And when I say, one *cannot* doubt, I do not mean a physical or logical impossibility, but a moral and *therefore* absolute impossibility. Insofar as I doubt his reality, I do not merely bracket somewhat the reality of the friendship; rather I destroy it. Friendship does not allow for an ontological abstinence, for an *epoché*. It implies an ontological affirmation. In the case of friendship this affirmation is not a postulate, but a necessary implication. But there, where the relationship to the other does not have the intensity of friendship, but is defined by the claim of each to "respect," there the moral claim becomes a metaphysical postulate, becomes the postulate of recognizing the other as "real." This postulate does not allow itself to be deduced from a law, but expresses nothing other than the unmediated demand of the real to be perceived. But the perception of the living *as* living is, as Kant first showed us, an act of freedom. When Kant writes that teleological judgments are not constitutive of our experience, the meaning of this thesis is: I can at any time decide to view a living creature which I encounter as a mere machine, as a non-substantial reality. The unity of experience and the capacity for identifying temporal-spatial objects will not by destroyed by this. I can decide to act toward the world as I would to an empire of mere objects. And even when I, for the sake of a more comfortable life, deal practically with humans and animals as if they were humans and animals, but then only to the extent that it seems good to me and it does not disturb my interests, that is, without acknowledging an obligation to anything resembling unconditional respect, I reduce the living beings to something like toys or movie characters. The real recognition of the real is irrevocable. It cannot be divorced from faithfulness. It is not by accident that the Hebrew word for truth is the same word as for faithfulness. The affirmation of the reality of being a self is a free act. It is identical with benevolence. What we are attempting to say here has been expressed by Plato, when he wrote that the good is the ground of reality and the intelligibility of things, and when he characterized the theoretical affirmation of the idea of the good as inseparable from willing the good.

The real is perceived as itself only when it is perceived as a project. Only in the "benevolent" accompanying of this project do I realize its reality. It is evident that the concept of reality here is taken from the paradigm of the living. Is it being said then that all reality is to be thought of as a kind of living, to be thought of teleologically and thereby as a possible object of benevolence? We can only give a hypothetical answer to the question. To think of an object of our experience as being also independent of this experience, as a being in itself, means to think of it as analogous to the living, so that it is not constituted by the momentary perceptions which I have of it, but gathers together various states and happenings in a unity of identity with itself. But the perception of the world of the living and of the people who live along with us is in principle of the same kind as the perception of inanimate objects. We can identify a table or a molecule in the same way as dog. Not to confer any being on inanimate things beside their being perceived by us would land us in huge difficulties. On the other hand, we cannot say at all what identity, what "being a self" means, if it is not thought of as a process which is concerned with its own potentiality for being and a certain kind of "fulfillment" (Whitehead). The only alternative to this biomorphism appears to me to consist in denying the inanimate anything like reality and identity; conceiving it instead as a kind of potentiality for possible perception by which it first becomes real. The problem of anthropomorphism in the interpretation of the living repeats itself on this level. Whoever is not prepared to choose conscious life as the paradigm for interpreting the living in general must also deny the being-alive of the living and reduce it to an "objective" structure of material being. What one does not realize is that that which is called "being" in reference to materiality can in its turn only be understood from the viewpoint of the living.

Only being which has the character of being a self is a possible object of benevolence and only for benevolence does being a self reveal itself. When the Psalms bid the sun and the moon, rivers and seas to praise God, and when St. Francis does the same in the *Canticle of the Sun*, these are powerful expressions of such universal benevolence, since these creatures praise God by being what they are. But it implies that their being is not merely an objective being-there, but is a tendency, that is, that it is already "concerned about something," namely, its own potentiality for being, and that inanimate beings *make possible* something like involvement with themselves and are not just *passively* involved with living beings. From this stems the open question connected with the meaning of physics, especially that of quantum mechanics: Is it the case that before being fixed by our observation, the subatomic world has no fixed "nature" but is only potentiality, i.e., real only as that which it is observed as. This conception would lead to something close to the position of Fichte. Leibniz, however, believed that we have to recognize that the world possesses a character of spontaneity and subjectivity, in complete independence from the thoroughly determined, purely passive context of functions which physics represents to us. In this century Whitehead is a follower of Leibniz. Leibniz and Whitehead thereby establish a connection with the Aristotelian concept of substance. The paradigm of substance for Aristotle is the living being, and the paradigm of a living being is the human. But the concept of substance, gained from the human, is so formalized by Aristotle that it becomes the basic concept for reality. Of course, its application to inanimate objects is very formal and abstract, since all the intuitions which underlie this concept come out of the self-experience of conscious life. It is appropriate then that benevolence toward the world of inanimate being as "being a self" must also have a very abstract and metaphorical character. That means that the benevolence is always mediated through the "meanings" by which the inanimate becomes an element of our world, as mountain and stream, as snow and rain, as crystal and as shore, in short, as those things which we want to be as they are, without having to impute to this being anything like a natural being-out-for. The actual "substantial" reality of the inanimate world, if it can be spoken of at all here, would be the molecular, atomic, and subatomic reality. In practical life we can refer to this only indirectly and from the viewpoint of what is useful. The question of whether intrusion into the constitutive structure of these realities needs to be justified in some way, of whether they can or must be objects of some consideration in which something besides the "interests" of the living plays a role, is a question whose determination depends upon ontological predeterminations which would lead us beyond our present scope. These predeterminations depend upon our perceiving these realities. And if it is correct to say that they *are* that which is experienced, then these realities are open to interpretation only in reference to life, and it is their importance for life which defines their place in the *ordo amoris*. To acquiesce to this means: to wish well.

The ambiguity, which is our present topic, does not stem from a defect. It corresponds to the nature of a finite subject itself to *also* be a thing among things. And it accords with the especially human trait of needy love, which is never to be unequivocally divided into benevolence and desire. We *ourselves* would not experience the love of another as a pure kindness, if it were disinterested in the sense that the other did not want to have anything to do with us. This benevolence which is free from desire appears to us as the lowest level of *amor amicitiae*, not the highest. Concupiscence predominates in the relation with the inanimate. If we cannot relate it to ourselves or others like us, if we cannot give it some significance, then it does not appear to have any meaning. Something living, on the other hand, is related both to itself and to its instincts; things have significance for it. We could not experience it in its reality *as* living, if we did not understand it, that is, if we did not try in some way to *be* this other. And that means, if we did not wish it well, if we did not view its pain as something, which *prima facie* should not be (the reasons for this pain may always modify this *prima facie* judgment). Not to view it in this way means the same as not perceiving pain *as* pain.

Just as Buddha's identification with all who suffer was not a moral decision but an enlightenment, a sudden awakening, so is it with benevolence. Buddhist compassion is distinguished from benevolence by a different interpretation of the fundamental experience as well as by a different intention. Buddha's experience was the lack of reality of the self. I myself am as unreal as the other is to me, so long as I stand in the centrality of instinct, hung up on instincts. Love as *amor benevolentiae* is affirming not negating. *It affirms instinct, because it has freed itself totally from its dominance.* It is no longer instinct which turns itself against itself. The fundamental experience for love is not that of unreality but that of the real. Unambiguous reality is, however, that of the person. In love the other becomes as real to me as I become to myself in this same awakening. The other and I attain the reality of the image. An image is supposed to accomplish something. It is not supposed to dissipate something, but to show it, to let it be seen. To perceive it as an image means to perceive what it shows, to be shown something by it. What appears in subjectivity? Being, reality, and this precisely because subjectivity itself is not positivity but negativity, not a found fact, but reflection. Facts can only appear in that which is not a kind of positive fact. The human is the place of the appearance of being. Unconditional respect for the human is equivalent to affirmation of reality. And vice versa: Reality is not an objective characteristic of something, existence is not a "real predicate," as Kant has said. Being is that which reveals itself only to the benevolent. And this self-showing precedes all "Shoulds." It is the gift, which underlies every possible task.[1] For the benevolent benevolence itself is a gift. It is *eudaimonia*, the turning-out-well of life, which on the level of simply living and instinct appears to us to be subject to irresolvable antinomies. Only the life which is awakened to reason is capable of such a turning-out-well. Life is awake, if reason is no longer merely an instrument in the service of instinct, but becomes a form of life. Reason stops standing abstractly over against life, and becomes concrete and fills itself with living power – as creative fantasy and decisive

---

1   The play on words *Gabe* and *Aufgabe* is lost in translation.

willing: benevolence, well-wishing. In this reality shows itself as it is and that means: in a friendly light.

IV

The paradigm of acting from benevolence is any action by which we come to the help of human life which requires this help. This is not self-evident. There is then the possibility of seeing the paradigm of the ethical in omission, that is, in the renunciation of pursuing one's own ends without consideration of other living beings. We could see the paradigm of the ethical as the willingness to come to an understanding with others about the criteria for settling conflicts of interests. Or we could view the measures that someone takes to make the overall situation better or more beneficial for the greatest possible number of humans as the paradigm. But a fundamental state of affairs underlies all these paradigms: the teleological constitution of life, which is always concerned about something, and the neediness of the living, which, unlike the monad of Leibniz, does not unfailingly realize its *telos* but is constantly threatened with its failure and is not of itself equipped with the means of insuring its own self-preservation and the attainment of its essential end. Before all else, then, benevolence means the willingness to come to the help of life which is threatened. Hans Jonas has properly characterized the behavior of humans toward helpless children as the fundamental paradigm of moral behavior. Refusing to harm is only one, even if, as we shall see, one very specific way of helping. The question is: Can one also interpret the benevolence accorded to oneself as "willingness to help"? Isn't help essentially help from the outside? What then characterizes helpful action? First of all, indirectness. Help cannot take the place of the leading of one's life. Its goal is rather to make this leading possible. And we can do this for ourselves too. The unmediated pursuit of our instinctual goals does not resemble what benevolence expresses. In this pursuit we are completely given over to our environment and have not yet become actual, not yet caught sight of what is ours. It is only in reflection that the for-the-sake-of our will is revealed. Only when we see what is ours as a natural and rational being, can we come to the help of our *real* willing and begin to act responsibly with ourselves. So even in the relationship to ourselves, help is the category which expresses the ethical relationship, the relationship of benevolence. Help is neither a spontaneous expression of life, nor is it *poiesis*, making, creative activity. In any case it is not defined by means of these. It always presupposes a tendency, which is supported by it and which needs its support. All specifically ethical action is of this kind. It distinguishes itself from the immediateness of spontaneous expressions of life and also from technical or artificial actions, even when it is only a certain modification of these actions. The modification consists in an overcoming of the lostness in the end and of the forgetfulness in the for-the-sake-of, which is nothing other than "forgetfulness of being." The relinking of action with reality, the calling back out of forgetfulness has the character of helping, since it helps the agent toward that which the agent *really* wants.

The Platonic concept of the real will or of the "true interests" is indispensable for ethical practice, that is, for the practice of benevolence, whatever difficulties may be raised by this concept. This concept is based upon the experience of which we spoke in the first chapter, that humans often, according to their own criteria, want the wrong thing. That the living require help is not only conditioned by external circumstances, but precisely by one's own lack, especially by ignorance. Instruction is one of the most important forms of "helping life." This holds even when it is in the form of self-instruction, as learning or as reminding oneself of that which one tends to forget under the immediate suggestion of the instinctual goals of action. *Real* want is not then identical with an immediate instinctual goal. A certain type of psychoanalysis views as "real" that which presents itself in analytical introspection as the primary instinctual goal, and sees the correction of this by means of reflection and conscious willing as a construction by which humans are alienated from themselves. Were that so, the human would *really* be an animal which is in itself self-sufficient by means of a structure of instincts fitted for the environment, and for which something like a rational insight would only serve to disturb its security. But as we know, this is not the case. There is, as we have seen, no purely animal happiness for humans. The reality principle is not, as Freud thought, a condition dictated from the outside which necessitates the task of one's real will, since it cannot otherwise secure its own self-preservation. Reality is not primarily hostile to humans; rather it is that which they demand absolutely. This demand renders impossible any purely animal state of contentment. What leads human out of themselves, what leads them to the discovery of the other in their self-being and moves them to the sublimation of instinct is "deeper" than instinct itself. Essentially, the human *Dasein* has the character of anticipation. What we really are lies yet before us, and we need help to reach it. Friends have to come to our aid, we have to allow ourselves to be helped, because, "What we can do through our friends, we can, in a certain sense, do through ourselves." Only when we are helped do we learn to help ourselves, that is, to enter into that indirect relationship with ourselves which is constitutive for all rationality which is not strictly instrumental, that is constitutive for all ethical practice.

Chapter 10

Ordo Amoris

TO AWAKEN to reality means, first and foremost, that a finite being moves beyond the perspective whose horizon is determined by instinct, i.e., by the nature of its species. Before this moving beyond, its perception and activity can be understood as a function of the self-preservation of a system in an environment. The *animal rationale* discovers itself and the other as realities in a common horizon, a horizon which is in principle infinite – the horizon of being. Each thing which it encounters in this horizon comes to it as itself. Herein lies a peculiar paradox. Then, insofar as it is itself, it is unique, incommensurable, incomparable, remote, only identical with itself. But exactly in this it is somehow comparable, since it is related by resemblance to all those things which themselves are themselves and are identical with themselves. Benevolence has a similarly paradoxical structure. Benevolence is neither a function of instinct nor of the drive to preserve the self or the race, since it is precisely these which it relativizes. It is as universal as the horizon which it opens. It holds each being as something unique, incommensurable. And yet benevolent beings, as finite, have to establish commensurability and relativize that which they encounter, at least by the time they begin to act. As agents they are, then, essentially finite. To act is to be selective. Agents subject that which they encounter to their "viewpoint." They do not just let be; rather they engage reality, and they change it under finite perspectives and with finite consequences. They place one thing at the service of another; they call certain consequences "ends" while others are reduced to "side-effects" or "costs."

The universality of benevolence is a contemplative one, not active. In Plato one speaks of the love of the "good itself," in the classical tradition of philosophy of the love of God, and in Spinoza of *amor Dei intellectualis*. Augustine talks of *amor Dei usque ad contemptum sui* and sets this over against *amor sui usque ad contemptum Dei*. In a way that is radical without being empirical, the two loves divide humankind into two kingdoms. That the universality of benevolence understands itself as love of God means that universal benevolence is not simply possibility, the empty form of abstract generality, which first realizes itself by means of "cases." If the universality of benevolence were only of an abstract kind, directed toward something like "all humankind," then there would be no one for whom the fundamental benevolence would be actually valid. As a transcendental *optio fundamentalis* it always remains transcendent as regards its "categorical" application. It follows from this that the love, the *amor benevolentiae*, never really become real. As long as it remains general, the fundamental option, the "good will," is purely abstract. Where it does becomes concrete, it is no longer itself. The relationship between love of God and "love of neighbor," on the other hand, does not have a transcendental form and is not a case of categorical application; rather it concerns the presence of the absolute and its real symbol. The image is not an "application" of that which it portrays. It presents that of which it is an image. Behind a saying like that in the first of Letter of John: "How can someone say that he loves God, whom he cannot see, when he does not love his brother, whom he can see?" stands the thought of the image in which appears that of which it is the image.

I

We cannot direct our actions to God, only to finite beings – with the exception of the ritual forms of reverence, whose finite, particular, "conventional" gestures symbolically thematize the divine. But every unconditioned reference of acting, which grounds the ethical identity of humans, is symbolic. Therefore, all ethical action is ritualistic, not pure rational-purposive, action. It is a *presentation* of benevolence, and not benevolence itself. In this presentation the universality of benevolence is broken. The well-worn saying, "All things to all people" is a hyperbolic metaphor which, taken literally, is impossible to integrate with the conditions of finitude. One of the conditions of finitude is that no one can give without taking, whether it concerns time, energy, attention, or material goods. There is a way to try to ignore this condition: the cult of pure spontaneity. One gives oneself randomly – led by chance or passion – to a being, upon whom one concentrates all the benevolence one is capable of, be it forever, be it for the length of the passion or the sympathy. The incommensurability of *each* individual gets realized through the incommensurability of the dedication to *an* individual. It changes from being a symbol of the absolute to being an absolute symbol, which is not relativized by considerations of the interests of a third party, or by considerations of foreseeable secondary consequences, or by the fact that actions set precedents for others. We can call this kind of behavior a "fanaticism of passion." Its self-justification is the slogan: "Can it be sin to love?"

In reality this exclusive benevolence, which leaves out all considerations of justice, is anything but that awakening to reality, which could be understood as *amor benevolentiae*. Here the other is not the representation of the unconditioned; rather it is its replacement. Both the subjective arbitrariness in this love's choice of object as well as its absolutizing tendency show that this is the living out of instinctual spontaneity and that the other is not being thematized as himself or herself, but as an object of an inclination, even when it is an inclination to do good. In the end the reason for my devotion does not lie in the other, but in me. If it were in the other, then that love would not be a reason for ignoring all others, who in view of their incommensurability cannot be distinguished from the object of my devotion.

Looked at the other way, does this mean that the *amor benevolentiae* reaches its specific dimension only when it holds without distinction for everyone in the same way? That is, when every moment of contingency, fate, and underived individual inclinations is removed? If this is so, then benevolence itself would be reduced to the command of impartiality and the demand for generalizability, thereby losing its power to reveal reality, which was what first allowed us to catch sight of subjects, who could then be objects of a respect commensurate with our duty. The reverse is also true: For its part love would be merely a "pathological" tendency in the Kantian sense, a result of instincts, which then would not be in any position to reveal our being a self. Being alive and being rational would once more be separated. The "fact of reason" would be an alien element which breaks into life, without transforming it, only able to subject its expressions to certain conditions, without it ever being evident what reason could induce a living being to subject itself to these conditions. Then there must be an inner connection, rather than a mutually exclusive relationship, between the experience of a unique and particular love and the universality of benevolence. And indeed there is.

The original and purest forms of benevolence are completely contingent in relation to their object: affection, friendship, gratitude. Jean Paul has pointed out that the feeling of gratitude is essentially unselfish (*Quintus Fixlein, Sämtl. Werke* I, 5, pp. 208ff). An act of kindness calls it forth, but its aim is not further acts of kindness; rather it is directed to the giver himself. Every act of benevolence from finite beings has the character of gratitude. One notices that the calculating type is especially incapable of gratitude. Benevolence, which is in its origin contingent, shows its genuineness, that is, its cognitive character, its power to render reality accessible, in that it experiences the whole world in the one to whom it directs itself and sees everything in a new light. The initial contingency cancels itself in this. The one represents the whole. On the contrary, when love for the one leads to injustice against others, then the initial contingency becomes fixed, and even that one becomes only a contingent and temporary object of affections who can be turned away from, since the one as himself or herself was not actually intended.

Friendship as the exemplary and most intensive form of benevolence lies beyond all standards of justice in its origin. It is a free gift and a free choice. It is the center of all ethics, since in it that benevolence, which is the basis of all demands of justice, becomes visible in its pure form. To recognize someone as having legal claims means in some way to wish them well. But then if we ask what benevolence is, we can only refer to its highest paradigm, friendship. One can only have such a small number of real friends that our dealings with them never become the subject of considerations of justice. The place where "normative" ethics, the obligation to justify, begins is on the other side of friendship. For the finite being benevolence in its universality has to organize itself into a structure which corresponds both to the finitude of its perspective as well as the finitude of the objects of benevolence. In other words there exists what Augustine called the *ordo amoris*. Everyone has their own place in the *ordo amoris* of the other. Through reason's universality we ourselves realize that we cannot be as important to others as we are to ourselves. And because each of us know this, no one has the right to treat someone else as a nobody. Each one who is affected by the actions of others can demand a legitimate justification of the actions of the other. It is precisely because I am able to relativize my own interests, and precisely because I myself am capable of a fundamental benevolence, that I have the right to be the object of reasonable consideration when my interests are involved. The Kantian imperative, never to use persons as means but always to respect them as ends in themselves, has first and foremost the meaning that each of those who are affected by my actions and are not themselves the one for whom I perform the action, deserves respect to the extent that the question of the acceptability of my actions will have to be posed. This question is asked on account of the fact they are the subject of their own actions and so are potentially ethical beings. A positive answer to this question means the same thing as the assumption that the affected person as a rational being must be able to approve this consideration in principle.

We have not yet asked what form these rational considerations are to have, nor what role discourse and the actual consent of the affected person play in all this. We are only concerned here with seeing that one can be affected by the actions of others in three ways. One is affected when an action is performed directly for one's sake, an action which took place "to please" one. The reverse of this relation is hatred, in which an action is performed for the sake of the other; it is performed to hurt the other. Finally, one can be affected by an action which is not performed for one's sake, but in which one is still involved. The finitude of the agent makes it impossible to make everyone the direct goal of action. *Ordo amoris* means there is a hierarchical order of preference within universal benevolence. It is in reference to this order that we speak of justice.

II

Within this order of preference there are viewpoints which intersect and overlap and therefore have a role to play in the case of conflicting interests. Thus, we have relationships of greater closeness or distance. They are grounded in the sensuous, spatio-temporal make-up of life. From an ethical viewpoint this structure is not without its significance. If reason is the coming to itself of a living being, its awakening to reality, then practical reason is not some second reality next to that of the living organism, but rather the "form" of that reality. The centrality of instincts, according to which the world is essentially an environment, does not remain a matter of indifference to the rational being. Human interaction is not an amalgamation of rational beings who are transparent to one another and who exist in the realm of rational generalities. If this realm of rational generalities is not to remain empty, it presupposes the concrete vitality of particular individuals, whom we call persons because of their capacity *as* these individuals both to be benevolent and to relativize on account of this benevolence their own interests. The individuality and finite perspectives of the person are not to be equated with the irrational or with that which is to be overcome, but rather they are what make possible and sustain the ascent to the universal perspective. Persons *are* only as individuals. In this way the order of near and far is an ethically relevant order. That – *ceteris paribus* – family, friends, coworkers, neighbors, fellow members of a religious or civil community have a greater claim to be the direct beneficiary of our action than those who are further away or unknown or foreign must be expected by the latter. This follows from the fact that no one can give someone something without taking or withholding it from someone else. If priorities really are to be the expression of benevolence and not subjective arbitrariness, then they have to be grounded in insights which are accessible to everyone. Near and far are such rational relations, since the one who is faraway is, at the same time, in a relationship of nearness with others, from which follow corresponding priorities for him or her.

Standing before the alternative of saving the life of my child or of someone else, I would choose to save the life of my child. And I would need the forgiveness of the one, who by this decision, was lost. Forgiveness, not in its narrower, moral sense, since I have no guilt. And yet the tension remains between the infinite horizon of responsibility, which encloses the rational being and the finitude of the human as a living being, who cannot measure up to this responsibility. Often the only solidarity which is possible with another is the ineffectual wish to help. But even the intensity of the wish to be able to help lessens with the distance of the other. Benevolence itself diminishes. Some faraway person's need does not normally prompt us to decisively change our usual way of life or to disrupt our interests in order to free them from their situation. Every appeal here seems to land in a void. Something faraway is simply not as real for us. We are used to having the mass media show us daily in our living rooms the fate of faraway peoples. The world grows smaller. The faraway comes nearer. But this process tends to dull rather than effect solidarity. It produces a feeling of impotence. This dulling or rendering apathetic appears when the universality of reason directly confronts the particularity and finitude of individual life, without developing the mediating structure of an *ordo amoris*. To develop this is, however, a demand of reason. As rational beings we know that the reality of the other forms an independent center of life. For us as finite living beings, however, this knowledge is not vibrant; we do not experience it. We are in some respects only half-awake. Still, to be fully awake cannot mean that we cease to be living, feeling individuals. If that were so, then every impulse to solidarity would be quickly extinguished. From being half-awake we can only want to wake up in the sense that we make what we know experienceable for ourselves in that we develop an *ordo amoris*.

First, this implies a political obligation, consistent with our own possibilities, to help bring about political structures which, without leveling the distinctions between near and far, between citizen and foreigner, to a universal indifference toward all, still make it possible for *every* human to have somewhere, in the fullest sense of the word, a home. Human rights are not the rights of citizens; still it is a human right to have the rights of a citizen someplace. Second, it follows from the universality of benevolence that anyone at any time can become our "neighbor," that is, the one who on accident or on purpose ends up being in a situation of physical proximity. German penal law recognizes a duty to offer help to victims of accidents even when a person just happens to come upon the scene. The contingency of this meeting, which lies in the fact that someone turns to me for aid, is transcended by the mutual relation which comes into being when two humans regard one another. The other reveals himself or herself to me in this relationship as *real*. Although I did not seek this revelation, I cannot go back on it, without thereby separating myself from the benevolence through which the reality was first made accessible. This is the point of the story of the good Samaritan. The Samaritan is a foreigner who comes by chance across a man who needs his help. He is the one who happens to be close by. This situation does not somehow exempt one from the *ordo amoris*; rather it is a case for its application.

Still, it is not enough to push the general problems to level of the political and to add the Good Samaritan case to the traditional list of obligations, if at the same time one tries to avoid such cases and knowledge of others' needs. What counts is not so much diffuse universal information about human suffering, which tends to render it unreal, but that we allow some small part of that which we know to become real to ourselves. It is this part which constitutes the experience from which we can draw conclusions for action. How much this is cannot be determined by any casuistry. It was Kant's opinion that no one could do more than his duty and everyone must do that. Consequentialists of utilitarian and other varieties arrive at a similar result, when they understand moral duty as a duty of universal optimization. We will have to concern ourselves more deeply with this conception later. It is common to both conceptions to place imperatives, laws, or norms at the beginning of ethics – an "ought" then and not a perception of reality. The greatest models of love of neighbor did not live and act in the consciousness of doing something extraordinary, when they did that which in reality no one could have demanded of them. But the matter-of-factness with which they did what they did does not imply that everyone in their place must act as they did. This would be valid only for those who *were* like them. At most the question could be so formulated: Is there a duty to a certain habit of being? Certain ways of being do, in fact, so touch us that we spontaneously feel: "That is how one ought to be." But it is not completely clear what kind of "ought" this is, since one cannot successfully want something *to be*. At most one can through his or her doing unintentionally become a human being with such and such characteristics.

Aristotle understood his ethics as a teaching about virtues, a teaching about certain habits of being, certain behavior which had become "second nature." He did not set up any casuistic rules for generosity; rather he described the habit of a generous person, who *knows* in a given situation how much has to be given to whom. And Aristotle characterizes this knowledge as knowledge of the right mean between too much and too little. Thomas Aquinas took over this conception of ethics but added that for the *forma virtutum*, love, there is no such mean. Its measure is infinite. If we understand love in the sense of *amor benevolentiae* as the becoming real of the real for us, then the same conclusion emerges. The measure of this becoming real is not a mean lying between two extremes, but is itself an extreme: the spanning of an infinite space between the negativity of reflection and the positivity of being. For the being awakened to reason the metamorphosis of life through the Logos and the fulfillment of rationality with life is a process without end. To grasp this process as a task is itself a gift, the gift of being that has begun to awaken. *Amor Dei usque ad contemptum sui* and *amor sui usque ad contemptum Dei* – both of the "usque" respectively express tendencies, directions, and not "standpoints." No one can actually take the divine standpoint, and no one ought to try, since, as a denial of finitude, it would be raising this finitude to the level of the absolute. "Not to want what God wants, but to want what God wants us to want" is *ordo amoris*, the ordering of the ethical. And conversely, no one can consistently hold the position of solipsism, for in order to do this one would have to be of superhuman strength, a god. Even "egoism" remains a tendency with an "usque . . ." and so it is not a standpoint that anyone can consistently hold. Precisely because we are concerned here with tendencies, there cannot be anything like a "development" that leads to moral reason, only a development within moral reason or a development in the opposite direction. To reverse one's direction is the opposite of development. Conversion and development are incommensurable categories. Within the *ordo amoris* there is a growing wakefulness, but there is no development from being asleep to being awake.

III

Our relationship with the scores of different individuals is structured by the *ordo amoris* not only under the viewpoint of near and far, but primarily under the hierarchical order of the realities which we meet. What grounds such a hierarchy? An answer justified in detail could only be carried out in the context of an ontology. Still, in the context of ethics a justification cannot be totally dispensed with. There is no ethics without metaphysics. We already saw this in connection with the necessity of having to view the other as real, as a "thing-in-itself," in order to experience anything like an obligation toward this other. In the end the experience of this obligation is nothing other than that experience of reality, since this experience is not something which is purely theoretical. In pure theory we only have qualitative experience, never the experience of existence, of being a self, never, then, the experience of that which *per definitionem* is not an object.

But not everything which the self encounters has the same priority or the same clearness. Other humans are unequivocally given to us as "things-in-themselves," as real in the strong sense of the word. That our duties are, first and foremost, duties to other humans finds its reason in this fact and not in the biological solidarity of the species, since this has its effect, as we said earlier, instinctively and without reflection, and also because it is unable to ground an obligation for a reflective being. That others belong to the same biological species as I do is not a reason for me to respect or help them; rather the reason lies in the fact that, beyond all biological kinship, these others stand in a relationship with themselves, that is, they are selves. They are in some sense *real*, which cannot be reduced to being an "object," a "value of a bound variable" (Quine). A being, which refers to itself, is not just relative in its relation to others and in the experience of another, but as finite it is also essentially related to others and real only in this relation. But insofar as it knows this, insofar as it realizes its own relativity and, leaving its own centrality, relativizes itself, it overcomes this relativity and becomes a representation of the absolute. This is what is meant by the dignity of humans. A being which has at its disposal such a virtually moral, that is, absolute, perspective prohibits, by its being, being treated in any instrumental fashion which is not justifiable *to* the person himself, that is, which cannot be seen as the sort of action in which the person puts himself or herself at the service of someone else. But what does "prohibit" mean here? The prohibition which we speak of is not grounded in some further impersonal "ought" or an abstract imperative, about which we would have to ask why we ought to subordinate ourselves to it. This prohibition is identical with the perception of being a self. Plato's thesis that no one knows the good who does not also want it expresses the actual situation. *Amor oculus est.* We speak then of a prohibition rather than a command because the prohibition indicates the bare minimum of every command to come to the aid of someone in need, which in regards to its positive content is unlimited and variable.

If moral relationships are primarily those which subjects with self-consciousness have among themselves, what about those relationships with those who do not yet have, or no longer possess, or never had self-consciousness? Does the phrase "human dignity" have any meaning for these people, besides being a metaphorical expression for the biological solidarity of the species, which cannot be rationally grounded? In order to be clear about the inseparable connection between human "nature" and personality, it is enough to be clear about the fact that we can never empirically verify something like personality or a self. We only have empirical representations, primarily the human countenance and speech, of a personal "soul." These symbolic representations are able in principle to be simulated. The opposite also holds: There are cases in which the symbolic representation is not present without us feeling forced to conclude to the absence of self-consciousness: cases of aphasia, the disfiguring of the face to the point of being unrecognizable. We know that the same things could happen to us and that we could still be recognized as persons without such signals. An elementary insight lies behind this recognition, which was formulated by Aristotle in the following manner: What the essence or the nature of something is can usually be figured out from what it, for the most part, reveals of itself. Human nature is of the kind which for the most part realizes itself as life which is conscious of itself. Rationality is, so to say, its "normal form." To perceive a living organism means, as we have seen, to perceive it teleologically and that means to anticipate the completion of its "tendency." We can anticipate the completion of the tendency of the human organism only if we perceive it as that which comes to itself as conscious life. For every failure to achieve this "becoming real" there is a zone of darkness which we cannot adequately interpret. And therefore it is also impossible to determine the temporal origins of personality in human development. It is an essential part of being conscious that it cannot remember its origin. When we say: "I was born on such and such a day," we do not mean by "I," something which began when we said "I," but the living being to whom the spoken "I" refers and which precedes all saying of "I." It is an essential part of being a human person that it is grounded in that which is primordial. Respect for the person can only express itself in respect for everything which is engendered by the human.

A "transcendental-pragmatic" argument proceeds in the same direction. If talk of human rights is to have any meaning at all, then it implies that the claim to such rights is not bestowed by other humans but comes to the being which asserts the claim from the being itself. "From the being itself" can only mean: on account of its nature. If, for the grounding of human dignity, some empirical quality or other was required beyond the simple belonging to the human species, then the recognition of a human as human would be dependent on others who defined these qualities and decided on their presence or absence in individual cases. But that would mean that the real essence of human rights, namely the independence from such definitions and judgments of others, would be lost. Since human nature in its fully developed condition is for the most part the nature of a conscious being who is in relation with itself, the benevolence toward this being has to realize itself in coming to the aid of this nature–even in those individual cases where nothing about the factual presence of such a self-relationship can be ascertained.

IV

The question needs to be asked, whether the ethical relationship of humans, a relationship of benevolence and aid, also exists in the realm of relationships outside of the interhuman. This question must be answered in the affirmative. Benevolence toward a human is indeed, as we have seen, an affirmation of that type of being which "bound up" with the human as such. Whoever regards reality as a whole to be the senseless "being there" of *facta bruta*, cannot regard it as suddenly meaningful when, in the course of evolution, a being opens its eyes and in this moment the universal meaninglessness becomes aware of itself. Schopenhauer saw this correctly. Conscious life would only be the intensifying of the absurd. Looked at the other way, if meaning lies in the emergence of being, that is, in consciousness, then this meaning necessarily precedes this emergence. What one becomes conscious of must itself be thought of by analogy with being a self, which engenders "the possibility of meaning."

We see this most clearly in the case of animals who have such a central nervous system and so behave that we cannot avoid experiencing them as expressing a sensitivity to pleasure or pain. However such sensitivity is only perceptible by us in an act, which has the character of benevolence or its opposite, malevolence. We cannot say what a sensation is, which is not known in a self-consciousness *as* sensation. Our talk here is essentially that of analogy. But this talk is not only justified, it is unavoidable. We ourselves distinguish our sensations from the consciousness of these sensations. We become conscious, for example, of a headache, which we have been having for a period of time even before we were conscious of it. The question: "What was this headache before we became conscious of it?" is unanswerable, since the becoming conscious of pain is not the same thing as becoming aware of an event of the outer world. It is rather something in the pain itself. The pain enters into a new condition through our becoming conscious of it; it becomes more real. That we could not say anything determinate about the pain before our consciousness of it does not lie in the fact that it possessed a reality which was hidden from us, but that before we were aware of it, it was not fully determinate and therefore less real.

An animal cannot discover itself as a being among beings. It cannot move out of its own centrality. Hence, it cannot accept something like duty. When it does accept some super-individual function, this always occurs in such a manner that the performance of this super-individual function is itself a function of its own well-being. For this reason, the concept of expected agreement or acceptability, which is often used these days in the context of animal protection, is, strictly speaking, unsuitable. An animal's pain can be great or small. It can be passing or long lasting and recurring. But the concept of an expected agreement presupposes that an animal could agree to the pain which a human inflicts on it in view of the purpose which this infliction serves and that it would be "expected" of it to agree to this. But no one can expect anything from an animal in this sense. One can *inflict* on it something which is more or less terrible, and we can ask ourselves whether we can justify *ourselves* or not for causing such pain. Still we can only ask ourselves these questions if the animal has become real for us, if we have perceived it *as itself*. The considerations we then give to the proper expectations we might have, are themselves unavoidably analogical considerations. Only in this way does the reality of an animal reveal itself to us. Beyond such analogy, any attempt to say what animal life "really" is, leads into fantasy, of which, materialistic reductionism is the most irresponsible form.

Since the animal does not become real to itself, but remains in the centrality of the instinctual drives, its life does not become a whole. Pleasure and pain are not discovered in their life-serving function. The animal lives wholly within its circumstances. And so well-being for the animal is reduced to the way in which it experiences these circumstances, and is not referred to its life as a whole. Accordingly, the killing of an animal, like the doing away with any being, has to be justified by a good reason. But it is not something which is always reprehensible as is the killing of an innocent, unarmed human. In the killing of an animal we do not close our eyes before reality, since the life of an animal does not have any reality as a whole, but is only real from moment to moment. It only becomes a whole for *us*, when *we* have a relationship with it. The animal itself does not have a biography, and the longness or shortness of life does not matter to it. Reality is its momentary experience. It is to this that our benevolence and responsibility must refer. (From this also follows that we are not absolved from responsibility to animals which are being led to slaughter and cannot subject them to any and every degree of anxiety and hardship.) Of course, something else holds for the existence of the *species*. Here it is a matter of the variety of types which constitute the wealth of the world of humans. And in consideration of those who will come after us, we may not leave it in a *status quo minus*. Over and above this there exists something like a responsibility to nature for its own sake. What meaning can this have? It means that every species is a revelation of being in its own being alive, a way which allows reality to become real as one of its reflections. When we correctly understand respect for humans and respect for nature, then there is no way we can play the one off against the other, since the relationship of humans to the world is not primarily a relationship of maintaining one's self and metabolizing stuff from nature; rather it is a relationship of "belonging" of a primordial kind. In the consciousness of a rational being reality as a whole comes to itself, the whole of the world becomes "real" in a new way. The sadness which overcomes us when we hear about the extinction of hundreds of kinds of butterflies on a faraway continent has nothing to do with a loss of something useful. It doesn't even have anything to do with a reduction of aesthetical pleasure, since, more than likely, we would never have a chance to see this type of butterfly. Nevertheless, we are poorer through its disappearance, since our own being is fulfilled in reference to every reality which we ourselves are not. *Delectatio in felicitate alterius* – this formula of Leibniz overcomes the opposition between anthropocentrism and love of nature "for its own sake." To love something for its own sake is the specific form of human realization.

To what extent a non-living object can be the object of benevolence depends upon how we understand it, that is, to what extent we perceive it as real. But since it of itself demands of us no ontological decision, since it does not suffer on the account of any decision, it would seem that it is our perception which lifts the lifeless creature to meaningfulness and so to its reality. The brook exists as "brook" as long as there are humans, animals, and plants which together with it make up a world. Just so long does it have a place in the *ordo amoris.*

Chapter 11
Consequentialism

ARISTOTLE WAS OF THE OPINION that the interest in philosophical ethics was not a theoretical, but rather a practical, interest, an interest in how one should act. Fortunately, we do not normally need to wait for philosophy to know what is good or bad, right or wrong. Rather the task of philosophical reflection is to make transparent the principles which operate in this already existing knowledge. Nevertheless, this reflection on principles is not without its practical consequences. First of all, it has a critical function in that it uncovers the contradictions and inconsistencies that exist in our normal behavior as well as in our unreflected ethical convictions. It corrects these by means of a deeper insight. It leads then to a "purification of morals." Second, it serves to orient us in extreme cases and about new issues, that is, in those cases where traditional rules for acting and immediate intuitions are of no help. The fact that ethical counseling, ethical orientations, and even "ethics committees" are needed more and more these days is connected with the technical and cultural development which constantly opens up new issues by expanding the sphere of human action into areas which the accepted ethos does not "reach." At the same time these issues are often limit cases, cases which concern life and death. Here the translation of knowledge of principles into normative guidelines is not always something already accomplished by ethics, which then would need only a hermeneutic, as it is in an ethics like that of Aristotle. One is looking for a kind of principle, which – with the help of empirical statements – would allow for a verifiable deduction of normative sentences. *Eudaimonia*, "the turning out well of life," is not such a principle. So also contentment and subjective well-being fail to qualify, even if one adds having a good conscience to being content. For, as Kant rightly saw, one must already be someone who wants the good, in order to be able to have an idea of this contentment.

Still, we have to ask whether what up till now has been described as benevolence can be operationalized in a way which corresponds to the modern expectations of a normative ethics. Augustine's dictum, "Love and do what you will," appears to proceed from the fact that the right thing emerges of itself, when one has understood the principle of the good and has a basically ethical attitude. We can see though that this is not the case, since in order to do the right thing out of love, one has to know what is good for humans, and this knowledge is not simply empirical, but also normative, that is, an ethically orienting knowledge, which does not of itself emerge from benevolence. Augustine knew this, of course. By love he understood primarily love of God. From love of God followed for him immediately obedience to the divine commandments which are accessible through the light of reason and sacred Scripture. These commandments were in no way analytically contained in the command to love. There is, though, another reason why what we are to do does not follow immediately out of the principle of benevolence: The receivers of benevolence are so numerous that we cannot possibly come to the aid of each in the same way. The classical teaching on *ordo amoris* was an attempt to prevent the unavoidable "refraction" of benevolence from becoming a return to arbitrariness, that is, to delusion. This does not mean an "operationalism" in the actual sense of the word, but a structuring of responsibility. The filling out of this structure tended more toward balancing and moral fantasy than toward unequivocal instructions. The object of responsibility was, however, always a certain individual or collective object, the "neighbor," who was directly affected either by the action or its consequences.

I

As a contrast to this seemingly loose principle of order for normative ethics, a new moral principle began in the last century to recommend itself on the basis of two qualities: It understands itself as a principle from which can be deduced the unique way of acting which corresponds with duty for every conceivable situation and that without recourse to traditions, conventions, or customs. Moreover, this principle allows for the dissolution of all pre-rational tendencies toward taboos, and so of all the hindrances which stand in the way of a fully rationally developed, functionally planned society. In contrast to every ethics which existed before this, no way of acting is a priori excluded by this principle from being considered as a duty which is to be deduced. We are speaking here of the principle of utilitarianism or consequentialism, which is also termed by its exponents as the principle of teleological morality. Marcus Singer defines it as "the view that whether an act is right or wrong depends, solely, on its (actual or probable) consequences. On this view, an act is right if and only if it produces, or is likely to produce, at least as much 'good' as any other act open to the agent; whereas an act is obligatory if, and only if, it produces, or is likely to produce, more 'good' than any other act open to the agent . . . This, then, is the principle of utility, which, in one form or another, is common to all the varieties of utilitarianism. The different varieties of utilitarianism are merely different views of the proper way of determining the value or worth of the consequences, for determining what is "good" and how it is to be estimated."

As a supplement to this definition and in order to avoid misunderstandings, it must be added that the words "good" and "value" are to be understood here in a non-moralistic sense; otherwise the definition would be circular (an action would be morally good when it had morally good consequences). Further, there are in principle no limits to the morally relevant consequences. The fact that there exists a limited area of responsibility can only be grounded "universally and teleologically" in the further fact that things go better for "the whole," when *not* everyone is directly concerned with everything. But this "decentralization" does not change the fact that the actual object of responsibility is the whole world. This is the essential characteristic of consequentialism. It is misleading when it terms itself an "ethics of responsibility." Actions are defined by the effects which they have. Every ethics is an ethics of responsibility, since no ethics can disregard all effects. For then, it would have to disregard all actions. The difference lies rather in the object of responsibility.

We need to mention one variant of utilitarianism, the so-called rule-utilitarianism, which does not refer every action directly to the optimization of the state of the world; rather it requires only the following of those rules which, when generally followed, would bring more benefit than harm to the whole. The elector in Kleist's *The Prince from Homburg* argues in a rule-utilitarian fashion, when he condemns the victorious prince to death after the battle. The latter's violation of military obedience had indeed led to victory, but he violated a rule which usually needs to be followed for winning a battle. Rule-utilitarianism is an ambiguous position and not a real alternative to the so-called action-utilitarianism. Either it is an improved action-utilitarianism or it is no longer utilitarianism.

If it is an improved action-utilitarianism, then it would want to say that the agent has to weigh those consequences of the action which in the long run will either certainly or probably result in the strengthening or weakening of a beneficial rule. The consequences of strengthening or weakening have to be counted among the consequences of an action. The pedestrian who crosses on red since no car is in sight has to consider whether this example will perhaps result in a weakening of the traffic rules for a watching child and so, indirectly perhaps, contribute to a future accident. When it does not seem that the action would cause such a weakening of the validity of the rule, when, for example, no one is watching the pedestrian, then the violation of a normally good rule cannot be objected to on the basis of utilitarian grounds. And when it is not to be objected to, then it becomes a duty, since then there is an advantage without any disadvantage and it is a duty to multiply beneficial situations in the world.

It is something else again when rule-utilitarianism demands the observance of all beneficial rules without exception, that is, without consideration of whether the observance of the rule in a certain case is relevant to its being further observed. According to this version of rule-utilitarianism the obligation is no longer grounded in some remote usefulness of the action. Then utilitarian reflection only serves to test a certain internal correctness or falsity.

Kant's categorical imperative already contained such a test. But even with Thomas Aquinas we find again and again rule-utilitarian considerations, that is, the question how a certain way of acting would work itself out if it were to follow from a general natural law. Should it appear that such a natural law injures the preservation of the human species or consistently impairs its well-being, then it followed for Thomas that this way of acting is *contra naturam*, internally turned around and therefore morally objectionable, even when a concrete instance of the action does not have a disadvantage as its consequence and does not impair the general validity of a corresponding rule for others. In cases like this, considering a concrete instance of action in a rule-utilitarian light has the sense of an examination of a "deontological," a context-free, ethical norm. It is, then, no longer utilitarian. The grounds of justification for doing or leaving undone some individual action no longer lie in its real – direct or indirect – consequences. For in this kind of argument Thomas Aquinas makes a telling distinction between conventional rules of action and those which emerge from human nature. For him conventional rules, like traffic rules, are subject throughout to utilitarian considerations. They can be rescinded in those cases where the usefulness, which grounds the rule, is not likely to be realized or where it is outweighed by some drawback. However, the commandment of faithfulness in marriage, the commandment of keeping promises, or the prohibition against killing innocent humans are a type of "natural moral laws." They too can be justified in terms of their usefulness. Still, they follow from the "nature of things" and so structure a priori the ontological constitution of the human, that a person would lose himself or herself and separate himself or herself from the creator of the universe, if he or she were to arbitrarily subject this type of rule to a calculus of usefulness. With this type of command or prohibition utilitarian reflection serves only to test the content of the rule and not to relativize the rule's validity in individual cases. In this context Thomas is thinking of a generalizable ethics like the Kantian system.

Utilitarianism does have a certain appearance of rationality and plausibility. It appears to be rational since it–apparently – offers an unequivocal and verifiable moral criterion. But a deontological ethics of the Kantian variety does this also. What distinguishes the former from the latter is the natural character of its criterion, which is then further interpreted as the ground of validity for all ethical norms. There are, of course, radical differences within utilitarianism as regards the standard of judgment for the consequences of actions. Bentham designed a hedonistic calculus for figuring out the greatest possible happiness for the greatest number, whereby happiness was defined hedonistically, that is, in terms of obtaining pleasure or the degree of comfort. John Stuart Mill had already suggested including in the concept of pleasure a qualitative element, something that would correspond to the principle, "better an unhappy Socrates than a happy pig." Finally, George Edward Moore dropped completely the hedonistic criterion for judging the consequences of actions and introduced instead a concept of value whereby pleasure was just one value among others. But even Moore's "ideal-utilitarianism" clung to the fact that it was the intention to optimize the world which distinguished a good from a bad action. The internal ethical good of an action is bound up with a certain orientation toward instrumental rationality. The purpose of responsibility, the object of benevolence and of help, is not a certain human or a certain group of humans but always the whole of world-processes. An action is correct, and therefore morally good, if, looking at the whole, it makes this process richer in value-content than any other possible alternative action.

This "teleological morality" seems to have certain merits which recommend it particularly to modern civilization. Our civilization tends toward the gradual abolition of that structure of support which we have called *ordo amoris*. The relations of near and far are steadily leveled. The near – family, neighbors, compatriots – lose their importance and at the same time the far-away becomes perceptibly near through the media and the speed of travel. The question, "Who is my neighbor?" becomes harder to answer. Consequentialism seems with one move to solve all the problems which stem from this situation in that the object of responsibility is just one thing: the world as a whole.

Modern technology has so enlarged the scope of human action that the rule is no longer valid, "if everyone pulls his own weight, things will never go badly for the whole." First, it is no longer clear, what "one's weight" is, since human practice is constantly being revolutionized by science and technology. Second, and more important, the comprehensive whole, nature, is no longer a neutral medium which always absorbs and neutralizes the long-term consequences of our actions. The whole itself is in the process of being transformed, and we constantly contribute to this in one way or another, through action or omission. In light of this perspective also, it appears that an ethics would be desirable, which foregoes determining that which is "the weight" for each except through its functionality for the course of the world.

One can further assert on behalf of this kind of ethics that it fits in well with the technical model of action, which is dominant today. Moral points of view in this kind of ethics do not limit the instrumentally rational, technical orientation of action, but bring it to completion. It expands the horizon of ethics beyond a limited area of responsibility and allows us to ask whether the action, which is useful for a country or a business or some individual human, is also good for humankind as a whole in the long run. However, this question is, in principle, of the same kind as the normal questions for coping with difficulties. This type of ethics does not allow for any form of interaction or "dealing with," other than technical, instrumentally rational action, other than making, *poiesis*, which would be organized and justified in some other way. Here the ethical is not the human quality of the "dealing with"; rather it is any action which itself optimizes this "dealing with" in a rationally purposive manner. Accordingly, the ethical does not optimize human dealings themselves, but at most optimizes its advancement. (We see the preparation for this kind of reasoning in the theological handbooks of the nineteenth century, which allow, for example, sexual relations only when they – naturally within marriage – "serve" the mutual love but not when they simply give expression to it.)

Finally, consequentialism recommends itself by making any thought of God unnecessary, in that it takes up the divine viewpoint through the acceptance of universal responsibility. Thomas Aquinas said that each human had a specific area of responsibility and that God alone had to care for the *bonum totius universi*. Consequentialism does not avail itself of this lightening of responsibility. The sole moral criterion is, "What is good for the world as a whole." Since God is eliminated, so also is eliminated the distinction between that which God wants and that which God wants for us to want. We ourselves must now want what God, according to view of Leibniz, inevitably has to want, the best of all possible worlds. Thomas Aquinas thought it was impossible for God to want something like that, since a best possible world could no more exist than a largest possible number. Thomas thought of the creator more as an artist than as an accountant. One can say that a symphony from Mozart is perfect and could not be improved. There would be little sense in saying that there could not be any other symphony which was better. Leibniz postulates an absolute optimum, and it belongs to the definition of this optimum that only an infinite consciousness could carry out the corresponding calculus of optimization. Consequentialism demands the carrying out of this calculus for every action as the condition of morality.

II

An ethics of consequentialism imposes on itself a heavy burden of proof, in that its supporting thesis contradicts the moral intuition of most people and the ethical tradition of all cultures. The saying, "The end justifies the means" – long seen as the expression of a morally objectionable conviction – finds its theoretical explication in teleological ethics. For this kind of ethics the moral quality of action depends solely upon its suitability as a means for the goal of optimization. To object that immoral means could not, in fact, foster this goal misses the point: According to this theory one cannot know whether a means is moral or not apart from knowledge of its suitability. The morality is nothing other than this suitability.

This conception of morality allows no room for something which was characteristic of all hitherto existing ethics, that which the Greeks called *aidos*, shyness or shame, the feeling that humans have when there are boundaries set to their pursuit of goals. European literature is full of examples which show that not even the grandest and most important goals justify baseness, knavery, or betrayal. For consequentialism, on the other hand, "baseness," "knavery," "betrayal" are expressions which can be used correctly only when they are applied to actions which shall not contribute to the optimizing of the world. There is then no way of acting which can be so designated apart from knowledge of the universal context. Everything is allowed to the one who wants the best. In place of shyness, shame, and reverence we have the correction of the calculus.

In the fifties the Supreme Court of the Federal Republic of Germany determined that this view constitutes a real break with our European tradition of ethics, when it found a number of doctors guilty who had helped with the selection of mentally ill patients for euthanasia in the Third Reich (1933–1945). These doctors were able to make a plausible case that they had saved the lives of many sick, since they applied the criteria of selection comparatively loosely. The court did not accept this argument, but ruled that in the European-Christian tradition contributing to a murder is not justified even when it hinders other murders. Are then limits to the balancing of goods or not? The decision for or against teleological ethics can be reduced to this question.

The objections which we have mentioned above are of a preliminary character. One could call them persuasive since they rest upon intuitive rather than strictly demonstrated presuppositions. Still, one has to be clear that ultimately the only criterion for the settling of moral questions which is at our disposal is agreement with our elementary intuitions, so the following arguments which flow out of principles must also finally appeal to that which we already know before we are taught by philosophy or theology.

We have to begin by saying that consequentialistic ethics ends up in a self-contradiction, since, as a whole and in the long term, it leads to consequences which no one can want. Even rule-utilitarianism has as its basis the insight that the unmediated orientation of action to general usefulness is harmful, if at the same time that it weakens a useful rule, this damage is not outweighed by the advantage of the violation. So long as rule-utilitarianism is to remain utilitarianism, agents have to weigh case by case to what extent their action will set some precedent. And then they have to compare the advantages and disadvantages of this precedent setting with the direct advantages or disadvantages which are to be expected. But what follows in the long-term from an action is far beyond our knowledge, if we allow ourselves to be led by our fundamental moral intuitions. Reductions in the infant mortality rate can lead to consequences which are catastrophic, and no one knows whether the following generations will overcome them or not. And it goes without saying that we do not know which problems will appear as the most urgent to our descendants based on their scale of values. A universal calculus of benefits, no matter what its parameters of benefits may be, is simply beyond our capacity. Even the assumption that short- or long-lasting kindness will show itself in the long run as a step to greater benefits cannot, as G. E. Moore correctly wrote, be shown to be even probable. According to him we must simply postulate it. But why? Apparently not for utilitarian reasons, since here these leave us in the lurch. Such a postulate is meaningful only because we already consider a certain action to be moral *prior to* any such calculus and therefore hope that the moral taken as a whole and in the long run, will prove itself also to be the beneficial. This was the thought of Kant and Fichte, and so for them the reason for believing in a divinely governed world. It did not, however, have anything to do with utilitarianism.

Since the weighing of goods in light of elementary ethical rules of action fails us in the long term, the validity of even the most useful rule is weakened by utilitarian reflection. In a concrete situation the reasons which could induce someone to put aside such a rule can always win the upper hand over the reasons for following the rule. For the latter can become so weakened by reflection on the uncertainty of its benefits as well as the uncertainty of the effects in terms of setting a precedent that, in comparison to the certainty of the expected advantage, they no longer stand in the way of the original intention. But people who have the global goal of a better world before their eyes are dispensed by this from rules which have good effects only in the normal and generally prevailing circumstances. In cases where it concerns the whole, these rules ought not to present any hindrance. Looked at in this way, no other existing "human ethics" has concerned itself with the whole. No action was considered "above the law" just this one time. Rather, *every* agent and every human with whom we have something to do is a totality, which is unable to be mediated, and never merely a means, but a symbolic representation of the unconditioned. Consequentialism, which relativizes every individual in terms of the whole of an unimaginable world-process, has the effect of demoralizing people in the concrete situation and thereby contributes to the worsening of the world.

Even rule-utilitarianism does not constitute an exception. In its authentically utilitarian form it shares, as was shown, the weaknesses of utilitarianism. In its "deontological" form it would lead to an unbearable rigorism, precisely because consequentialism does not know the distinction between moral and technical norms. Actions are moral, according to it, when they are suitable for the realization of some certain goal of optimization. Acting becomes producing. Someone keeps a promise, not because he made it and because the person to whom it was made has a claim on its being kept, but rather he keeps it in order to further that advantage for human life which comes about from the general trust in promises being kept. This means that the precept to keep promises is structured in the same way as the precept for the pedestrian not to cross on red. The utilitarian sees both as precepts which have only a pragmatic sense and whose violation is always allowed if the purpose of the rule is not vitiated by the violation. Rule-utilitarianistic deontology, on the other hand, has to claim unconditional validity for both types of precepts. In fact, however, the two types differ fundamentally. A traffic rule is an abstract prudential measure, and our compliance with it sometimes protects certain concrete persons, sometimes – when it concerns the effect of setting a precedence – it protects an undefined circle of people, and sometimes it protects no one at all – at night, for example, when neither auto nor watching child is anywhere in sight. A promise though is always binding for a concrete person. It grounds a relationship in which being a self becomes visible. It may well be that in certain situations a more pressing duty suddenly exempts one from the duty of keeping a promise. But that can only be the case if it can be expected that the other person would not demand it to be kept, when the agent has the right to presume the subsequent agreement of the other. In any event it would destroy the meaning of promising if an additional calculus of benefits were necessary for their being kept. Promises given to someone dying would always be something tenuous, since breaking this promise, if it did not hurt anyone, would be justified by any slight advantage. Those who hold consistently to a teleological ethics teach that in fact one does not need to keep such promises. The conclusion that one should not make them in the first place is false from a consequentialistic viewpoint, since the promise consoles the dying person. When the duty to be truthful is only an expression of a function of benefits, then it can eliminated. Viewed "teleologically" it is correct to make the promise and then not to keep it. But this teleological view misses precisely that which constitutes the essence of the ethical, the becoming real of a reality for the agent. Once the dying person to whom one makes a promise has become real, the subsequent calculus of benefits can only appear as a frivolity. Morality places limits on rationally purposive action. Its rationality is not simply the completion of purposive rationality. The boundaries consist in the fact that the purpose itself is made present as an "end" in the self-being of the other. The Greek word *telos* means both: purpose and boundary – in this case then the end of all further calculations.

Utilitarian ethics, because of its tendency to relativize, causes not only the self-being of the other, who is affected by our actions, to disappear, but also the self-being of the agent. That is, if the morality of an action is a function of its suitability to make the world better (and not the reverse, that the improvement of the world is a hoped-for consequence of actions which can be acknowledged on other grounds as moral), then morality becomes an affair for experts with the most comprehensive calculus of benefits. Any individual who opposes certain demands and is not prepared to commit any crime must be denounced standing in the way of the improvement of the world with these ideas of humanity and its dignity . That which they see as a crime is not a crime at all when it contributes to the progress of humanity. And it is not the business of these people to judge, since they are not experts on whether or not an action does in fact so contribute. And so the transformation of moral imperatives into technical ones results in a declaration of incapacity of the individual, who naturally cannot judge what is good or bad in *this* aspect. The agent and the patient are rendered unreal in the same fashion. Two abstractions take their place – namely, "the world" and "science."

How will the utilitarian answer, if a version of Nietzsche's thesis is argued, that the morality derived from willing to act in a way which brings about the universal best is itself detrimental to the universal best and leads to the gradual degeneration of humanity? Or to Mandeville's thesis: *Private vices, public benefits*? If these theses were true, *every* ethics would be in a dilemma. But their truth cannot be proven, and so long as it is not proven, moral persons can hope that they are false, since they know what good and evil is, independent of answering these questions. The consequentialist, however, cannot know this apart from answering these questions, since if the theses were to be true, then good would in fact be evil and evil good. Even the mere possibility that something in Nietzsche's thesis could be true makes it necessary to suspend all morality, since the dreamer in his or her egocentric existence is perhaps better for the world than the one awakened to reality.

III

The consequentialists' pretended claim to a divine viewpoint begins by asking too much of humans and ends by asking too little. The excessive demand is as much theoretical as it is practical. We have already discussed the theoretical aspect. We have to know what we cannot know in order to know what we should do. The practically excessive demand consists in the fact that everyone in every moment is compelled, in order to act morally, to do the best possible to bring about the best world. For in this conception the moral viewpoint not only limits us in our free and, in a certain sense, arbitrary pursuit of finite and particular goals, it also prescribes all of these goals for us: They must be, each and all, means for the overall goal. There is no *adiaphora* and hence no morally neutral action, no creative free play: Every act of play stands in need of justification. The theologians, who have appropriated this view for themselves, have, consistent with this, denied the traditional Christian distinction between the commandments and that which goes beyond them, the "counsels." The tension between reason and life is set aside, in that it is incumbent upon the agent as duty always to act as pure reason.

It is exactly this though, that leads to asking too little of a person. The goal of optimization can only be defined by external values, if the position is not to become circular. That is, it can only be defined by values in which being a self does not appear. And these values can only be those connected with biological life or those which are aesthetic in nature. Consequentialistic reason orients itself according to these values. It exhausts itself in its instrumental function in the service of life without becoming the form of life itself. To put it pointedly: As a rational being the human is not organic and as an organic being the human is not rational. This is valid also for the way a human treats himself or herself. As an organic being the person is part of the world which is to be optimized. The way one treats oneself has to be governed by the following double-rule: (1) Perfect your capacity to contribute to the bettering of the world as an instrument of the rational will. (2) As a part of this improving world, take care of yourself by making it as good for yourself as an organism as possible – whereby, by definition, moral perfection, being morally awake, does not belong to this definition of well-being. The two imperatives remain unmediated, and one cannot see how a choice between them should be made. As a moral agent I am a pure rational being bound to the goal of optimization. As part of the world which is to optimized, my sought-after perfection can only lie in the development of myself in an non-moral sense. The unification of reason and life cannot be thought of in this way, since moral rationality does not belong to the world which is to be improved, and so does not become the form of life. It could only become this as love. But love exists only over against the self-being of determinate concrete persons and not over against an abstract "all." But when an agent has caught sight of the reality of being a self, then this experience includes himself or herself within its boundaries. The concrete becomes a representation of the unconditioned. The distinction between "transcendental" and "categorical" fall away. When this occurs, the primary response is not an abstract will to optimize, but an attitude which could be better characterized with words such as reverence, shyness, respect, and letting be. The real goal of all moral action shows itself as already present before we begin to act. The impulse to come to the aid of someone flows out of this letting be. But any aid which proceeds from this impulse, even with all the necessary technical perfection, will remain within this attitude of reverence before that which is, which, since it is, precedes what should be and should occur.

Chapter 12

Discourse

CONSEQUENTIALISM, as we saw above, cannot render benevolence concrete. It cannot provide for something like the construction of an *ordo amoris*. In this kind of thinking the incommensurable self-being of the other is lost. This self-being gets reduced to a mere moment in an imagined totality of goodness. For the agent each individual does not grow more, but rather less, real. The only thing which is real in the full sense of the word is a "whole," which is, however, in reality only an abstraction. The consequentialist seeks to leave behind the perspective of the organism in its finitude, which is an essential component of any *ordo amoris*, and to take on something like a divine viewpoint. But it seeks to do this without the power which traditionally belonged to this viewpoint, namely the capacity to integrate all perspectives and, at the same time, still to notice the fall from the sky of the sparrow. The reason why the consequentialist thinking goes against our moral intuitions so blatantly is, in the end, that it authorizes the agent to do away with all traditional, cultural, and natural norms, if the idea of the totality of benefits demands this. The end justifies, according to the circumstances, *any* means. Outside of himself or herself, the agent need give account to no one. Radical consequentialism is actually a form of solipsism. The consideration of some other viewpoint besides one's own is only justified if this viewpoint appears to the agent as a means to optimize the world-process. For this end, to rephrase the famous words of Kant, everyone is to be viewed only as a means and no one as an end. Each person's status as a subject is respected by consequentialism in the sense that it has to be demanded of all rational beings that they subordinate and even sacrifice their well-being to the optimization of the whole. But if one's idea of optimization does not happen to coincide with that of those who actually exercise influence on the way things go, then this sacrifice can only be viewed by the person as irrational fate.

I

In face of this, an attempt is being made by what is known as "discourse ethics" to renew the Kantian thought of rational generalization in such a way that the position of every rational being as a subject is guaranteed. This is, of course, only possible when a command for universal optimization does not exist, and so the interests which dictate actions of individuals do not stand in need of justification and have particular goals as their content. In Kantian ethics even intentions to improve the world count as particular goals, since it is within the discretion of an individual to bring their ideas in conformity with such goals or not. The specifically ethical does not consist in such goals, but in the respecting of a certain condition to which all individual purposes are subordinated. This condition is the acknowledgment of the other, i.e., unconditioned benevolence toward *every* rational being. This benevolence does not supersede all natural purposes, all goals of instincts and actions, nor does it reduce them to mere means in a strategy of optimization which accords with duty. Rather it relativizes them by having the agent grasp himself or herself as one among others, who does not rob the others of their possibility to pursue natural or arbitrary goals. This benevolence does not demand that one make others' goals one's own, but that one validate their self-being and strengthen their possibility to promote their own purposes.

Discourse ethics is an attempt to operationalize the Kantian concept of practical reason while rendering it less individualistic. The concept of morality and its legitimacy are to be grasped from a coherent principle. According to Kant agents should ask themselves whether they could wish that the maxim of their action would become a general legislating maxim. Still, the result of their reflection could be based on self-deception. It could easily mirror an individual's special interest and thus be an "ideology." Finally, this result depends on the extent to which the particular situation of the agent is taken up in the maxim. "Regardless of circumstances" would mean not to speak of determinate actions at all and to renounce all operationalizing of the principle of benevolence. The result would be a purely nominalistic situation-ethics. The reverse strategy would lead to the same result; an overly exact description of the action dealt with by the maxim would mean that it applies only for this case and all generalization would remain purely formal. It seems that no principle emerges from Kantian formalism which would allow us to determine the degree of individualization of determinate types of actions or situations to which our moral rules could refer.

Finally, it needs to be pointed out that asking what one would want as a maxim of general legislation allows not just the particular interests of the agent to play a role but also the agent's temperament. This problem is present in John Rawls's suggestion that we make the initial choice of a political system under the "veil of ignorance." He would have us ask, "In which system, under which distribution of opportunities, do we wish to live?" without knowing what position in this system we ourselves would have. In no way does this necessarily lead to an unbiased choice. Humans are treated here as gamblers. Some gamblers tend toward prudence and so choose a system in which, even when everything goes wrong for them, they end up relatively well off. Others wager everything, risking the miserable life of the under-privileged for the chance to become a potentate. In order to choose a just order, one must already *be* just. The justice of the choice cannot be construed from a calculation of one's own interests under fictive conditions.

So the proposal has been made to replace this individualistic consultation of one's own practical reason or even the individual ability to wish for a general order of distribution with the result of real discourse with all who are affected by the consequences of my action. The principle of benevolence demands not only the consideration of their well-being, but their being allowed to speak in the defining of this well-being and in the working-out of norms which are to be acceptable to everyone. No one can decide this acceptability for another. For someone to do that would be tantamount to presupposing a non-personal instance of reason, in which each participated. In fact, in the theoretical sphere we accept the possibility of each person representing reason as such. One person alone can work out a mathematical proof and understand its compelling power a priori for every thinking being. Plato thought of practical reason as such a super-personal instance. This conception presupposes something like a general human nature which is thought of in a teleological fashion, i.e., all of its strivings can be measured with the same standards so that when we need to make these compatible with each other, each rational and just thinker can in principle make the decision alone but still representing all others concerned. It is primarily the anti-teleological nominalism of the modern period which suggested re-interpreting classical rational ethics as discourse ethics.

II

This kind of discourse has to fulfill three conditions, if it is to function as the equivalent of the monologue of reason itself. First, it must be free from domination. The unjust distribution of opportunities for advancement, which exists in real life may not exist in it, since the criteria to be developed here are those by which the justice of this distribution will be tested. In this discourse of justification each concerned party has to articulate its interests without pressure and has to have an equal chance to contribute to the re-working of these interests into a compatible whole. Indeed, and this is the second requirement, all concerned have to be in command of the necessary competence; they must be clear about their own interests. They have to have the intellectual capacity "to be disposable" to justice. Finally, the third condition is a certain moral qualification of all participants. They must be prepared to really open their interests to a new formulation. Otherwise, those who cling most stubbornly to the immutability of their formulations would enjoy an immediate advantage over those who are prepared to compromise. Moreover, to these moral qualifications belongs sincerity. The proposals for discussion may not be simply tactically or strategically intended as a way of gaining an advantage over the other in the long run. Rousseau saw this problem quite clearly when he distinguished the *volonté de tous* from the *volonté générale.*[1] The *volonté générale* is not articulated when all citizens simply formulate their private interests and then let the average value prevail. Rather, each person has to be ready to propose that which he or she is convinced is just. Then the just is not the average of the interests but of the convictions of justice.

When one considers these conditions of ideal discourse, it is easily seen that discourse cannot take over the role of rational self-deliberation, but rather that it presupposes it. Actually, no one who holds discourse ethics requires that morality be measured by the outcome of real discourse. The discourse which serves as a criterion is rather a presupposed, contrafactual, ideal discourse whose result we have to anticipate in our moral deliberations. Real discourse, which has practical questions for its object, is never free of domination. It privileges those, for example intellectuals, who can speak well. The farmers of the area around Münster who hid Jews during the last war, were not moved to do so by discourse, but by a compassion strengthened through Christian morals. They did not allow themselves to be talked out of it by historical "proofs" that the Jews were the vermin of history. *Good people close their ears to such things.* Moreover, what distinguishes a discourse rooted in justice from a group-dynamic process with all its hidden mechanisms? Michel Foucault has demythologized discourse. Under nominalistic presuppositions, which underlie the paradigm-shift from reason to discourse, discourse becomes subject to the very same verdict to which reason, which has come to terms with itself, is subject. If no general-

---

1   *Volont'é de tous* means roughly the will of all, while *volonté générale* is translated as "the general will." Cf. Jean-Jacques Rousseau, *The Social Contract and Discourses*, tran. by G. D. H. Cole, revised and augmented by J. H. Brumfitt and John C. Hall (London: Everyman's Library, 1973), 203 *et passim.*

ity, in reference to which particular interests could transcend themselves, exists, then discourse has no common object, i.e., there is no such thing as justice. There would be only particular opaque interests and their ever-present repression. Discourse would be merely another form of violence, violence with words. Every distinction between violence and speech has a hidden Platonic presupposition. Without this there is only that "continuum from debate to civil war," about which Ralf Dahrendorf speaks in his *Praise of Thrasymachos*.

Finally, the more recent investigations into the history of science have shown that even the theoretical sciences do not turn out to be "free of domination"; rather they show that the great *peripeteia* of this process, the paradigm-shifts, are based on non-theoretical factors and move more according to Darwinian laws. If over against this we wish to maintain in a contrafactual manner the idea of domination-free discourse oriented only by truth or justice, then we have to ask the question how this gets distinguished from other group-dynamic processes and what allows us in reflection to anticipate a moral norm in its result. For, if we can anticipate the result, then it appears that there is no need for discourse to occur. The anticipation of its result is nothing other than the result of that rational self-deliberation which is supposed to be substituted for by the fiction of ideal discourse.

III

What has been said about freedom from domination applies in a similar fashion to the other criteria of ideal discourse, i.e., moral competence and sincerity. In those cases where these conditions are capable of being fulfilled, the task, which was presumably to be solved through discourse, would already be accomplished. The readiness for discourse about justification does indeed possess an eminently moral meaning; only this meaning does not lie where "discourse ethics" seeks it. Its meaning is not that of producing norms, but of examining them. This function cannot, however, be fulfilled by fictive, ideal discourse, but by factual empirical discourse. Ideal discourse, whose result I have to anticipate in order to reach ethical action, does not really accomplish anything beyond the exertion of proper moral reason. This discourse remains under the same suspicion of ideology as any other. Real discourse, and only real discourse, can examine the anticipations of fictional ideal discourse. Only in real discourse do we open ourselves to others in their reality, to their viewpoints, which are often completely contrary to ours and which we could not anticipate, so long as we were dealing merely with the "idea" of the other. That we can enter into discourse about justice with the real, and not the ideal, other, and that this discourse can have as its result the transformation of individual interests, presupposes a space protected by legal authority which is constituted by a common source of history and nature.

What we bring into this discourse are not incommensurable, opaque, natural interests and wishes, which are then to be either satisfied or suppressed but which cannot be ordered, made into a hierarchy, and in certain cases even transformed; rather we bring proposals which are already oriented toward justice. It is concerning these, and only concerning these, that rational discourse is possible. This is the reason for the obligation of representation in a law suit. The attorney does not represent the interests of his or her party, since these are facts of which one takes cognizance, but about which one cannot discuss. The lawyer presents rather a proposal for a solution which already has the *form* of an impartial judgment. We know that it is, in fact, not as impartial as it appears. The opposing party also makes such a proposal. The discussion does not concern the interests, but the alleged impartiality, of the proposals. This impartiality is what is examined and the result of *this* testing is the judgment. Thus, real discourse has the function of examining the alleged impartiality of our moral judgments. The readiness to submit our own judgment to such a testing is the test of the sincerity of this claim. What especially counts here is the readiness to discuss one's own estimate of what is acceptable with the people, concerning whom one made the estimate. This does not mean that their judgment has to be the final word, since they are also able to think sometimes more and sometimes less correctly. If, in questions of acceptability, the consent of the people affected were decisive, then the surest means of evading any burden from the action of others would be *never* to consent. In this case such a consent would unavoidably be forced in one way or another.

Thus regimes, which are based on the ideology of freedom from domination force the consent of their subjects. For the same reason torture was the necessary consequence of the medieval principle of not punishing anyone for capital crimes unless the person had confessed. The consent of the concerned parties cannot give the definitive solution in normal discourse; rather their reasons must be heard and further tested in moral self-responsibility and be brought into one's *own* formation of judgment. Discourse is never an instance of moral decision, but always remains a phase in the formation of personal moral judgment. Those who in principle remove themselves from discourse with those who are affected by their actions stop distinguishing reason from idiosyncrasy. The general validity, which they claim and which they also keep from the test of really including other perspectives, remains a pretension. On the other hand, those who understand discourse as an instance of normative decision, mix up the formation of moral judgment with the process of political decision. In democratic, constitutional states legal norms do indeed gain their validity through an act which stands at the end of a discursive process, albeit one which in no way corresponds to the criteria for ideal, domination-free discourse. As a rule, respecting these norms can be a moral duty. But the conviction which obliges me to obey these laws is not itself, in turn, a legal norm produced from discourse. Otherwise, we would end up in an endless regress. When it is more than conformity out of fear of punishment, this obedience is grounded in a fundamental benevolence, in which the reality of myself and the other becomes real to me. Readiness for discursive agreement about the good and the bad is only one, and then not even the first, of the material consequences of this benevolence.

The secondary position of discourse in the area of moral judgment formation becomes clear when looked at from two other viewpoints. One concerns the relationship between speech and action which comes into effect when time is short. This relationship gets expressed in the old saying: *Ars longa, vita brevis.* The consequences of this insight are made most clear through the example of medicine and medical treatment. Diagnosis, therapy, surgical operations are, on the one hand, moments in a scientific, epistemological process which is indifferent toward the life of the individual patient. This process moves unflaggingly forward. Success and failure, knowledge and error can all be equally fruitful for it – indeed failure even more than success, since science is stimulated all the more by falsification rather than by verification. The perspective of the patient, that is, the medical perspective in its truest sense, is completely different. Here failure is definitive and mistakes are fatal. Therefore, the ethos of a physician and that of the medical researcher are not identical. What we as patients expect of physicians is actually twofold. On the one hand, they must constantly control and improve their medical arts through medical science. They must participate in the discourse of the science. On the other hand, as patients, we do not wish that the doctor be a mere instrument which carries out what science has taught. We do not put our trust in an anonymous community of discourse called "science" but in a certain human being, who, as participant in this discourse, still takes responsibility for what he or she appropriates from this discourse and what he or she sees as advisable in this case. This cannot be simply deduced from some so-called state of the science.

Here another thought presents itself: There must be yet another discourse which is cognizant of these practical decisions and their ethical aspects, which is cognizant of that which benevolence demands. The so-called ethics committees are supposed to advise the physician in decisions which touch on life and death. In fact, there is a danger here. The becoming real of the other for me is, and remains, a strictly personal process which is inseparably bound up with the activation of one's own self-being. Counsel can indeed be given. For the objectification of benevolence leads to typical situations which, detached from the immediate need to act, can be reflected upon and discussed. Physicians have to have taken part intensively in such discourse in their training, and they need to take part in it over and over again. But to think that an ethics committee would be the subject of relevant decisions, that the physician could delegate "the ethical" to them, is already a misunderstanding, since the composition of these committees is completely contingent and their decisions are dependent upon what can be agreed upon with a majority consensus within a certain time frame. There is only one way to overcome the contingency: in full consciousness to accept this contingency in the figure of the one with whom I actually stand in a common situation – for example, in the figure of the physician – and so not to discharge the other from their responsibility, which the dimension of the unconditioned, of conscience, requires of him or her alone. When we are in this position we are reduced to a hope: that I will become real for the one who has responsibility for my fate. For every community of discourse which is unbounded, and that means freed from the immediate situation which calls for action, I necessarily become a "case," and it makes no difference if here that means an "ethical case." Ethics is not an *ars longa*; ethics has to do with *vita brevis*.

IV

The second viewpoint which makes clear that discourse is not an example of something which produces elementary moral norms is the following: That which is decisive has to have already occurred, before discourse begins. We saw this already in the context of the criteria required for making discourse morally relevant. The whole of morality is already contained in these criteria. A mutual recognition of the participants in the discourse underlies every discourse. The more real they are to each other, the more relevant the discourse but, at the same time, the less necessary, since precisely this recognition was the decisive step, from which the rest followed. *Dilge et quod vis fac*. The displacement of the burden to discourse is dangerous because it limits the benevolence to the participants. In labor negotiations the unemployed are not present in the same way as the workers and management. If, nevertheless, a responsibility for them is perceived, then it is a responsibility to those who are not party to the discourse. Certainly, as citizens the unemployed are present in the wider political discourse. But what about children, the mentally ill, the future generations who will be affected by our decisions but who are not present in any discourse which concerns their interests? What about the responsibility for the life and death of the unborn? Later participants in the discourse will only be those who are allowed to live. And what about the responsibility for the remembrance and furtherance of the work of those who were before us? Discourse ethics cannot ground the responsibility for those who cannot participate in the discourse. This responsibility is *anterior* to discourse. And responsibility, that is, that practical benevolence which is called "help," forms the basis of all discourse. Discourse can only be a consultation about how to concretize the help. The fact that discourse proceeds endlessly has significance here also. In order to act, we always have to leave discourse, view it as finished for ourselves and make up our minds about what we see as the result of the discourse. Discourse *accompanies* action; moral action is not the result of self-contained discourse. And for its part discourse is embedded in a legal framework, which first makes it possible, in that it protects it against violent influences.

Mention must be made of a further presupposition of ideal discourse which is, generally speaking, not discussed in the present theories of discourse: the presupposition of a certain degree of homogeneity. Reason alone is not sufficient to bring this about. Let us imagine a discourse between ourselves and a rational being from another planet, a discourse which concerns conflicting interests and the attempt to produce a settlement through the making of a hierarchy of interests and of common compromises. That all participants are rational means that they are in a position and prepared to perceive the self-being of the other as well as to relativize their own wishes and interests, that is, transcend the centrality of merely being alive. Despite this readiness, it would still be possible that the problem of what is acceptable would be irresolvable on account of the fact that we would not have any intuitive access to the pre-rational drives, wishes, and needs of the others. We would not be able to gauge what was irreplaceable for them, what was of vital importance and what made life worth living. We have – and this is what renders the common understanding impossible – neither a common history, nor do we share with them a common "nature." Discourse presupposes such a commonality; it cannot produce it. A being who is not sensitive to pain could perhaps consider it to be a remarkable contrivance on the basis of its use as a signal, but it cannot know in what this signal consists, that is, what it would mean to actually feel pain. It cannot grant a high value to efforts to avoid pain, and it would not be prepared to share in costs for anesthetics. If the commonality of human nature consisted only in the capacity for speech and thought and not also in a certain elementary commonality of immediate evaluation, discourse would not be able to replace it. Differences in taste become capable of negotiation only because the sense of beauty itself is general. A person of no religious persuasion can give high value to the respect for the religious convictions of others because he or she is not as irreligious as they may think, but rather has an idea what it means that something is seen as holy by another human. The consistent materialism of the Marquis de Sade has systematically strangled the capacity for this idea. But even here, a small remainder of this idea must survive so that the sadist can find enjoyment in the desecration of the holy.

A common esteem for things is not produced discursively; it is presupposed if an agreement over what is good and bad is to be at all possible. The value ethics of Franz Brentano, Max Scheler, Dietrich von Hildebrandt, Nicolai Hartmann, and George Edward Moore, which understood values as the primordial, intuitively given basis of all morality, are often suspected today of destroying all rational ethics because of their appeal to subjective evidence and of thereby rendering impossible the most important task of ethics, the resolving of conflicts through consensus. First, it has to be said that the resolution of conflicts is not the primary task of ethics. Ethics is primarily the reflection on the conditions for a life which turns out well, and then it is the teaching of the practical consequences of benevolence, i.e., of the *ordo amoris*. In certain circumstances the ethical, far from solving conflicts, intensifies them. Whoever champions the cause of the abolition of slavery, whoever stands against the legalization of abortion or stands for the humane treatment of animals disturbs the present consensus and brings out conflict. Ethical reflection is not concerned with the resolution of conflict as such, but with the *correct* solution, and there can be disagreement about what the correct solution would be. But, so runs the objection against value ethics, the appeal to something like the self-evidence of value is incapable of leading to rational argument since it is not to be distinguished from idiosyncrasy. For the one this is self-evident; for the other not. In fact, any conversation would already be over with this appeal. Without going into the ontological question of the self-evidence of value, let it suffice to point out here that in the end every discourse is bound to founder if it does not lead back to certain insights which are not subject to dispute by the parties involved. Value ethics believed it had worked out and presented such ultimately uncontested insight, insights which are hidden by superficial differences in the perspectives which are grounded in particular interests. What these insights are themselves can be put aside for the moment. It is enough to make clear that without a certain homogeneity of the moral perception, the will to rational understanding and rational equalization cannot effect anything.

Kant clearly saw the analogue to this in reference to the legislating of theoretical reason. He wrote that the categories of the understanding could not structure our experience at all if nature did not come to meet them half-way. The principle of causality would be an empty principle if nature were not so constructed that it presents itself in *certain* laws of causality, laws which we cannot deduce a priori and without which the "a priori" of causality would remain without consequence, like a divining rod where there is no water. So also in the practical field. Discourse can no more lead to a material norm of action than reason, which it wants to represent, if those who are to speak with each other do not already find themselves in agreement about certain elementary values.

And when they do not agree, discourse cannot replace this agreement. For those who have not had certain elementary moral experiences, who have not learned a certain basic trust, who possess neither a sense of honor nor a sense of shame, who have never experienced the attitude of respect or the feeling of thankfulness, for these, whose participation in a discourse about norms would probably be useless, discourse is not something to which they can contribute, but rather destroy. If it is possible at all to make up for fundamental experiences which were missed, then this can only be accomplished in a completely different way, that is, by treating the person in such a way that he or she experiences an unconditioned benevolence, behind which stands the *courage to act unilaterally*, that is, precisely the renunciation of that reciprocity which is constitutive of rational discourse.

The introduction of an intuitive self-evidence into ethics is suspected of being what the eighteenth century called fanaticism: the establishment of a particular perspective as the instantiation of the unconditioned. In comparison relativism appears to be a form of moral universalism, since it allows to each *its* moral truth. The opposite is actually the case. Relativism is an extreme moral position, which, far from representing or producing consensus, falls out of the consensus of all peoples and times, since, if there is anything which binds all humans, it is the distinction between good and evil. This distinction produces conflict. It underlies a lot of the cruelty which humans have perpetrated on other humans. But it is also the only refuge of the victims. On the other side of this distinction there is only cynicism. And the greatest crime of this century, the slaughter of millions of humans, did not occur because these millions were supposed to be "evil" but because they were supposed to be objectively harmful, that is, because they stood in an antagonistic relationship, on the basis of the class or race to which they belonged, to the supposed interests of their executioners. Relativism, which forbids naming the deeds of these executioners evil in a universal sense, would be the ultimate betrayal of the victims. Whoever says one may kill even his own mother, so writes Aristotle – showing the boundaries of discourse – deserves not arguments but rebuke.

Chapter 13

Action or Functioning within a System?

I

THE QUESTION, "Is this right?" – meaning 'Will it help make my life as a whole?' – is only meaningful given a theoretical presupposition. The question presupposes that there is such a thing as action, that is, that action is what the agent believes it to be: the conscious and willful realization of an intention. Further, this implies that judging an action by its immanent aspect, that is, its subjective sense, is to judge it according to the viewpoint which is *essential* to the action. But does this essential viewpoint really exist? Doesn't every action have many aspects, just like any other occurrence? One person is affected by it differently from another. The one action exists in various system-complexes[1] and derives a different meaning from each. The therapeutic measure of the physician has one meaning for the patient, another meaning for the progress of knowledge of medical science, and still another for the economic situation or the psychological well being of the physician. Moral judgment of an action refers to its subjective meaning, that is, to that which makes it an action. The judgment views this meaning as autonomous, as not requiring a further context in order to be understood or evaluated. This autonomy of an action's meaning is another word for what we call freedom. If this autonomy of meaning is an illusion, then so is freedom. For, to act freely means to know what one does and why one does it. In those cases where our action was intelligible or capable of being judged only from a context which lay hidden within ourselves, we were not free and only thought that we acted. The meaning we gave to our action was not constitutive of the judgment of the action and so was unessential.

---

1   I have chosen to translate (with a few exceptions, most noticeably in the title of the chapter) the various terms which begin with *System*, such as *Systemzusammenhang, Systemtheorie, Systemstruktur,* etc., by prefixing the word "system" to the appropriate word in English. It makes for some rather ugly neologisms, but is less confusing than using the adjective "systematic," which has a different meaning.

But wouldn't it be conceivable that an autonomous meaning of action exists, such that it could not but require that the essential meaning for the judgment of the action be given by something else? No power on earth can hinder us, according to Sartre, from giving a meaning to our action in this way. But this meaning remains simply a meaning for us; it cannot compel someone else to let it play a role in their judgment. Precisely because the agent is autonomous, so too is everyone else. Agents can never succeed in making the for-itself into an in-itself. Simply because one knows oneself to be free is no reason for that one also to be acknowledged from the outside as free "in-itself." This view would equate freedom with the existence of a dimension of interiority. But in this sense an animal is also free. Neither the fact that its activities have a biological function nor that we are able to lead it beyond this, when it is useful for us, alters the reality that the animal itself is after drive-satisfaction so that pleasure and pain give its activities a meaning which cannot be negated by another meaning. But the animal is subject to manipulation precisely because it is shut up in this subjective meaning. It is at the mercy of others precisely because it does not perceive the meaning which its activities have for others. And these others can reduce the meaning which its action has for its self to something unessential.

The specific autonomy of human action is constituted by the knowledge that our action has various meanings for others and in other contexts. These other meanings can enter into the meaning which we ourselves give to our action. That is, we can take them into account. These meanings and contexts are in some non-necessary way connected with one another. Such a connection is brought about only from the viewpoint of responsibility. To the extent that it remains a matter of subjective arbitrariness whether or not agents want to accept the objective meaning of an action in their considerations, to that extent they remain dreamers. Since the agent is in a speech-community with others, the dream cannot be respected. To acknowledge agents as members of the speech-community means to view them as accountable, and this, in turn, means to credit them with responsibility for that which their actions means to others. To judge their actions under this aspect, that is, morally, means not to judge it according to objective consequences without consideration of their intentions and knowledge, or to judge it only according to that which was thematic as the agent's intention. "The principle which says, 'Disdain the consequences of actions' as well as the one which says 'Judge actions by their consequences and make them the measure of what is right and good,' – both are the product of the same abstract understanding."[2] To

---

2   G.W.F. Hegel, *Grundlinien der Philosophie des Rechts,* §118. Eng.: *Hegel's Philosophy of Right*, trans. T. M. Knox, (London: Oxford Univ. Press, 1967).

judge actions only according to their consequences means not to view them as actions at all but as a kind of natural occurrence. To act means to pick out from the infinite number of consequences certain ones as "purposes," in relationship to which the others are reduced to secondary consequences. Further, there are those secondary consequence for which we bear responsibility and others which escape all possible foresight. To judge an action as an action, that is, to judge it morally, does not mean to measure it directly by the totality of its consequences, but to judge it in light of the agent's perception of responsibility for the consequences, that is, how the agent subjectively took account of the objective content of his or her action.

For it is only in the eyes of the agent or some other person rendering judgment that the consequences become integrated into a whole. Integration into a whole is always perspectival. To expect a strictly non-perpectival, i.e., a divine, standpoint of the agent in this integration is the error of consequentialism. Nevertheless, no agent can demand to be judged only according to his or her express intentions.

In fact, the unforeseen but accepted consequences, even that which was not thought of, even inattention and forgetfulness, become part of the responsibility of the agent, if the agent is to be acknowledged and understood as free. This might seem surprising, since unawareness, forgetting, and not paying attention are obviously not psychic events, not actions of the will. If, nonetheless, we are to judge them as moral, we do so because the locus of freedom is not primarily the individual action, but the constitution of the person, the degree of wakefulness to reality. That this being awake, this attention, is itself once more to be answered for is a paradox which has caused philosophy trouble over and over again. For it appears to ensnare the problem of freedom in an infinite iteration. If freedom is grounded in being awake to reason and if, on the other hand, we bear responsibility for this wakefulness itself, then this appears to lead to the postulate of a "freedom before freedom." Without going into this problem with the necessary nuances here, the following direction presents itself *prima facie* as a solution. There is no way that the primordial wakefulness can be thought of as the self-achievement of the subject. Rather, it is constitutive for the subject's personality. The highest degree of wakefulness – also the highest degree of benevolence – is identical with the highest degree of freedom, whereby this freedom has left behind all moral indifference. It can only be indifferent toward the moral *adiaphora*. Moral indifference, freedom for good or evil, can only be thought of as a result of a fall in which finite freedom has not kept its wakefulness. The morally negative decision can only be thought of as a secondary decision. Humans are free to pull themselves back from wakefulness to reality into the particularity of *amor sui usque ad contemptum Dei*, but they are not so free as to reverse this direction. Rather, they need a "liberation" for this. More does not need to be said about this here. We are only concerned at this point to show that the unintentional consequences of action are also relevant to its moral evaluation, since the acceptance of these qualifies the intention itself. The saying that the end justifies the means is not only false; it is the motto for the school of insincerity. For if this were true, then the best person would be the one who most succeeded in deluding and manipulating himself into repressing the actual goal and making it into a secondary consequence of other actions which he had successfully set up as the goal of the action. In the language of jurisprudence one calls this rightfully, *dolus eventualis*.

In a certain sense the problem of our actions' secondary consequences is the central theme of all normative ethics. That all humans want the good by nature was a tautology for the ancients. The good meant primarily the pleasant. Equally old is the discovery that the pleasant can have harmful secondary consequences, and then it is not good. And if one defines the good as the beneficial, then it becomes possible that it has secondary effects which are beneficial for the one and harmful for the other. Only pure evil, "diabolical" evil, has evil as evil, the bad as bad for its goal. Normally, evil consists in inattention to, or surreptitiously looking away from, what we bring about and accept. We cannot make all the consequences of our actions the center of our attention, even if we tried. Selection through the focusing of our attention belongs to the essence of finite action. The ordering of the degrees of attention, the distinction between justified and unjustified neglect of consequences, the boundaries of what we will as the means and what we ought to accept as the secondary consequences, this is all the affair of that *ordo amoris* which sketches out the structure of moral responsibility. In principle *all* consequences of an action of ours enter into this *ordo amoris*, since benevolence, when it is not the expression of subjective arbitrariness but the being awake to the reality of self-being, should not exclude anyone or anything. Nevertheless, this benevolence is determined by a finite perspective and only becomes real when it is conscious of this perspective and accepts it in freedom. Only by the acceptance of the totality inherent in the subjective intention and by the conscious integration of its own particularity in a totality does the meaning of an action become "absolute." This means it is no longer merely an element which misunderstands itself in a totality of "non-sense." And only this turns it into a real action, as distinct from a natural occurrence.

II

Today this self-understanding of the agent is endangered in an unprecedented way. Endangered by a line of reasoning that has both a practical as well as a theoretical form. Its practical form runs along the following lines: Through modern scientific technology the latitude of consequences of human action has become so large that the traditional distinction between the goal of an action and its side effects has been blurred. The accumulated consequences of individual actions affect nature in a way which has brought about a completely new situation. Nature is no longer the unchangeable ambience within which human action takes place and which, over the long run, absorbs and neutralizes all the consequences of this action. We need only think of the ever-increasing rate of extermination of this planet's natural species, which is the unintended but accepted consequence of the modern form of economy. These consequences affect the irreplaceable heritage of all of humanity and therefore so surpass the importance of individual goals of action, whose secondary consequences they are, that these actions now appear to us to be defined primarily and essentially by these consequences and not by the subjective goals. The perplexity lies in the fact that this is only the case if we view the consequences as accumulated. For it is usually only this accumulation which leads to these effects. Therefore, the specific importance of the individual action seems to disappear. It seems essential to the action that it is a part of an ensemble, which the agent does not have in view. And this further reduces the specific importance of the action.

Added to this is the already mentioned theoretical reasoning which changes the self-understanding of the agent. Science – the natural sciences but even more the human sciences – constantly interpret our action as an element of an ensemble which the agent never intends. The computer predictions on election night make the deliberations and considerations of the individual voter appear meaningless in the light of the trends which show themselves. The most personal forms of lifestyle, love, child-rearing, work, religion, and attitudes toward death become not only the object of statistical investigations but also of sociological, system-functional interpretations, which expropriates the agent from his or her self as soon as the agent becomes aware of the interpretation. They are in the situation of the Hopi Indians, who heard the ethnologist's interpretation of their rain dance. At that moment the dance's latent function for the preservation of the identity of the tribe becomes essential, the goal of the action becomes a mere means for this essential function. The colonization of our life-world by science appears to have made the concept of action, and with it the human, obsolete. There seems to be only systems without subjects, in which the human appears under different aspects, without the possibility of being able to refer to "reality." Even the scientist is not a subject; science itself is not the uncovering of meaning; rather it is merely a subsystem of that system called "society."

There are two reactions to the above: self-objectification or the withdrawal into the fanaticism of the passions. These ways are more closely related to each other than might first appear. Self-objectification takes the system-functional perspective as its own, thus abdicating the role of subject. Humans cannot help being a feeling, acting, and suffering being; they cannot stop valuing, distinguishing between good and evil, better and worse. But they have learned to withdraw or to bracket these intentional achievements which are constitutive for the reflective life. They have learned to speak about themselves in the language which objectifies, and so demeans the human, and to re-interpret their own intentional acts as merely subjective states. In principle they consider themselves like all the others to be dreamers and everything from wakefulness to be only the dream of being awake. Their dream has then no real meaning, but it has a function within the complexes of organic, psychic, social systems. Since this way of bringing such complexes to bear on something like meaning is a relapse into that subjective perspective, which itself has long been exposed on a theoretical level as illusionary, there remains the sole goal of making the functions as frictionless as possible and removing the possible tensions between these and subjective experience. The only thing that matters is that one feel good. Hedonism is the ethics which corresponds to functionalism *beyond freedom and dignity.*

The fanaticism of the passions is the apparent antithesis of scientism. In it individuals refuse to acknowledge at all the "objective" meaning of their actions. They enclose themselves in their subjective experiences: They act, suffer, value but do not yield to any relativizing of that which is real to them. They demand, like Don Quixote, all the world to be put in chains if they will not admit that Dulcinea of Toboso is the most beautiful woman in the world. This "fanatical" indifference to any exterior view of the *amour fou* contains within itself relativism, like a fatal poison, similar to the scientistic task explained above. Insofar as fanatics refuse to perceive the meaning of their actions which goes beyond their perspectives, they make clear that they do not really believe in the reality which they defend. Privately they realize that their views do not stand up to scrutiny "from outside," and therefore they do not subject them to this test. They dispense with convincing others; it is enough that they are convinced and that no one contradicts them. But even this shows that they are not really convinced. They are like the dreamer who is already aware that he dreams but tries to put off waking up in order to be able to think of the dream as reality a bit longer. For they too believe that the "true reality" is that which expropriates the agent from him or herself.

The first one to pose this problem of the opposition between a scientific *Weltanschauung* and the self-interpretation of the agent was Kant. His solution consisted in holding the scientific form of objectivity to be the dream and the self-understanding of the agent to be the revelation of the true reality. Action as an occurrence in the world is indistinguishable in principle from natural occurrences. It stands in causal and functional sequences by which it is fully determined. But this being determined does not touch the heart of the matter, the action. By the same token, neither does inner experience reach it. For, according to Kant, this is also a form of "dreaming," and we cannot distinguish which one is real. The agent's insistence on his or her self-understanding could be simply fanaticism. We can only judge whether it is fanaticism or not, that is, whether their dream is more real than that of another, if we are truly awake. This being truly awake occurs only when we are met by the reality of the person, be it a stranger or one of our own, who claims unconditioned respect or "benevolence." This reality does not reveal itself primarily in order to demand this respect, but it is only in light of this claim – the "fact of reason" – that we become conscious of our freedom as a "thing-in-itself," as the true reality. The question, irresolvable on a theoretical level, about what "is really true" will be decided at that point where theoretical and practical philosophy, where metaphysics and ethics originally are one, in the conscience. I should not view the other as a mere "appearance," if I am aware of the claim which originates in his or her reality, and I should not view myself as a mere appearance, if I experience myself as the addressee of this claim. On the other hand, I can only meet the claim through actions which are oriented toward the other as appearance, since it is only this which I can affect. For Kant then the appearance of the human is a representation of its actual, "noumenal" reality "in the sense world." This means: The functional complexes within which we have to deal with other humans cannot ground an unconditioned claim. On the contrary, through their multiplicity they relativize every functional grounding of such claims. Still, they are not in the position to bring the unconditionedness of the moral to naught. What we call "the dignity of the human person" is not derived from some system. But it is also not just the dressing room which a differentiated social system needs in order to make possible the necessary role changes of individuals. It is much more the reverse, that our technical civilization has to protect through codification that which was self-understood in every archaic society, even if it was never a securely guaranteed element of life.

All systems in which humans live have a characteristic ambivalence regarding the self-being of the individual as the true reality of humans. On the one hand, it is they that first develop that which the human is and can be. Human dispositions and capacities unfold themselves only under highly developed conditions and in a high degree of differentiation of the social sub-system. Only there do science and art and a culture of subjectivity, all of which underlie our talk of self-being, exist. But insofar as this differentiation into a multiplicity of systems makes necessary a plurality of roles, it also makes it possible for humans to distance themselves from these roles and to define their identity independent of them. Rousseau was the first to describe this possibility of distancing as alienation. The person who has to live in many houses is not at home in any of them. It seems, then, as if any assignable determination which constituted the being of the human, would be one of these houses and that humans could stand in a kind of ironical relationship to world and to themselves, by refusing to take anything seriously or to attach their identities to a finite content. All necessity dissolves into optional possibilities, and that which can still be meant by the concept "progress" exhausts itself in the constant expansion of these possibilities. But this expansion depends upon individuals subjecting themselves to a certain homogenization of needs so that these needs correspond to the system. Further, it depends upon them perceiving the options which fall within the spectrum which this system offers to them. For example, they have to tolerate the fact that all the ways in which one can fill one's life get presented exclusively in the form of satisfying needs. People who do not accept this inversion of intentionality, since it concerns something of great importance to them, drop out of the system. They are misfits, infantile or fanatic.

In such a view the unconditioned aspect of morality also appears to become obsolete. At most it gets reduced to an *optio fundamentalis*, a purely mental attitude of benevolence, which never quite finds empirical embodiment, but instead leads to the demand for behavior which is in keeping with the system in some autonomous, practical field. But this demand can be grounded just as well within the system and comes close to being simple interest in one's own well-being. This does not yet constitute an objection. Thomas Aquinas writes that love does not find any adequate empirical embodiment since any action which occurs out of love, could have occurred without love. This corresponds to the saying in Letter to the Corinthians: "If I give my body over to be burned, but have not love . . ."

For its part, this moral, fundamental option, which is without consequences, can be coordinated with a social subsystem, namely the "philosophical-theological complex," within which it is a certain *façon de parler*, a certain way of self-interpretation. The moral attitude becomes real only as a certain way of placing oneself in a real relationship to the totality of system-structures in which one lives and so to assert one's self-understanding over against one's system-functional interpretation. The system-theory itself is a prime example of such a relationship. System-theorists, e.g., the biologist, the psychologist, or the sociologist, do not find themselves outside of the systems which they analyze. They practice their science and thereby belong to that system for which the medium of truth is constitutive. Nevertheless, this medium cannot be defined by the social subsystem called science; rather the former is presumed by the latter. Insofar as they practice theory, system-theorists refer intentionally to the whole of reality. For the system-environments are also the object of their study, especially since they, for their part, have further system-characteristics. Of course, this is a completely formal relationship to the totality of reality, which can be concretized only in the form of individual analyses. Still, proper to this relationship is some characteristic kind of unconditionedness, which is contained in every truth claim. Indeed, system-theory can only function as an instrument of radical relativism under the presupposition that it itself is not subsumed in it. Otherwise it would cancel itself. Minimally, the action of producing theories has to understand itself as an action, which is not "expropriated" by a latent function. But then there is something moral in this theoretical action, an implied practical moment of unconditionedness – what we call truthfulness. Truthfulness is a practical relationship, a relationship of recognition and fundamental benevolence. Practical solipsists can contrive and assert the arbitrary. For them, will to truth and will to power are not in principle distinguishable. If I am not to understand the expression of another as a serious communication, at least in the sense of an experimental thesis which is subject to testing, then I cannot comprehend it as a theoretical communication at all. The recognition of the reality of the other is contained in every seriously intended theory. The reverse also holds: In every action, which corresponds to its concept, we refer to the whole of reality. In fact a merely partial meaning is only the appearance of meaning. Action, then, can only be what its concept means and what the agent understands it to be, if comprehensibility and intelligibility are the encompassing structures of reality. This depends on the following sentence being true: "In the beginning was the Word." This does not somehow mean that agents have to redeem this tacit presupposition of all action and so set themselves in a relationship of understanding to the whole of reality. Action is finite, as is human understanding. In action we throw ourselves into reality. We start an incalculable chain of occurrences going, over which we soon lose any influence. Even the system-functional complexes, within which our action comes to be, cannot be taken in by us. Philosophy in ancient and medieval times was not disturbed by this thought, since the institutional framework of our action appeared to be given ahistorically. The system-functions of action were all manifest, comprehensible, and, accordingly, the responsibility of the agent. The saying of Goethe, "You need act correctly only in your affairs. The affairs of others will take care of themselves!" expresses the basis of all traditional ethos. That the order, within which something takes care of itself, is not independent of our action, but rather is stabilized or destabilized by it, and that this depends, in turn, upon our judgment whether we want to stabilize or destabilize it, is a modern thought, the thought of the Enlightenment. The thought of system-theory is post-Enlightenment. It goes back to the "affairs of others will take care of themselves," but it views the order, which constitutes itself out of itself, as a dynamic order. It changes itself through human action, but in such a way that the intentions of agents could not anticipate the direction of this change. It is precisely the essential system-functions which are latent and cannot be integrated into action-intentions.

This situation is made acute by the fact that nature is no longer the comprehensive framework of our action, in which its long-term consequences are unfailingly neutralized. Nature, too, has a history, and in this history human action plays a greater and greater role. But this role is for the most part not intended. It does not enter into the meaning of the action. The mere omission of actions which appear to us as likely to be irresponsible does not lead to the solution of problems. For pre-modern philosophy omission meant the same as: Everything stays as it is. But when the world is understood as a process, in which nothing stays as it is, then it appears as if agents are always responsible for the way things go. At every opportunity for omission agents have to ask whether the other alternative would not be more responsible. A global responsibility for reality as a whole is loaded on to agents at the same time that it is made clear to them that they cannot bear it. The unintentional secondary consequences of their action keep cropping up. And what's more, the greater the range of planning, by which we had hoped to get a handle on these consequences, the greater they become. Agents are in a causal relationship with the whole of reality, but they cannot overtake this relationship and derive from it meaning for action. Their action seems to degenerate into one natural occurrence among others. In light of the systematic excessive demands on the agent, the only possible consequence of the abandonment of the classical, humane concept of responsible action appears to be resignation, withdrawal to immediate satisfaction or to a use of power which is uninterested in justification.

III

In contrast to the whole pre-Kantian tradition, Kant himself believed he could save the imperiled concept of action and/or freedom only through moral experience. The older tradition started from the basic experience of the intelligibility of being. In each experience the partial meaning of action was embedded in a universal meaning-structure, which underlies all reality. This universality of meaning became questionable when an anti-teleological science broke it up into an infinity of casual sequences without the possibility of closure. In this situation the totality of meaning is given only in that unconditionedness which is demanded of us by every individual personal self-being. In moral experience it becomes clear that reality is not a infinite process without the possibility of closure, within which "self-constructing" system-structures form, transform, and destroy themselves, but rather that all processes and structures are only variations of a monad-like realities. For self-being alone is it valid to say: "Everything is predicated of them, but they themselves are predicated of nothing" (Aristotle, *Metaphysics* 1017b14). Leibniz too understood correctly that in each self-being the whole universe represented itself. In this way every self-being is without context. To refer to it in action means to transcend all system-structures and the process of nature, since the meaning of the whole displays itself in every individual who becomes real to us in the full sense of the word. That which distinguishes action from natural occurrences is grounded in moral experience, that is, in the unconditioned aspect of benevolence and its self-interpretation is made superior to every system-functional interpretation.

That being said, no practical question has yet been answered. And the answers, which would be forthcoming, would certainly not have the character of pleading for an ethics of immediacy, which simply ignored the way in which action is bound up with structures and the responsibilities which flow from this. On the contrary, *that* responsibilities emerge at all from the structural and functional complexities shows that system-functionality is capable of being recovered by a theory of action and transformed into moral responsibility; but this presumes a monad-like, unconditioned aspect which is capable of being grounded only by the thought of representation. Responsibility has to involve itself in institutional agencies. No one is concerned with just a single person. And even granting that in certain respects each individual is incomparable, we cannot do otherwise than to make him or her comparable in reference to our finite actions. Principally, we are able to make a hierarchy of the various system-contexts in which humans exist, since we can refer them to self-being, and they can be brought into a scale of responsibility according to the weight and urgency of the interests, needs, and convictions represented in them. Individual agents cannot directly intervene in the system-structure which predetermines all action, in order to transform it from the point of view of personal responsibility. But they can work together with others so that such a structure becomes a political matter.

The area of the political is the area in which the original self-understanding of action asserts itself in the face of the predominant system-structures of a highly differentiated society. To politicize something means to thematize those decisions which underlie all the so-called necessities in question, or to transform the spontaneous givens into objects of decision. Looked at from the point of view of the goal of expanding the latitude of freedom, such freedom is ambivalent. It is possible to thematize something only on the basis of a non-thematized horizon of the self-evident. It is possible to act only on the basis of a background of normality, which is not called into question. The thought of a permanent discursive justification of all the structural givens of human action fails to recognize one of the elementary presuppositions of such justification. Nevertheless, it makes a difference whether this framework of self-evidence and normality actually has the self-evident and the normal, or the absurd and the abnormal, for its content. In appropriate instances this distinction has to be capable of being proven discursively. It can be proven by the fact that agents implicitly affirm this framework in their actions so that the meaning of the action can be extended, so to say, into the context of meaning which is implicitly given, or else it finds itself in contradiction with this framework. In the latter case the agent is no longer one with himself or herself, since they accept *nolens volens* this framework in order to act at all. In the former case the agents can affirm the unthematic, systems-stabilizing function of their action without calling their friendship with their own selves into question. All the same, the reverse does not hold here, i.e., that correct action would be impossible in a false context, and that action, in which agents stabilize circumstances against their will, would be inevitably depraved so that in such situations only revolutionary action could be acknowledged as free. This reasoning process is much more characteristic of totalitarianism.

One can best characterize totalitarian thinking as defining all action, without consideration of the intention of the agent, in terms of the function it possesses in reference to a certain system-framework of boundaries, regardless of whether the function is to stabilize or destroy the system. And when an action does not have any visible reference, for example, an everyday, a scientific, or an artistic activity, then it is defined by its lack: The agent should have done something better, i.e., something that was more relevant to the system in this time. There is only one meaning, and it coincides with a certain system-framework or a certain interpretation of history. The placing of the duty of the wife of a criminal over against the duty of the judge by Thomas Aquinas is an example of a non-totalitarian view of action. Not every action has to move within the same system-framework. The judge has the *bonum civitatis* to care for, while the wife cares for the *bonum privatum familiae*. The judge should so little contest the wife's right to this as Kreon should contest Antigone's right to bury her brother without consideration of the reasons of state. Otherwise, the judge puts herself in the place of God instead of wanting "that which God wants her to want." This is, however, circumscribed by a circle of responsibility which is always limited. The saying, "Act correctly in your own affairs," remains valid as the necessary presupposition for the possibility of the existence of something like unconditionedness in morality

Participation in the reflection on the conditions of the framework of our existence has become such an element of modern political life that complete abstinence from this requires justification. But even this participation as moral is qualified by the same maxims which limit and concretize responsibility. "Being informed" or merely "having one's say" or strategic manifestation of one's concern are not identical with the perception of concrete responsibility. For the one who has perceived this with competence, the meaning of their engagement can no longer be made dependent on the outcome. Moral action is that action which lives in each moment from the presence of a totality of meaning.

Without a religious implication this thought is somewhat difficult to retain. Thomas Aquinas starts characteristically with the thought that it is the same God "who wants what we should want," and who relieves us from total responsibility for the course of things, since he himself cares for the *bonum universi*. In the necessity of an ultimate trust in the convergence of righteousness and the salvation of the world Fichte saw the "reason for our belief in a divine world government" without which all human morality must fall apart. And Jean-Paul Sartre noted in his *Cahiers pour une morale*, that the atheist has to make the starting point that the end justifies the means. The morality in which the agent is concerned with his own righteousness instead of the course of things would be something other than egoism only for believers, since only they have their own existence as something to answer for, whose meaning is not at their free disposal.

Actually, an unconditionedness which transcends all system-reference is not primarily the result of an already-made metaphysical or religious decision. Rather, such a decision is much more the consequence of a unbiased reflection on our elementary moral intuitions. Kant continues to be correct when he says that outside of the thought of the unconditioned the concept of action cannot be saved from the clutches of system-theory.

Chapter 14

Normality and Naturalness

I

CONSEQUENTIALISM and discourse ethics are—like all ethical theories, at least in their origins—responses to a crisis of tradition in our life-world. Such traditions, mores, and normative orientations have the function of mediating the unconditioned quality of that benevolence in which the reality of self-being appears to the many-conditioned situations in which finite action occurs. In these situations benevolence has to "break" itself up in order to realize itself externally. To a certain extent, these structural determinations of our expectations and duties place a "language" at the disposal of benevolence. Over and above this, they have the function of making social life largely independent of the presence or absence of benevolence. That same politeness, which can unite respect, affection, discretion, and delicate consideration toward each other, can also be a veil behind which calculation and antipathy can so hide themselves that the difference reveals itself only to those who really want to see it. First and foremost, social traditions serve the existence of the social system. They stabilize the relationships of the near and the far; they set the standards for the distribution of burdens and compensations. Such standards are always subject to dispute from the viewpoint of justice. That is, they are controversial in the discourse of justification. Plato distinguished arithmetical from proportional justice. He was of the opinion that it would only be possible for God to realize proportional justice, that is, to attain real commensurability between the "merit" and the reward. In this world proportional justice has to be tempered then by arithmetical justice, that is, by the fiction of the equality of all humans. Marx distinguished two principles of justice. One was measured according to performance, and it was valid for the phase of socialism. The second was the communistic principle of "to each according to his needs," which presumed the definitive overcoming of scarcity and thereby also presumed the fiction of equality.

Moral education is always a handing-on of a canon of social rules and expectations of behavior. But it is also a handing-on of good examples, of people who broke out of the ambiguity of these rules and, by being awake to a higher consciousness of reality, gave an expression to their benevolence which transcended the rules and often did this at the cost of their own fundamental interests. Over a period of time such examples can help to bring about what was called in previous centuries, "the purification of morals." Today, for example, the behavior of the good Samaritan is the legal duty of every traveler, at least as far as first-aid is concerned. Custom is unavoidable for the embodiment of benevolence, but an *adequate* embodiment can never be give by custom.

Precisely for this reason custom, convention, is indispensable for human action. It establishes the normality which is constitutive for all living beings. In the realm of inanimate material there is no normality. Each movement is exactly like every other, the result of a parallelogram of forces. There are no movements which can be characterized as normal or "natural." In the same way there is no such thing as a "break-down," except for an external observer of the occurrence, who perceives the deviation from the expectations or from that which usually occurs. But in reality this deviation is as much a consequence of the same laws and forces as that which normally occurs. This is not the case with the animate. The well-being and pain of a living being are not the consequences of the same type of occurrences. The growing of a tree and its getting bent in a storm are diametrically opposed movements. Simply to perceive a living being as a living being presupposes the distinction between normality and deviation. For the thirsty fluid intake or its lack are not neutral physical facts; rather they have a meaning in relation to the normal condition of the living: They mean to drink or to die of thirst. There is meaning only where there is something like normality. We will see that normality, which we characterize as "the natural," is also constitutive for the ethical. But in light of the lack of instincts which would adapt the human to a particular ecological niche, this normality is too rudimentary to suffice to orient our actions. The room for action would be so large that it would place excessive demands on agents. They would have to spend so much time weighing alternatives that they would never actually be able to act at all. In view of the multiplicity of these alternatives, we would not be able to have any horizon of expectation with reference to others. We would have to regard almost everything not just as possible, but as equally probable, and this would make human interaction and cooperation almost impossible. Custom is one such second normality, which is mediated by upbringing. If, indeed, there was already in fifth century Greece an argued critique of the reigning *nomos*, of the reigning custom, then this critique took the form of measuring the *nomos* by a standard of normality which was of an earlier origin and located on a more elementary level; it was measured by the standard of *physis*, that is, the *natu-*

ral. The conventional normality, so runs the objection, is sheerly conventional. Mirrored in it are the special interests of those who are in the position to establish these conventions. These can be either the interests of the stronger, who by such conventions deepen their *de facto* power over those being ruled, or the interest of the weak, who want to restrain the powerful by the invention of moral norms. In conventional normality each person appears only in a certain role, to which a certain behavior corresponds. Still, human nature with its elementary impulses always and irrevocably underlies these roles. The liberation of these impulses served the critique of culture of ancient Greece as well as the Enlightenment of the eighteenth century.

It was primarily those thinkers who took up the critical concept of nature in order to make it into the basis of a new theory of culture and ethics who were determining for the whole tradition of European philosophy: Plato and Aristotle. They showed that the abstract confrontation of an individualistic, asocial human nature against a social convention does not correspond to reality. If one can show that the wish of humans to survive and to live well is only attainable in a life in society, then sociability belongs to human nature. And yet the social instincts of humans, unlike those of ants, do not suffice to make social living possible. Still, reason, which allows us to see the necessary and to understand social conventions, also belongs to our natural fitments in a constitutive way. One cannot understand the natural and the rational as opposites. To see that the very stability of our expectations of behavior as well as the behavior itself cannot be guaranteed by constant reflection, but instead requires tradition and custom, means that tradition and custom are, in turn, rational precisely because of their function of relieving excessive strain on reflection. This insight does not mean a return to unexplained traditionalism. On the contrary. Precisely because tradition and custom as such are rationally justified by their function, so also is their content accessible to the critique of rational reflection. We can distinguish between rational and irrational conventions precisely because conventions as such are not irrational. In both Plato and Aristotle the standard of this distinction was, once again, nature. That which is right by nature is not something set over against all of human laws; rather it is a superior standard, according to which human ordinances can be measured one more time. Thus, for example, ordinances, which do not favor the elementary, natural goal of preservation of the species, are unnatural ordinances which cannot meet the demand for rational justification. The same goes for a constitution which does not recognize some of the people who live under it as subjects, people whose self-realization depends upon this recognition. One could try saying that such a constitution would be natural for those who have the status of citizen under it and is unnatural only for the others. But that presupposes that reason is not included in human nature. To treat beings with whom one can speak as mere things, i.e., to treat them as beings to whom we do not owe an account if our action affects them, is against the "nature of reason." For, to speak with someone means to grant them accountability.

Having had at its disposal since the time of the Greeks and the time of Christianity a standard on which every existing normality has run aground, European history has become the history of the constantly recurring crises of the existing normality. The historicism of the nineteenth and twentieth centuries was the first to place this standard in question. The natural came to be considered a merely illusionary glorification of historical norms and conventions. If that were so, the only alternative which would remain would be the one between a traditionalism which defends a certain contingent life-form and language game as not being open to question and immunizes it against any critique, and the demand for permanent revolution against every form of normality which establishes itself, since normality as such would be repression. Still, one has to constantly ask: "Repression of what?" The answer always reverts to an abstract and absolute concept of freedom, understood as liberation from all laws which are not established by freedom itself. This means liberation from nature. Thus, the connection between sexuality and preservation of the species, for example, appears to be a connection which has to be dissolved in the interest of self-determination—without consideration of the natural conditions of this preservation. Radical emancipation from nature would only be conceivable as suicide, that is, as that action which, in canceling the conditionedness of our existence, also cancels that existence itself.

II

At this point three possible counter-arguments emerge. The first one grants that the quality of being conditioned cannot be totally eradicated from human existence, but still holds that in the course of history it can be progressively whittled away at. The crucial point being that nature, a necessary condition of subjectivity and freedom to be sure, is in no way constitutive of these. The natural, as the condition, and therefore the boundary, of freedom cannot ever normatively prescribe its content. Nature, understood as the essence of that which is the case, does not contain any answer to the question how we should react to that which is the case. Or nature has already decided our actual behavior; the behavior is, as a matter of fact, determined. In neither case is the appeal to nature of moral relevance.

The second argument, which I call the physicalistic, challenges the assertion that nature could be a standard for distinguishing anything, since everything is nature and so nothing is unnatural. Voltaire lets nature exclaim: *Je suis le grand tout.* (I am the great all.) Everything which happens is the result of the natural forces which bring it about. Nature is what we call the essence of the laws and forces of the world. The unnatural means the same thing as the impossible. The storm which breaks the tree is as natural as the growth of the tree. Deviations from statistical normality are as natural as the normality itself. And if it happens to be us who clear the rain forests, then this is no more unnatural than when a primordial catastrophe—catastrophe being what we would call it—destroyed the forests.

The third argument, which I call the cultural-anthropological, begins from the fact that humans are beings who are not "by nature" determined by instincts, but who have to create a kind of second nature through culture in order to survive. A moral orientation belongs to this second nature. This orientation is not free from socio-cultural influences which are conditioned by time and place. This orientation clearly transcends nature and so cannot be measured by something like an allegedly invariable human nature.

The second and third arguments draw opposing conclusions from the opposition which the first argument posits between ‘being’ and ‘ought-to-be’. The physicalistic argument does not allow any room for moral self-determination. Everything is nature. What one imagines to exist beyond nature, primarily then any thought of freedom and self-determination, is an illusion which itself is subject to a naturalistic explanation. The other, the cultural-anthropological, argument goes in the other direction and emasculates nature by making it mere material for human practice. The one thing it cannot be is the interior standard of human practice. The adventure of spirit, culminating in the technical civilization, is not limited by any natural telos. Nature may place a limit on this spirit and bring it to naught in the end. But then this limit is merely external. It is not, contrary to what the word telos suggests, an internal limit which gives meaning. Aristotle says that death is not a telos. But even human nature belongs to the objective world and is responsive to manipulation by spirit. It is not a degradation, but a humanization when it is separated from its natural spontaneity and regulated by humans. As Rousseau might say, the homme de l'homme occupies a higher place that the homme de la nature.

As opposed as these two arguments might appear, they belong together and mutually produce one another in the form of the two poles of the modern Weltanschauung which have been mutually opposed for the last few centuries: naturalism and spiritualism. That same consciousness which recognizes nature as its own construct and for which human nature is only an objective and instrumental quantity which can be freely manipulated in service of a world-less subjectivity, completely reduces itself to something natural, i.e., to being a product of evolution and a material aggregate, thus making itself into an object among objects. At the same moment that hermeneutics and philosophy of language regard the immanence of linguistic understanding and self-understanding as insurmountable, they render themselves defenseless against some external interpretation of this immanence. Such an interpretation sees language as a mental phenomenon of physical processes which are free from meaning. These processes are what they are only by the fact that they so appear to the exemplars of the species homo sapiens. One wants to say along with Karl Valentine: "A thousand years in circle," or to think of the fable of the rabbit and the hedgehog. Quine tried to make the virtue of a scientistic holism out of the necessity of this circulus vitiosus, in which the various specialized sciences eternally reach toward each other in their remaining questions. In the one case nature is spiritually emasculated; in the other spirit is naturalistically reduced. Only one thing is never to occur within the framework of the modern Weltanschauung: Nature is never to have a spiritual dimension, or is spirit to have a natural one. The ethics which come out of such a civilization are either utilitarian or consequentialistic. For these kinds of ethics there is no *intrinsic* rightness and certainly no intrinsic falsity in actions. The morality of an action is a function of the totality of its consequences in comparison to the totality of consequences of some other possible alternative action. In principle, the prohibition against torture, against cheating, or the breaking of promises is not different in kind from the prohibition against crossing the street on red. There is no inner nature of action, which limits the universal and preposterous commandment of optimization. Every concrete human responsibility is only a variable element within the single actual responsibility of the agent, the responsibility for the optimizing of the course of the world.

In fact, ever since the sixteenth century modern thought has tried to eliminate the concept of nature, of physis, and to replace it with a mechanistic one. For in Greek philosophy physis meant anything but the pure objectivity of a passive material. Rather, it meant a self-being thought of in analogy with the self-experience of humans, its import being the demarcation of a natural being from all others, the demarcation of a living system, as we would say today, from an environment, and indeed an active demarcation, a self-assertion and self-realization out of one's own drives. According to Aristotle physis is the essence of anything which has a principle, a "beginning of movement" in its own self. In this sense though physis is a concept which, from its origin, has served to distinguish. In the Corpus hippocraticum it serves to distinguish the healthy as the normal from the sick as the abnormal. Here normality is not, however, a statistical concept. If 90 percent of all people were to have headaches, they would not therefore be the healthy by which the other 10 percent had to measure themselves, but the reverse. For headaches are opposed to that natural tendency to self-preservation and well-being, which is characteristic of all natural beings. And since human customs, human nomos, such as the constitution of human society, can either correspond or not correspond to these elementary natural tendencies, Sophists like Archelaos, Antiphon, and Hippias von Elis could oppose nature and convention, physis and nomos. Above all they could call the nomos of tyranny unnatural. It is a widespread misunderstanding that the concept of that which is right by nature is based upon a naive ignorance of the variety of human cultures and customs. One can see this mistake even in Pascal. The opposite is correct. The concept of that which is right by nature only comes into being in connection with the discovery of this variety. For it is only the variety of customs and cultures which allows the asking of the question, whether we have at our disposal a standard which will allow us to distinguish better customs from worse. Those of us who think that torture should not exist do not mean merely to say that we ourselves would not practice torture or that torture represents a stain upon a civilization; rather we wish to criticize a civilization in which torture is not considered a stain. And Aristotle found that a polis of free citizens would be the natural style of life for these citizens, on account of the fact that for him the free and the natural were practically synonymous. The free movement of a being goes according to nature—in contrast to the forced movement which is thrust upon the being, against its nature, from the outside. Thus, we still speak of someone dying a natural death when they die of old age, rather than an unnatural death resulting from violence from outside the person. In this sense the growth of the tree is a natural movement, but its being felled by a storm or a lumberjack unnatural, the being eaten unnatural for the antelope but the eating natural for the lion. It is only with modern physics that the difference between natural and forced movements in the realm of the inanimate have been done away with, since it did away with the concept of nature as an internal principle of movement. Each movement is merely the passive result of a parallelogram of forces, connected to the principle of inertia. Leibniz constructed what one could call a mirror-image metaphysics which also abolishes this difference: In the Monadology every movement comes from inside. Everything which befalls a monad, every accident and every pressure, belongs to its self-definition so that what Angelus Silesius said applies: "There is nothing which moves you. You yourself are the wheel, which runs on its own and has no rest." But this metaphysics is not only without consequence for the natural sciences—which is perhaps one of its advantages—it does not give us any defense against physicalistic reductionism in the setting of a theory of action. Because it explains the failure to attain instinct-goals as being equally appropriate as their attainment, it can no longer conceptually grasp the experience of the failure.

The ancients knew the concept of hamartia tes physeos, the concept of peccatum naturae. By this they thought that something could come from the inside and still be false, that is, not be natural. This applied to all living beings, or at least to all highly developed living beings. How would this be possible? It is possible because the inner-outer distinction—as opposed to the windowless monads of Liebniz—is not a impermeable barrier, but is a boundary of constant exchange, a metabolism with the surrounding nature. This exchange does not occur according to purely mechanical laws; rather there holds sway a moment of living spontaneity. Living persons do not simply endure mechanical operations; they react to an interpreted world. They translate, as Niklas Luhmann says, what is at first an exterior complexity into an interior one. At this point they can either be deceived or deceive themselves. Deception, however, is more closely related to what we have called forced movement than to what we have called natural, since the attainment of the goal of the drive is thwarted by it just as it is by force. For every being for whom there exits anything like perception between it and the surrounding world, there exists also the possibility of false perception. On the basis of this falsity exits the possibility of activities which, although they stem from internal drives, still miss the meaning of these drives. This is equally valid for human action. Someone, of their own free will, drinks from a glass. The lemonade has been poisoned. Can one say: He did what he wanted? Apparently not, since he did not want to poison himself. But there are other possibilities. Someone knows that a drink is poisonous. But he has a terrible thirst and drinks no matter the consequences. Did he do what he wanted? He immediately satisfied his appetite; he quenched his thirst. Nevertheless, the objective function of thirst is the preservation of life. When drinking destroys life, we cannot simply say: The person did what he wanted. And we also cannot say: His action was natural. Even in the latter case it is based upon a deception. The appetite does not interpret itself. Only the human person, only the rational being interprets it. In the case of the drinker who could not control himself, the interpretation did not prevail. He does not want to know about it. He does not actually act; rather he hands himself over to the appetite. He does not do what he wants; rather he gives up wanting. His knowledge of the poison was only an intellectual knowing, and so it was weaker than the appetite. Appetite is never simply given to us in external perception. Appetite is interior. In the appetites a being isolates itself from the rest of the world. We can characterize an externally perceptible behavior as appetitive only when we interpret it by some kind of analogy with "being-out-for" which is the structure of our own self-being. And we can do this because our own "being-out-for" is experienced by us as something which underlies all self-consciousness and all conscious positing of goals, that is, it is experienced by us as something natural. And so we do not have any reason to think of that which we experience as thirst, as being completely different from that which induces the dog to run to the water bowl and to drink.

III

The position appetite holds vis-à-vis our acting is not at all describable by the `Is-Ought' schema. On the one hand, human action is not simply an event of the appetites. Rather, action begins at that point where we control ourselves as regards our appetites and do not simply hand ourselves over to them. If I am hungry, I do not have to eat. I can have reasons for not doing so. I could have something else urgent to do. I could be on a diet. It could be Lent. Or someone could be involved in a hunger strike. Hunger does not necessitate eating. Still, hunger is not a neutral fact which stands in need of a further premise in order to become a reason for acting. We do not need a major premise of the type that says: "When I am hungry, I should always eat, so long as there is no other important reason not to." In response to such a maxim, one could ask: "Why should you do that?" An appetite distinguishes itself from other facts in that it itself already has a vectorial character. It propels, it makes one inclined *(inclinatio)*, and that means it is itself a reason for the actions which serve to satisfy it. If we, as free beings, were confronted with a world of pure matters of fact, we would not be able to discover in these facts any motives for acting. And we also would not find any reasons to form maxims, which could lead to directions for action. External facts are only able to be occasions of action for us as natural beings, as appetitive beings, who are already oriented toward something. But is an appetite a *sufficient* reason for an action? Is the fact of being hungry a sufficient reason to eat? Often it is, namely, when there is no other reason which opposes it. What kind of other reason? That cannot be decided beforehand. It is sufficient that one wants to prove to oneself that one is not at the mercy of an appetite. Fichte speaks of a drive for freedom which consists simply in the wish of a free being to be conscious of its freedom. The appetite itself is only a sufficient reason to do something to satisfy it when we make it to be that, when we accept in freedom the vectorial meaning which lies in it. And we can do this only when we perceive this meaning *as* meaning, not as *factum brutum*, but as something which is available to interpretation, which is already a kind of speech.

Interpreting an appetite does not occur by itself. The interpretation does not belong to nature. Rather, it is what we call the rational. Only in the light of reason does nature *as* nature appear. An animal has hunger, but the natural purpose of hunger, namely self-preservation, is not revealed to it, nor is the natural purpose of the sexual appetite, preservation of the species. The meaning of the appetite is only uncovered when it loses its immediate power of compulsion and is understood as something which is translatable into speech. An animal without appetite does not want to eat. The need which demands satisfaction does not exist. But we think of hunger as a natural signal, as a function of self-preservation. We do, in fact, eat to appease the appetite, but we are concerned when we have chronic loss of appetite, since for us hunger is a means for the goal of self-preservation, and eating is nourishment. On the one hand, the self-preservation of a free being is, for the most part, guaranteed by powerful drives, while on the other hand, it is constantly tied to free acts, to eating and drinking, which, in distinction to breathing, do not occur "by nature," that is, by themselves. *Inclinatio* is not *necessitas*. What is the consequence of this? Eating and drinking, as free actions, as *actus humanus*, which the scholastics, following Aristotle, called them, enter into a cultural context. They are cultivated, culturally remade. In many cultures the cooking of meals is, as Claude Lévi-Strauss has shown, the basic paradigm of culture itself. Eating and drinking become the meal, the family meal, the meal with friends, the marriage banquet. In religion it becomes a sacrament, and even eternal life is presented by the image of the heavenly marriage banquet. The *finis primarius*, the elementary natural purpose of taking in nourishment, becomes almost invisible in this cultural remaking in the new functions of eating and drinking. This can take place because the fulfillment of the natural purpose occurs of itself, so to say, and is not systematically set aside by us. For it is only as this elementary action which insures the physical preservation of free persons that eating and drinking can acquire their basic social function. It is the multiple functions which first give it human meaning. When the Romans of late antiquity, having eaten enough, prolonged their feasts by vomiting their food in a vomitorium, they did not, by this uncoupling of the cultural from the natural function, raise eating to a higher, more humane level; rather it sunk to something lower. In the place of sustenance came consumption without consequences. It is precisely because humans know the natural function of an appetite that they can set it aside.

Animals do not know this natural function, and thus they fulfill it as a rule. The latency insures the function. Functions which are manifest carry less insurance. They can be set aside. This uncoupling of the attainment of pleasure from the objective good to which it belongs was already one of the central themes in Plato's *Republic*. Eating is essentially something which is enjoyable in that it fulfills a natural function. If we imagine that humanity would satisfy its atavistic need for social and festive eating and drinking by the communal chewing and swallowing of good-tasting but indigestible material while insuring its nourishment by a small daily injection, then we begin to see the consequences. There wouldn't be any more eating and drinking, since neither of these two actions deserve the name. A central element of human culture would be eliminated. For this element is inseparable from it elementary natural function. The word "culture" comes originally from agriculture; culture is nature humanized, not abrogated.

The connection between humanity and naturalness is no less clear when we examine the relationship between sexuality and the preservation of the species. Whether in the long run the perpetuation of the human race will be assured when it is uncoupled from the satisfaction of the sexual drive, no one can yet say. It seems to me unlikely. Human sexuality, as a basic, natural element has been integrated into a personal relationship by a humane and personal remaking. This has meant an increase in both intensity and in meaning. Thomas Aquinas was of the opinion that the pleasure of sex for the Edenic human, that is, for the perfectly humane human, was the highest possible, since perfect sensibility belongs to perfection. But the systematic detachment of sexual pleasure from the natural context of its function of passing on human life would rob love between the sexes of its specifically human dimension. Spiritualism on the one side and naturalism on the other would make what is actually human disappear. When Max Horkeimer wrote: "We will have to pay for the Pill with the death of erotic love," he had this connection in mind. There is another side to all this. It is conceivable that the perpetuation of the human race will be safeguarded in the future by the state, in such a way that it bypasses human reproduction and uses the test tube. (The words of the secretary Wagner in Goethe's *Faust* have already taken on an unexpected actuality: "That old style we declare / A poor betting in foolish fashion."[)] One has to make clear to oneself that test-tube reproduction differs from begetting in that it is an action which is a rational means for a goal, a *poiesis*, and not the natural consequence of relations between humans. "Don't imagine," so wrote Gottfried Benn, "that I was thinking of you when I was with your mother. Her eyes were always so beautiful when we made love." A manufactured child, one that comes into being by *poiesis*, is a creature of its parents or of the doctor or of the state in a qualitatively different way from the child which owes its existence "to nature." The former really could ask those who have forced it into existence, how they can answer for this. And what should one say in reply? No one can answer for the life or the death of another human. One can have a sufficient reason not to want to have a child. But a sufficient reason to have one cannot exist. The existence of self-being is the existence of a being for which reasons are reasons. It cannot itself be further grounded by other subjects. Without entering into casuistry we can still summarize by saying: The natural growth of the human and the dignity of the human are indissolubly connected, and the humanizing of natural appetites does not consist in denaturing them, but in their conscious integration in a human and social life-context.

People have raised the objection against the concept of a natural law or a natural moral law that the human is a rational being by nature. It is not nature but reason which is the proper standard of action. So instead of natural law one should rather speak of rational law. I have tried to show that nature first becomes aware of itself as reason. The law of nature does not consist in imitating non-human nature. In fact, in non-human nature there is a variety of kinds of parasitic relationships, of exploitation of members of the same species within a population, of perversion of appetites, not to mention the fact that the prey appears to the beast of prey as nothing more than an object of the appetites and remains completely hidden as a center of appetites. One could put it pointedly by saying that only in rational action does the concept of the natural fully come into its own. But not in such a way that reason simply takes the place of nature. Human reason is receptive. Of itself it is merely form. And it is often objected against reason that its imperative is merely formal. It does not advance the argument to refer to the form of the character of the human being an end in itself. First of all, this is also empty. If Kant has nevertheless made this operational and deduced from it concrete, substantial consequences, then he obtains these consequences by presuming as obvious that humans have something like a nature and that this nature is not just an instrument of its freedom, but is the representation of its personality in the "world of appearances." In this, their nature, humans have to be respected, if they are to be respected at all; in this, their nature, they and their dignity are inviolable. One cannot spit in a human's face and then claim that one did not want to come into contact with him or her as a person. Above all torture is completely irreconcilable with respect for humans as persons, not because it hinders them from harmful action, for this hindrance can be necessary, but because it forces them to abdication as free subjects, it reduces them to instinctual beings and wants to beat them down to a subhuman kind of reaction. To affect the body of a human always means to affect a human.

IV

Humans are not world-less subjectivities who then have something like a natural organism at their disposal. The human body is the human itself. To oppose nature and person is to fail to recognize that finite persons themselves have a nature in which they represent themselves and in which they are visible and vulnerable as themselves. Given that even the physical self-preservation of the human organism depends upon free actions, upon eating and drinking, then an ethical prohibition presents itself. It cannot be compatible with respect for humans as the subjects of freedom to force nourishment on them against their express will and thereby to make the physical sustenance of humans an affair of external coercion, since this sustenance is by nature a result of free action. For the nature with which we are here concerned is the nature of a rational being. To violate it is to violate human dignity.

Without such a nature human reason as practical remains completely formal. It would truly never get from facts to orientations for action. Its formal maxims could be filled by anyone with arbitrary content.

Still, nature of herself does not produce anything that resembles an "ought." Tendencies is all that she has. As Fichte once said, her productivity is finished once she has brought forth appetites. Appetite *as* appetite, nature *as* nature, discloses itself for the first time to a rational, that is, reflecting and free, being. It is precisely when one distances oneself from nature through reflection that one can recognize her in freedom and allow her to become a source of moral insights. The recognition of the self-being of a natural being, that is, what is right by nature, does not happen by nature. By nature everything which a natural being encounters is merely environment. Every animal lives in the center of its world. As physical beings, even optically, we too are constantly in the center of the world. But as rational beings we know that every other person is also the center of a world. Precisely in that we know this, we step out of the center. Humans can think of themselves as those who are important or unimportant for the other.

This stepping out of the center position in one's experience does not cause the natural to disappear, but allows it to make its appearance. One's own nature as well as that of other humans comes forth. To respect others as persons means to affirm them in their nature. According to Kant then, the primary expression of morality is not promoting the morality of others, but promoting their happiness.

Two consequences emerge from these considerations. The first concerns the question of finding criteria for when a natural being is to be respected as a person. The second concerns the problem of possible manipulation of human nature. When is a living being a human? A preliminary answer is: When it belongs genetically to species homo sapiens. This answer appears to be biologistic. If respect for humans were only a kind of biological species-solidarity, then this answer might suffice. But such a species-solidarity either exists as a biological fact or it does not exist at all. In the case of someone who wants to break out of this solidarity it does not help to point out that such solidarity appears in the animal world. In fact, the specifically moral respect which we owe the human is not owed to the member of the same species, but to the person, the rational, potentially moral being who is capable of free self-determination. This respect is owed to the being who withdraws itself and takes on a perspective which is beyond its own centrality and can accept demands. That is why it can demand to be taken as a subject and not to be used as a mere object. But then who is a human in this sense? How do we know that a being is really a person? Because it is capable of rational self-determination? But then shouldn't there be a test for this? It is closer to the truth to answer the question by saying: A speaking being is capable of rational self-determination, that is, a being with whom we can enter into mutual symbolic communication. Is this enough? What kind of communication does this have to be? Can't I enter into a certain communication with my dog? Perhaps even a communication which is more intensive than one with a severely debilitated person or with an infant? Who defines where the human begins to be a person. In the Aristotelian tradition the answer was readily available. One concludes from that which a species "usually" displays to that which is the essence of a thing of this kind. From a healthy, adult human one can read off what the essence of every human is, the essence of even those in whom this essential does not show itself. The essence, which often but not always shows itself, is that which we call the "soul." The soul has to be respected even in those in which it remains concealed. This answer is full of presuppositions. It is not compatible with nominalistic premises, for example. But the following considerations, which we could call transcendental-pragmatic, lead us in the same direction. If there is to be anything like human rights, then they are only possible given the presupposition that no one is entitled to render judgment whether someone is a subject of such rights. For the logic of human rights entails that the human is not a member of the human society who is co-opted on the basis of certain qualifications; rather that each enters into the society on the strength of one's own claim. But on the strength of one's own claim can only mean: on the basis of belonging biologically to species homo sapiens. Any other criterion would make the one a judge over the others. Human society would become a closed shop, and the thought of human rights would be undone at its very basis. Only when the human is recognized as a person on the basis of that which he or she is by nature does the recognition apply to the self and not to him or her as someone who fulfills a criterion, which others have established for their recognition. From this it also follows that any temporal boundary for the initial recognition of the human as human is merely conventional. But any merely conventional boundary is, in reference to the fundamental rights of humans, tyrannical.

Criteria for the judging of genetic manipulation of humans emerge from what has been said. In order to make the path clear for this kind of manipulation it has been asserted that humans, as they exist today, are the result of a spontaneous evolutionary history and that planned human activity would not be any more a cause of a reduction in quality than random mutations caused by cosmic radiation. Why should the homme de l'homme be worse than the homme de la nature? Again the answer can only be a "transcendental-pragmatic" one. Humans are not transcendental subjects who have at their disposal an instrument, namely their body, which, should the occasion arise, is to be improved upon. For what purpose is it to be improved? For human purposes. But human purposes emerge from the nature of the human, as contingent as that may be. We do not have any critera to distinguish a noncontingent part of ourselves, called person or subjectivity, from a contingent part which would then be disponible for arbitrary reconstruction. In the service of which purposes shall we carry out this reconstruction? For we would transform the purpose by the reconstruction. Such a transformation of human nature, for example for the purpose of making the human more fit for an interplanetary sojourn, means to degrade the future human to a mere means for the satisfaction of the purposes of the present manipulators, for the satisfaction of their creative fantasy or their idea of what human happiness consists in, for example. The dignity of the human is inseparably connected with its natural spontaneity. Its nature is contingent, certainly. But any consciously planned reconstruction of human nature would not avoid this contingency; rather it would make it unbearable.

To come to the aid of humans means to come to the aid of natural beings, who are what they are. It does not mean to make something else out of them.

We do not need to come to the aid of angels, unless it be that we enlist their aide. The hope of breeding them is absurd.

Chapter 15

Responsibility

I

ONE CANNOT DEDUCE benevolence from some imperative. It precedes and grounds every moral imperative. But this does not mean that all moral obligation and every moral norm is grounded in an ultimately irrational, absurd, subjective "option." Benevolence is not some absurd option, but the result of a perception, the perception of reality as self-being. Whoever has had this perception finds himself in a peculiar, paradoxical situation. On the one hand, he understands that it is not he himself who grounds this, his own perception. That would be as if this perception were preceded by something like a moral decision, when in fact every moral decision is grounded in this perception. He can only understand it as a gift, and indeed as a gift whose absence implies that humans have not yet awakened to being human, that, in spite of all their intelligence, they still dream and that in this dreaming state they remain culpable to everyone for everything. This culpability is grounded in the fact that humans, as beings who are capable of speech, encounter each other as beings who demand to be perceived by the other. On the other hand, looking upon one's earlier lack of perception as one's own fault is part of being awake. According to Kant, the immaturity, which the enlightened one has left behind, appears to him or her as a her or her own fault. If the perception is a gift, then it appears to be in a contradiction with itself. This contradiction cannot be solved here. It has occupied thinkers in Europe from the days of Augustine up to the religious wars of early modernity, and it ceased to occupy them only because it came to be counted among the questions which Kant said human reason has to ask but is incapable of answering. In any case, the moral phenomena would be falsely described and thereby overlooked, if the contradiction were to be solved in such a way that one gave up either holding people accountable for evil or the gift-character of the good. Whether we perceive the reality of the real is not only *our* affair; it is a *demand* placed upon us, and we bear responsibility for whether we meet this demand or not. Our actions are true or false depending upon whether they meet this responsibility or not. As was already shown in the beginning of this book, actions can be right or wrong in three different ways. An action can be right or wrong in view of the purpose which it is supposed to fulfill or foster. It can also be right or wrong in view of the whole of our life and its turning out well. For actions together with their purposes are parts of this whole. *Eudaimonia*, the turning out well of life, revealed itself to be ambivalent. Clearly, it cannot be made the goal of action in the same way as other things can. It is only the life of a rational being which comes together as a whole in such a way that it is possible for it to turn out well or fail. But then it is precisely reason which makes it impossible for us to grasp our own life as a finite totality and to see its fulfillment in terms of the "external costs" which it involves. The second principle of thermodynamics teaches us that constructing and maintaining a finite system as an ordered structure is paid for by an increase of disorder in the whole. For a rational being such costs are not "external." The context, in which the living being stands together with all the living, indeed with all beings, does not remain external to the agent. It enters into the definition of the turning out well or ill of one's own life.

Out of this emerges the third dimension of being right or wrong, the moral dimension, in its narrower sense. It is the dimension of dealing responsibly with reality. It is once more opportune here to have recourse to the Aristotelian distinction between *poiesis* and *praxis*, the distinction between making and dealing with. Making is subordinated to its goal. It is even defined by this goal, but at the same time the thing which is made is the end of the making. The goal to be achieved is indifferent to the process which brings it about. That the means which brings something about are something besides just means, that they *themselves* are something at all, is a viewpoint which stands at odds with the purposive rationality of the machine. Pure making is, then, an abstraction, even if our civilization is ever more thoroughly ruled by this abstraction. Every *poiesis* is, in fact, embedded in a *praxis*, every making in a life-context, and this context constitutes itself in dealing with other living beings. As it is, the process of making almost always contains within itself elements of dealing with. The "means" are also things with which we deal and with which we are in a relationship which is not purely instrumentally rational-purposive. Even tools possess a certain independence, in the sense that they are usually not used up in a single production process, but remain available for many such processes. To use them always implies to treat them with care. But "to treat with care" is the most elementary form of moral behavior. The spread of purely purposive rationality at the expense of using something carefully, e.g., the rampant spread of disposable items, has fateful consequences for the forming of moral attitudes. There is a loss of reality for things insofar as they are reduced to that which they are here and now in the context of my goals or purposes. For the first time in history modern civilization has attempted to reduce the earth itself, the land, to the function of a means, and subordinated it strictly to the viewpoint of increased productivity. The consequences of dividing the cultivation of nature from the element of how we deal with her are gradually becoming noticeable. When our dealings with nature are purified of all rationally purposive, "poietic" elements, they appear to become a higher form of life. In fact, however, they become mere "leisure values" and so are themselves submitted to rational planning and denied their authenticity. The objection that the careful handling of things is, at best, a function of the overcoming of scarcity and, as such, has nothing to do with morality, fails to recognize that scarcity is most deeply connected with morality. It is scarcity which first allows us to become conscious of the preciousness of the real. But preciousness is the manner in which the reality of the real appears to us: as "glory." Immorality could be described as the behavior of a person to whom nothing is precious. The finitude of human consciousness is such that superfluity reduces and chokes off the feeling for preciousness. Our limited capacity for paying attention causes everything to become less important when there is a lot of it; when it is easy to attain, it becomes less real, except in the case of our own selves since there is only one person whom we experience in the first person, as "I." 'Dealing with' does not mean acting in such a way that only the agent is the goal, and he or she establishes or pursues goals, but means rather that he or she is in a mutual relationship with another, and this other develops itself in this relationship in his or her own teleology and so appears as himself or herself. The 'dealing with' uncovers that with which we are dealing. Reason as awakening to reality, benevolence, in which the real becomes real to someone, comes to existence in our dealing with others and remains tied to this dealing with others. 'Dealing with' comes before reason. Animals deal with each other as dreamers. The difference of the other *as* other has not yet opened up for them. On the one hand, the animal is completely outside itself, completely in the world. But precisely for this reason the other never appears as its self; instead it appears only as the meaning which it has as an element in the animal's environment. It is "there" only so long as it finds a place in the imaginative and emotional schema at hand. The maternal love of some animals extends to self-sacrifice, but only so long as the offspring have a "top priority" in the instinctive schema of the mother. If this schema is extinguished, then the offspring is from one moment to the next no longer there for the mother.

Normal interhuman dealings are also marked by such schemata. But since these dealings are mediated by speech, the self-being of the other is always potentially present in them. The other's coming to consciousness occurs by way of responsibility. Responsibility corresponds to care, which transcends all instinctual solicitude for self-preservation. We speak of "welfare." Welfare refers to the self-being of those with whom I deal and who are affected by the consequences of my individual or collective action or, under certain circumstances, by the consequences of my omissions. For the duty to provide welfare, which comes from the perception of reality, grounds duties to act too. One can only speak of responsibility and welfare in reference to a being whose character is teleological by nature, that is, one for whom what occurs has a meaning. One cannot give aid to a being who has been reduced to just existing. It is what it is, and it is that so long as it is. Nothing more is to be said about it. One can do nothing for or against an existent. But then every concept of a non-atomic individual totality already contains such a teleological element. Such a totality distinguishes itself from a contingent conglomerate which is only to disintegrate again, in that we view the former as the *telos* of the working together of its parts, as something which can turn out well or ill, can be maintained or destroyed. Only when we think of such "projections" does it make sense to speak of responsibility, since only then are our interventions in the events of the world dictated by something besides our own interests or pure arbitrariness. Only then can we distinguish moral from immoral actions at all, and not just the practical from the impractical, the advantageous from the disadvantageous to the agent.

Hans Eduard Hengstenberg defined moral action as "objectivity." This is correct granted the following two presuppositions: 1. The "object" over against which moral action is to measure itself has to be conceived teleologically, that is, has to be thought of as a "project." 2. It has to stand in a relationship to the agent. This relationship may be a relationship of dependence, such that it, in order to be what it is, requires help or is capable of being affected by action from the outside, and so is vulnerable. Or it may be that a relationship of expression is possible between myself and the object, a relationship of admiration, of respect, of reverence, of contempt or of indignation. As a rule the relationship of expression is connected with a bringing forth of real consequences for the being who is affected by the agent. Only the religious relationship has a purely expressionistic character, which means that it is only symbolic, since its object is without need and invulnerable. But there are also relationships of expression with animals. When someone gives his animal a name, he expresses a relationship which recognizes the substantiality of the animal. It is another case when animals are reduced in a calculated way to the status of means of production and excluded from all responsible handling. That there are laws to prevent cruelty to animals gives expression to the will to maintain, against this reductionism, a form of responsible dealing with non-human life.

II

It is appropriate to deal responsibly, not only with everything for whom something is good, that is, everything which is capable of confering meaning on something, but also for everything which has a meaning which goes beyond unmediated and complete consumption, everything then that is "good for something." All of these things deserve care and sometimes assistance. What one is responsible *for* and *to* whom one is *responsible* do not thereby coincide. We are responsible, that is, we owe accountability for careful dealing with things which are good for something, to anyone who, as a center of experience, confers meaning, that is, for whom something can be good or bad. Responsibility for an inanimate reality is a responsibility to all who could need, enjoy, or contemplate it. The inanimate first comes to its own reality, to its position in self-being, in this being experienced. We have responsibility for everything which could mean something to a self-being. This is a responsibility to every being which confers meaning, which knows itself as such and can, therefore, demand accountability. In principle we are accountable to everyone who is capable of posing the questions: "Why?" or "With what right?" And we owe them this for everything which could be of some value to them. The riches of the world are the common patrimony of all, comparable with the capital which provides interest for people to live, in that they possess the usufruct until the inheritance is passed on further. But this image can be misleading. For all the natural beings of the world do not exist just as potential material for human use, but primarily as something given, which are "there" with us, and through this belongs to the riches of our world. Kant's statement: "Act so that you never use the humanity in your person or in the person of another merely as a means, but rather always at the same time as an end" needs to be expanded: Nothing real ought to be reduced to the status of mere means for an individual goal, whose being is not already of itself merged in such a function.

The distinction between being responsible for and being responsible to, between the object and the addressee of responsibility, is easy to see when we talk about the world of inanimate nature or the world of tools and objects of art. It is not so easy when we talk about those forms of life which we ourselves can only grasp as such, for who care about their own being or that of their species, and who thus already confer something like meaning: animals and plants. They first show themselves to us in their own reality when we let ourselves get involved rationally in their being alive. As regards higher animals this means perceiving the fact that their well-being is not something externally established. Rather, to judge from their behavior, it is already experienced by them as subjective well-being, and its absence is experienced in the form of discomfort, pain, or suffering. Pain and suffering are not positive, existing objects in the world. One cannot begin to describe or define pain without the aid of negative concepts. As a signal of a life-threatening event, pain refers directly to something which should not be. But negativity is not something found in an object; rather it is essentially something subjective. We cannot perceive the suffering of others at all, except that the sufferer ceases to be a mere object for us and becomes instead real *as* self-being. (It is this thought which lies behind Schopenhauer's putting compassion at the center of his ethics. Still, it was accompanied by the anti-intellectual prejudice that reason is only an instrument of self-preservation and not itself being awake to reality. Therefore, the other *as* other cannot possibly become real for us; rather the other's becoming real could only be the canceling of his otherness in an unmediated, sympathetic identification with the sufferer.) Real perception of suffering is not possible in the form of merely neutral observation. It is always connected with an attitude, be it connected with the tendency to alleviate or to do away with the suffering or to be with the sufferer, or be it connected with the opposed tendency not to do just these things. The merely neutral 'taking cognizance' of pain is in reality an act which is opposed to rational benevolence. To see a beetle lying on its back struggling and to turn it over are one and the same for the benevolent, and they require a justified reason to break this unity. Of course, such an action is without moment for the whole of the world. It is a matter of happenstance that the struggling beetle had a benevolent human nearby. But that is not an objection. A human does not have responsibility for the countless sufferings that go on in the animal kingdom. Humans did not make this kingdom; they cannot rule it. They cannot even wish to do away with the pain since it is a function which is important for life, and to do away with the life-threatening situations to which pain is a reaction is already excluded, since the preservation of the life of the one is inseparably connected with the threatening of the life of the other. Also it is not possible for a finite rational being to perceive the self-being of every individual living creature, nor is this their task. The example of seeing the beetle is meant to express the following: When we are speaking of the experience of others, perception and taking an attitude are inseparable. To undo this inseparableness by reflecting on the meaninglessness of individual cases which are perceived by chance is to dissolve it by means of a solipsism. The truth is that there is no "whole" in reference to which the individual does not count. Subjectivity, negativity, and the pain of various subjects do not accumulate. It is the essence of experience that it, as a totality closed in on itself, confronts the whole of the world of things which can be accumulated. One sufferer may suffer more than another. But the suffering of two sufferers is not "more" than that of the one. Objects accumulate; subjects – and their pain – accumulate only insofar as they always have an objective side for other subjects or for each other. But in that which makes them real, in their being a subject, they stand beyond all calculation.

We have already seen that the animal is the object of responsibility, not its addressee. We are responsible for it, not to it. Still, the gesture in primitive cultures of asking for forgiveness from the animal being hunted has a deep meaning. In it the symbolic recognition of the self-being of the animal is contained and with it the need to justify its being killed. Thus, we speak with animals in our language, whose grammar is inaccessible to them, and thereby manage to express more truth than the one who deals with animals as objects. Analogy is the only possible way of perceiving non-human life.

To whom then do we have responsibility for such life? The answer can only be: to ourselves. Action ceases to be *actus humanus*, if it intentionally makes itself blind. The dignity of humans is grounded in the fact that they step out of that position of centrality in which everything which is encountered is merely their "environment" and only appears in the meaning which it has for their self-sustenance. The perception of the interiority of others is that which makes them to be a representative of the unconditioned. Now the perceived interiority of an animal is not such an unconditioned, since it does not have the power to relativize itself in its particularity. Thus, it is relativized from without, indeed it is relativized by humans. Not every pain of every animal can demand a human's attention. Responsibility always comes out of real perception, out of the face to face encounter, which brings us, perhaps completely by chance, to be the "neighbor" of the animal. The only animals for whom we have an inherent responsibility are those we have domesticated, those that live, not in their natural ecological niche, but in the environment which we have made for them, those we have made dependent upon us. We are forbidden from treating them as mere objects by our own self-respect and our claim of being something which occupies a higher position than an animal. Something similar holds for the sufferings of animals which are the result of our own intervention in nature. The worst of these interventions are those in which animals are already condemned through breeding to suffer in their "natural" life-form, simply because they are this kind of animal. Such interventions are shameless, "unconscionable." They lack that which, since the time of the Greeks, has been a synonym for morality: modesty, reserve, *aidos*. To ask what degree of sparing human beings harm could or would justify some infliction of pain on animals, leads to a casuistry, which, important as it is, goes beyond the scope of this book. As a general principle let me state the following: First, not just any human advantage, no matter how small, can be used to justify any animal suffering, no matter how great. Second, there is a degree of suffering which we living beings should never, under any circumstances, inflict. In order to determine this degree, the length of the pain in relation to the life-span and life-form of the animal has to be taken into account. Without a doubt there are ways of treating animals which are more cruel than ending the life of a bull in a bull fight, after years in free pasture – the enjoyment of this being, however, as problematic as it may be. Precisely because we cannot negotiate with animals about our responsibility for them, we have to have a discourse of justification about it with ourselves. And an index of the sincerity of this discourse is the free-will refusal by the people, like animal keepers or scientists, who come into unavoidable conflicts with the vital needs of animals, to be their own judges in these conflicts, but who agree to, or even demand, an outside control over their activity.

Curiously enough, our responsibility for animals is least injured by their being killed. This too is irresponsible when it occurs without necessity or good reason. But since the animal lives from moment to moment, since its interiority, from everything which we can guess, does not integrate its life into a biographical unity, the length of their life cannot really be the final issue. The animal is not awakened to reality, to being. It does not know the antagonism between being and non-being, only that of being such and such or being other. Therefore, the responsibility for animals concerns the how of their life and not its existence as such.

Its existence is of consequence as long as it concerns the species or forms of life which make up the riches of reality and belong to that patrimony which we, given that we live from it, have still to care for. This holds for the botanical world also. The question whether this responsibility is for its own sake or the sake of humans is falsely formulated. Of course, we do not have responsibility *to* plants. They are less addressees of justification discourse than animals. We ourselves are the addressees. But does that mean that they would be worth protecting only for the meaning which they have for humans? What meaning do they have then for humans? For now let's discount any meaning in terms of serving as food or as medicine or as a provider of oxygen. If we took account of only these meanings, then perhaps a massive reduction of the variety of kinds of plant life would be justified. But we enjoy this variety. Its diminution distresses us even when we only hear about it and that goes all the more for the variety of animals. What kind of interest is it, which we take in this variety? It is a "rational interest," that is an interest which cannot be referred back to anything like a need. It is an elementary relationship of humans to that which *is*. One can call this interest aesthetic. But what have we gained by that? Kant spoke of the enjoyment of the beautiful as "disinterested delight." By "disinterested" he means: not to be referred to one's own needs, "unselfish." To care for something out of consideration of this interest, this joy and this sorrow, does not mean to care for something "for the sake of humans." Rather it is characteristic of rational beings to be able to take an interest in that from which one "gets" nothing. "The soul of the human is in a certain sense everything," wrote Aristotle. It follows from this that "everything" which is not reproducible in kind and not reparable falls into the scope of human responsibility.

III

Responsibility presupposes, such is our claim, a 'to whom', an addressee, someone who can both demand accountability and be open to reasons. The only beings we know who demand such accountability are humans. And it is not just other humans who make this demand, but ourselves too. That part of ourselves which demands an interior discourse of justification and is above making deals, we call the conscience. But conscience is not a monological device which releases us from the duty of accountability to others. On the contrary, it is the readiness to give an account in principle to everyone who is affected by our action that renders the claim of one's own conscience credible and distinguishable from arbitrariness or private ideology. In principle we are responsible *to* every human. But are we also responsible *for* every human? What can "responsibility for humans" really mean? Does the object and addressee of responsibility immediately coincide here? That cannot be. For we have seen that the content of responsibility is both the support we give to beings which are understood teleologically, i.e., the living, for their capacity to be, and the care with which we deal with them. The human is the addressee of responsibility as the subject of freedom, as an agent. Action is, as we have seen, distinguished from all natural occurrences in that it refers indirectly to reality. It is itself already a type of "coming to the aid of" and presupposes a "nature" which we as agents come to aid. Eating as an action, as *actus humanus*, is not the same as the feeding of an animal. It is not the drive satisfying itself, but presupposes a relationship to the drive, to hunger. The latter provides the goal, but first agents have to make this goal their own and thus come to aid of the natural drive. Helping a person is, therefore, something different from helping an animal. It always means: helping a helper. We have to justify our help *to the person* himself. We are not to circumvent their freedom as a subject in order to help them as a natural being. An example of this is forcible feeding. Certainly, it can be justified when someone is in an unconscious state, and so incapacitated as an acting subject. Then we, as their representatives, so to say, have to perceive their interests, and so we presume that if they were in possession of reason they would accept them as their own. But when they are capable of an action such as eating, and for any reason whatever do not satisfy their hunger and do not wish to preserve their life, then no one has the right to seize control of their life by circumventing their freedom. *They* have the responsibility, and we have it only insofar as they need our help to fulfill theirs.

From this indirect relationship to the nature of others, it follows that the first and unconditioned responsibility toward *every* human being is a negative one: to avoid and to renounce influencing them in such a way that does not respect them as persons. All positive duties are conditioned; they are binding under certain circumstances and with circumstantial restrictions. The duty not to break into the sphere of freedom of others by affecting them as natural beings, which would ignore them as persons, is valid unconditionally and regardless of circumstances. Of course, there are cases when we have to physically resist someone in order to prevent him from harming others. Such resistance, which hinders the other from a certain use of freedom, does not violate his dignity as a human being; it only keeps from him what he has no right to. It is another case when the body of someone is worked over with the goal of forcing him, by means of unbearable pain, to actions to which one cannot move him with reasons – not even with the reason of saving his own life. Torture is always and under all circumstances an action which degrades the tortured person as a human being. Things which one can prevent only by this means are things that one cannot prevent, and no one has to answer for the consequences of his not being able to prevent something.

Our responsibility for and to humans is grounded in the claim of every human being to be taken by every other rational being not just as an object, but as a self-being. That this claim cannot at every moment be made good by everyone toward everyone is due to the finitude of humans, and this finds its rational expression in that which we have named, following the tradition, *ordo amoris*. However, from the universality of our reason as a capacity for perception and from the virtual dependence of every human on the support of his fellow beings for the ability to realize his nature as a person, as a subject of freedom, it follows with equal force that everyone can come into the situation where anyone else becomes his neighbor. In Genesis the Fall is spoken of twice. The first is in paradise, and the second is the fratricide of Cain. After the first God asks, "Where are you?" and after the second, "Where is your brother?" Cain's answer, "Am I my brother's keeper?" only gives expression to the way of thinking which is presupposed in the murder. Humans do not stand over against each other as autarkic subjects of freedom, who would be subjects for themselves but objects of indifference for each other. They are rather dependent in a twofold way upon each other. First, humans do not possess their own sphere of self-expansion which remains inaccessible to others, but we all have a common sphere, nature, in which we constantly impinge upon one another and therefore are responsible to one another for the consequences of our actions.

The institution of private property structures this responsibility, in that it excludes each from a certain limited sphere of the other. But this does not mean that this sphere should be acted upon only indirectly, namely in the sense of always being helpful to the owner; on the contrary, it means that owners have a greater responsibility, since they have at their disposal more possibilities of action by which they can help or hurt others. Besides, the arrangement of ownership always remains provisional. In emergencies it, as mere convention, has to yield to the demands of physical survival of others. The only inalienable boundary of others' freedom is the human body. And even the human body requires the joint help of others. We are dependent upon each other not only in the sense that we have a common earth at our disposal for the advancement of our being. We also need each other to become real as free beings. There is no person without interpersonality. The young infant becomes a speaking being, i.e., one who is capable of self-determination, only after others have taken over responsibility for it. Precisely this taking-over of responsibility is not grounded in a principle or in a maxim, but in a perception. The mother is there for the child because the child is there and needs the mother, without some principle having to step in to mediate.

IV

There are two limit-cases which are apt to make clear for us the nature of responsibility at its foundation, the responsibility of humans for themselves and the responsibility for the life of another. If we do what our natural interests demand, we are constantly aware of a responsibility for ourselves. We are aware of it also if we subordinate the satisfaction of our primary interests to those exigencies which emerge from the perception of the other as a being with finality. For our dignity as humans first constitutes itself in this subordination. But what about those interests which do not render themselves conspicuous in the form of subjective needs? What about the requirements of our own health or the development of our powers and abilities, which are not conveyed by needs, but which cause new needs of a modified kind to come into existence? Whoever is given to himself only as a drive-object and has not yet perceived himself as subject will never see the obligation for such a development. He will not understand *to whom* he should actually have such a responsibility. Who is the addressee of the so-called duties to oneself? What meaning does the talk of a responsibility to oneself have? The addressee of this responsibility and its object, the "to whom" and the "for whom" of the responsibility seems to dissolve into one another. And so it appears that to speak here of responsibility would be merely a *façon de parler*, since it is up to the whims of agents whether or not they dispense themselves of a responsibility which only they can give to themselves.

The decision as to whether the talk of such a responsibility can be meaningful or not is a metaphysical one. It depends upon what we understand a person to be, that is, what we understand ourselves to be. Moral experience is the experience of a peculiar kind of unconditionedness, similar to the experience of truth. This experience cannot be grounded in the contingent fact of existence of an exemplar of the species homo sapiens, without revealing itself thereby as a misunderstanding, an illusion. Every sociological, psychological, or biological deduction of the phenomenon is equivalent to its destruction. Only given the presupposition that finite subjectivity understands itself as the locus of appearance, as the image or representation of the unconditioned which it itself is *not*, can the thought of a responsibility to and for oneself be thought.

Certainly, there is a potential responsibility for oneself to other humans, i.e., to those who depend upon my existence and my powers and capabilities. This responsibility is likewise inseparable from the thought of an unconditioned. It can be made plausible that we are obligated before others to certain actions and omissions from the nature of the interaction of rational beings. But this interaction already presupposes the reality of certain rational subjects who are capable of action. The thesis that these subjects have an obligation to the others for their own being appears to fall short of what could constitute something like obligations in the first place. The social obligations of property can be made plausible, but can a duty to acquire property so as to be able to fulfill the social obligations? In any case, a duty not to bring oneself to a state in which one is a burden to the others seems plausible. But even this duty is problematic without the thought of the unconditioned. For the following thesis can also be held: For that which I do or do not do with myself, I owe no one an account, so long as I do not claim the help of another. If that other freely gives me his help, that is his business. The state of affairs is altered then in that moment when the one for whom my life is important becomes real for me. In that moment – the moment of benevolence – I am no longer a drive-object for myself, but it becomes important to me what I am for the other. But what is gained by that? To what degree is the meaning which I have for another whom I wish well more important than that which I have for myself? The care for myself as part of the world of the other is a part of the benevolence toward this other, but it is not something which I owe to him over and above what I owe to myself. The thought of bearing responsibility to anyone, oneself or another, for being the kind of person that one is, is realizable only if the addressee of this responsibility is understood symbolically, that is, as the appearance of the unconditioned, which he himself in his empirical existence is not.

The other limit-case, which makes clear what is at issue when we speak of responsibility, is the above-mentioned case of responsibility for the life of someone whose extinction would mean no harm or loss to anyone. Respect for this life presupposes anew that the "value" of human life is not relative to someone else *for whom* it has value, but that it is to be respected "plain and simple" without any such relative "meaning." What that means cannot be explained at all or can only be explained in concepts which do not stem from ethics in the narrower sense, but belong to a theory of the absolute. A theory of responsibility can be grounded only within this framework. It is also only within this framework that it can be made intelligible why human responsibility is always limited to one or the other kind. The unconditionedness present in the phenomenon of responsibility appears difficult to reconcile with the restriction of its scope and with the fact that its object clearly cannot be the optimization of the universe. It also appears difficult to reconcile it with the maintenance of the distinction between an action and omission and with the asymmetry which lies in this distinction, that the morality of a way of acting does indeed depend upon the situation, while at the same time certain ways of acting are always immoral, and so we do not have to answer for the consequences of not doing them. All of this becomes intelligible if we are clear that the subject of this responsibility is one with the absolute "to whom" of this same responsibility only in a symbolic way and that the responsibility of a finite being cannot be responsibility for the contingent totality of the future courses of the world, which are modified, or could be modified, by the action. Precisely this expansion of responsibility to include the contingent infinity of all possible consequences would destroy its unconditionedness, which is grounded in the fact that human action makes the good symbolically present as the unconditioned.

Chapter 16

Forgiveness

"TO AWAKE TO REALITY" is more than a metaphor. The movement from dreaming to wakeful consciousness occurs anew in the emergence of benevolence as existential reason, and reason perfects itself in this movement. But can reason really perfect itself? This image of awakening as the fundamental human movement to the truth comes from Gautama Buddha. And if one thinks of it as being accomplished in the way of the Buddha, then one can also think of its perfection. With the Buddha the perfection of awakening is to be extinguished. The essence of the self, of the "something," is desire. Perfectly extinguished desire is the extinguishing of the self and of the something. The perfectly awakened, the Buddha, is the one who, actually and radically, comes to his end in death, since death merely clears away what has already been extinguished, the appearance. The Buddha is therefore the "exalted" because he has overcome the centrality and perspectiveness which is characteristic of all life. That is why the gods and humans gather round him. He becomes the center because the truth is present in this middle point, that is, in this nothingness. The dying Buddha snapped sharply at the monk who was standing before him trying to cool him with a fan. He prevented the gods who were present from seeing him, the perfected one.

I

The awakening to nothingness is perfected when nothingness is attained. But the awakening to reality? Can it also perfect itself? Isn't it in its essence a desiring? If moving out from the centrality inherent in being a living organism into practical reason does not lead to the annihilation of being a living organism, an annihilation of desires, and so of centrality and perspective, but rather to their discovery and affirmation, then antagonism seems to be inevitable. Hölderin comments on the love of Socrates for Alcibiades: "Whoever thinks the most deeply, loves the liveliest." But if Socrates were like Alcibiades, then he wouldn't be Socrates. And what he loves in Alcibiades is inseparable from the fact that Alcibiades does not at all live the way Socrates teaches to live.

187

If love in the sense of *amor benevolentiae* is the becoming real of the other for me, then another contradiction presents itself: I would only be able to understand the other if I were to become the other. But then I wouldn't be me anymore, and accordingly would understand neither the other nor anything else. When Emmanuel Lévinas defines the metaphysical relationship with the other as "desire," as *désir*, he gives expression to the unfathomable infinity of the affirmation. This identification with the other would be capable of completion only if we were to grant the presupposition that we are both equally nothing. But, as a rule, the pains of another remain less real for me than my own. And yet this has to be experienced by us, insofar as we are awake to reason, as guilt. To acknowledge without shame the degree of our apathy toward the reality of the other is a sign of cynicism. The guilt which we speak of is not primarily of the moral order, that is, a violation of an "ought," which is grounded in the claim of another. The *ordo amoris* limits our obligations in a way which is compatible with the conditions of our finitude. But when we have begun to awake to reality, we no longer feel completely at ease with these conditions. When Anaximander speaks of the injustice for which things have to do penance for one another, it is this lack of ease which underlies it. And we show ourselves to be "awakened," to be thinking, in that we, unlike things, do not allow ourselves to simply displace and be displaced by them; rather we relate the displaced one with the one who does the displacing. That is, we, as the ones who displace, think about the one displaced, and understand and affirm the whole as a process of maintaining a balance of "justice."

Since we understand and affirm this balancing even when it is to our disadvantage, we seem, as rational beings, to be like onlookers of our own selves. We remain who we are. We live by hampering and disrupting the lives of others, but we do not rebel against the fact that, in the end, we have to clear the field. So long as reason remains with this attitude, it has not yet started becoming – as benevolence – the form of life itself. Can it become that at all? We saw that reason apparently cannot transform life without further ado: no life without centrality and no life except at the cost of other life. But the insight which teaches us this is not a neutral observation; rather it is accompanied with regret. And above all it is accompanied by the wish that our conduct which is burdensome to others still might not transform us in their eyes into a mere object or an enemy. What we hope for is forgiveness. Before they cut them down, aboriginal peoples asked the trees for forgiveness. There is a presupposition behind this request: that it was the necessities of life which made them fell the tree. In many languages one asks forgiveness when one causes a slight physical inconvenience to another on the way to reaching one's own goal. It is at most a mere form of politeness. It does not express that we regret our action, but rather that we regret that the circumstances of our advantage are tied up with their disadvantage. Of course, this does not require that we be forgiven. What is actually meant by this oft said, "Pardon me," is that we stand closer to ourselves than to another. We express that we know and feel this and that the other, when we infringe on him, is nevertheless more real to us than can be seen from our actions. We acknowledge others at the same time as we move to elbow them out of our way. We see that this cannot be otherwise, but we depend upon the fact that they also have this insight, so that insofar as they are real to us, we cannot be at peace with ourselves, as long as they do not forgive us our finitude. We saw above that *amor benevolentiae*, the acknowledgment of the reality of the other, exists only as acknowledgment of the other in his natural being alive, that is, in his centrality. This acknowledgment can only be grounded in the fact that the other has already transcended this centrality. But the potential for this transcendence lies in this living centrality, which, therefore, is not the ground, but the object of acknowledgment and benevolence. We could also say that the form and the content of the acknowledgment of finite beings coincide. Accordingly, this acknowledgment always contains a moment of forgiveness, forgiveness for the fact that no one fulfills what is promised by their being. A hidden splendor lies in everything. But this forgiveness – in a pre-moral, ontological sense, as it were – is at the same time acknowledgment. For the finite naturalness which we have to forgive is also the *being* of the one for whom the forgiveness is intended; it is the ground of their self-transcendence. In it lies the splendor on whose account we are benevolent to a being. Forgiveness, in this fundamental, pre-moral sense means that we are just to our own kind and respect them in their worth only when we do not take them completely seriously. To take a human completely seriously means to annihilate that person, since to be taken completely seriously puts too much of a burden on us. Reason opens up to us a dimension which we are forced to acknowledge cannot be exhausted by us. No one is perfectly awake. Naturalness *is* unconsciousness. "They know not what they do" is a comment on all human action which is not a pure expression of love, and is at the same time the argument for the request: "Forgive them." In answering the question why God made humans after the fall of the angels, Ambrose of Mailand said that after this experience God wanted to deal with a being whom he would be able to forgive.

I call the forgiveness of which we speak "ontological" because it has as its object our being, the fact that we are as we are. To use an expression taken from moral discourse for this seems to be misleading or merely metaphorical. Given that we did not make ourselves, it would seem that this being the way we are is exactly that for which we ourselves cannot be held responsible. Where is the addressee of the forgiveness? Had I made myself, I would have to think of myself as creator of myself without nature, and that means without any of the "mitigating circumstances" which would make the forgiveness possible. But if I think of myself as nature, then I would still not be the addressee of forgiveness, since then there is nothing to be forgiven. I do not have to answer at all for the fact that I am the way I am. But when it is so formulated the alternative clearly misses our specifically human experience. In our experience nature and freedom are connected with each other in a way which is not capable of being analyzed. As a matter of fact we do indeed make each other and ourselves responsible for being the way we are. And when Kant and Schopenhauer speak of an intelligible character, then they are giving a theoretical rendering of the way we experience ourselves. The intelligible character, that is, a human's individual nature [or individual character: *Sosein*], from which necessarily flows his or her action, is understood by these two thinkers to be a result of a prior decision to be thus and not otherwise, a choice which precedes all possible experience. The experience which underlies this interpretation is indeed distorted by the interpretation. Empirical subjects are understood as not being responsible while intelligible subjects are responsible in an unlimited way. The possibility of forgiveness is thereby also eliminated. Empirical subjects can only be interpreted in a naturalistic way. They do not need to be forgiven. Intelligible subjects cannot be forgiven, since they know exactly what they do.

If we give an unbiased description of the underlying phenomena, it appears more like this: We are not aware of any choice which underlies our daily makeup. Rather, our naturalness, which is centered in and prejudiced toward ourselves, appears to us as the fundament out of which the point of view of reason arises like an emergence from sleep. But in this wakeful view that primordial, that apparently innocent *amour de soi*, becomes something of which we are ashamed, as if it were really not primordial, but rather already the result of a culpable inattention. The phenomenon of attention and inattention is perhaps the best paradigm for what we call good and evil. We hold ourselves and others culpable for inattention. But what kind of culpability is this? If the inattention were intentional, then it would not be inattention, but just a pretense of inattention. It would be an intentional closing of the eyes. But the behavior of being caught up in desires is in fact well described as an intentional closing of the eyes, with the exception that the closing of the eyes still has a trace of action in it. Allowing attention to be lost is, however, a non-activity, a renunciation of that original activity, in which I allow reality to become real for me. In order to attain the object of desire, the agent does not want to know what he or she in reality does. Plato was completely correct: Whoever does not do the good is ignorant of it. But this ignorance feigns being "natural." In all evil hides an insincerity, a lie. We know that if we had been "awake," we *could* have known. And insofar as we are beginning to see, we accept the previous "not having seen" as culpable.

The theoretical interpretation of this phenomenon goes beyond our intent at this point. And there is also the question, whether a theoretical interpretation is in principle impossible or not. The ancients did not face this question directly. They traced the fact that a person does not do what the *recta ratio* commands back to an incapacity, an ignorance, a bad nature, a bad upbringing. Christianity was the first to bring a new view to things, in that it interpreted the blindness itself as a consequence of an unwillingness. "They do not come into the light, so that their works are not revealed" is how it is described in the Gospel of John. In the letter to the Romans the ignorance and error concerning the last things is presented as the consequence of ingratitude: The heathens could recognize God, but they do not want to thank him. But this means that when the phenomenon of which we speak, the paradox of culpable inattention, first became thematized, it was not the object of an anthropological theory at all, but the object of a contingent history, the history of the so-called original sin. This is the narrative of the genesis of a context of entanglement, which makes being fallen the point of departure for every individual, although it "in itself" is already the consequence of guilt. To acknowledge it as such and so to see the normality of the *conditio humana* as a ontological anomaly is itself already the consequence of a conversion. And no one can credit themselves for this conversion. One easily sees how both the teaching of Kant and Schopenhauer on the choice of the intelligible character as well as Heidegger's theory of fallenness are attempts to transform the doctrine of original sin into a theory and to metamorphose the radical contingency of the myth of the fall of humans which the Bible narrates into something like an a priori constitution of the human's essence. But one see also that the myth explains more than the theories which are supposed to interpret it.

Let's go back to the description which underlies them both. We were speaking of that naturalness which cannot be itself the sufficient reason for the remaining in it once the horizon of reason has constituted itself. To remain in it becomes insincerity and evil. But since the naturalness is still the lasting ground of everything good, we end up in an ambiguous situation. No one can give an ultimate judgment about the direction of their motives or the motives of others. For we can always bend even the most noble motive back to the centrality of the self: to the satisfaction of being a person who has such motives and is capable of such actions. The saying in the first letter to the Corinthians about those who give their bodies over to be burned and distribute all they have to the poor, but have not love, is aimed at this fact. But neither can anyone give an ultimate judgment on whether another is responsible for their actions or for their individual character, from which these actions flowed, since we can never exactly know what we mean by responsibility or accountability. What is natural about "remaining in naturalness"? We have to attribute this remaining to others as persons, if we are to acknowledge them as a free subjects. But we cannot attribute it to them, if we wish to continue to respect them as free subjects. The act, which moves this contradictory situation into moral unequivocalness and brings about a unity of attributing and not attributing, is forgiveness. In "ontological" forgiveness we allow others not to fulfill the promise which they as a rational beings *are*. We allow them the perspectival limitation of a finite *ordo amoris*, in which we are less real to them than we experience ourselves to be and which is, therefore, identical with ours only in that they know their own finitude and perspective, acknowledge them, and hold themselves to the conditions of co-existence with other orders of benevolence.

II

And what happens when another does not do this? There the topic of forgiveness begins to take on its specifically moral sense. But first we have to talk about the ontological sense, since the moral version of forgiveness of injury and evil is only possible on the basis of the forgiveness which has been discussed up to this point, that is, on the basis of that forgiveness in which we forgive each other the finiteness of a determinate "nature." But since this "forgiveness" only exists on the level of reciprocity, its real human meaning remains hidden. It can be interpreted in a naturalistic sense, as a systems-structure of the common living of finite beings, who are not and do not wish to be anything other than nature, so that the talk of forgiveness is nothing other than the imaginary construction of an equally imaginary superstructure. Its specifically human sense first becomes unmistakably clear when the order of its reciprocity is destroyed by an infringement of the one upon the other or, what amounts to the same thing, when one never reaches the realization of the reality of the other, i.e., never attains to the benevolence which is to be expected. What happens in forgiveness? The one who forgives perceives the reality of the other, his self-being, which goes beyond the individual character, which was visible in the action or omission, and she allows him to distance himself from it. The forgiver does not fall victim to the appearance of the dilemma which, since the time of Hume, has accompanied the concept of personal identity and seems to make the thought of forgiveness impossible: Either the action is a direct consequence of the being of the agent and is thus imputable to him and is not to be separated from him. He is as he acts. What could forgiveness mean then? Or the action proceeds from a freedom which has no nature. Then it is the consequence of the unique self-determination of the one affected, and there is no subject to whom this act could be imputed in a continuous identity which encompassed all the free acts. Not only is the subject who is accountable missing, but so also is the addressee of forgiveness. Forgiveness presumes that there is a subject of accountability for actions, that is, someone who reveals himself in these actions. On the other hand, it also presumes that this connection between the subject and the action is somehow able to be broken. It presumes then that the agent can, after the fact, recover himself or herself from the individual character which appeared in this action, but still without disposing of the responsibility that he or she was such a person which could and in fact did do this. On what basis is such a "self-recovery" possible? It is possible by a further step along that way of awakening to reality about which we have constantly been speaking. The human begins to see that which he or she has been in a new perspective. What from earlier position appeared to have to happen necessarily no longer appears so; rather it was his or her own fault to have been in this position. But taking this step, in which guilt as guilt is accepted and simultaneously distanced and overcome is not accomplished alone. The heroic utterances of Heidegger about wanting to be guilty remain a *façon de parler*. It comes out of Dasein's being isolated in principle, as that is thought of in *Being and Time*. But a guilt, which humans would want to have, is not really conceived of as guilt at all. Reason, in whose light alone a concept like guilt can come into existence, is hereby pulled back into the centrality of care against its will, where what matters is its own ability to exist. Reason cannot develop its own claims nor open up its own dimension. To look guilt – not just fallibility – in the eyes means to want to overcome it. And that is possible only with the help of others. Clinging to one's own guilt, as well as the attempt to exculpate one's self, remain in the circle of self-preservation, in the circle of "that's the way I am." And when the one pins another down to "that's the way you are," then the road to freedom is closed off. The guilty party is dependent upon forgiveness. The discovery of this dependency is the first step on the return to the truth and not to the self-accusation of the one who emphasizes: "I cannot forgive myself that." The same hubris is in this statement as is in the action which he cannot forgive himself for. Of course, no one can forgive himself. One can only let oneself be forgiven and accept the forgiveness. The result is gratitude. But gratitude is benevolence in its purest form, free from all danger of hidden hubris.

Forgiveness, which makes it possible for the other to step back from or beyond his being such an individual is itself not so free from the danger of hubris as allowing oneself to be forgiven. There is forgiveness in which the forgiver wants to appear – even toward herself – as a rational subject who is invulnerable to the limitations of the other. She does not allow herself to be really affected because the other does not appear to her as her equal in being, that is, does not appear to her as real. Forgiveness becomes just another word for the ultimate unreality of other, who is not qualified to give "satisfaction." Real forgiveness presupposes real injury. It has the character of a restoration.[1] Its unique moral meaning resides in its being a kind of creation. In contrast to the basic acknowledgment of the subjectivity of the other, it cooperates with the one whom it acknowledges to let him or her become real. It follows then that this emancipation of the self-being from the passivity of "that's the way I am" is only possible with the help of the other, who, in the act of forgiveness says: "No, that's not the way you are."

This description is not yet sufficient. For it could now appear as though the benevolence which is restored in forgiveness is valid for the abstract self-being of the other and not for his particular nature. But we have already seen that benevolence toward another self-being only realizes itself as benevolence when it is directed to his nature, to his being alive and to his natural concrete particularity. Yet now it seems that forgiveness would only be valid for the person insofar as he distances himself from this concrete particularity. Yet again, we have to deflect a dualistic misunderstanding of this distancing. "Person" is not to be thought of as reason, which the ancients then contrasted with the human's sensuous nature, so that the particular qualities, the individuality, ended up on the side of the irrational, which was then to be overcome. To speak of "person" is to take cognizance of the fact that human nature *as* nature realizes itself only when it "awakens," when it transcends its centrality, or, put more precisely, when it consciously grasps the self-transcendence which is essential to it and does not "turn it back" into an instrument of a merely natural self-preservation. This *curvatio in seipsum* is evil itself and is not just the individual character; rather it is the fixation of this character to go against its own natural dynamic meaning. What makes forgiveness necessary is not that someone is the way he is, but that he says:

---

1   The original German is *Widerherstellung*, which can mean either restoration or rehabilitation. Spaemann uses it in both senses. My translation will reflect the nuance being emphasized.

"That's the way I am" or expresses this in his action. In forgiveness the self-being of the other is not separated *in abstracto* from his individual character; rather the opposite: Actual forgiveness affirms the nature of the other and restores it to its human teleology. It even discovers in the negated action the positive possibility, whose perversion the action was. It does not demand that the other hold himself or herself in contempt in its particular naturalness; rather it demands that the other discover himself or herself. It always contains a moment of excuse, which means the revelation of a mistake: "You didn't *really* know what you did." The ambiguity of this not knowing, about which we have already spoken, the ambiguity of the inattention, allows this not knowing to be viewed from outside as "nature" and so to be excused, while it is overcome from the inside in that the agent accepts culpability for it and so makes himself dependent upon forgiveness.

The ambiguity of not knowing, the impossibility of dividing freedom and nature into two different moments, makes possible a certain promise of forgiveness, even where the agent does not distance himself from that individual character out of which his action proceeded. I do not see the world with his eyes. I see his blindspot, not mine. And even my being certain that he is in the wrong does not mean that he appears to me as a part of nature. I can reprimand him and appeal to his "better nature," to the teleology of his nature which is aimed toward awakening. I can and must defend myself from him. It may be impossible to have community with him on the level of rational communication. But to hold him in contempt, that is, to define his self-being in terms of individual character, means I would have to know him in a way which I can know neither him nor myself. Even when the rehabilitation, which is contained in every act of forgiveness, is impossible, the suspension of judgment is possible. Not a suspension of judgment about the way of acting, but a suspension of judgment about the agent. His full reality as a self-relationship never gets fully represented in any of his objectifications. In suspending judgment the one to whom the injustice occurred or who had to witness it asserts his own transcendence to reality over against the "contagion" of evil. Suspension of judgment is the minimal form of benevolence, which cannot be taken away from anyone.

III

To look at forgiveness from the viewpoint of rehabilitating the human in his self-being is to look at it from the same viewpoint from which philosophy has always viewed that which seems to be its opposite: punishment. The formula from Hegel's *Philosophy of Right* which characterizes punishment as "rehabilitation of the criminal" has often been criticized. This thought is already found in Plato's *Gorgias*. There it says – from the mouth of Socrates – that the one who has done wrong has to seek out the punishment as a "cure for his soul." Punishment has always been understood as restoration, that is, as the restoration of an order, the restoration of the balance of justice. And not just in the sense that the one who perpetrates harm has to "indemnify" the one harmed. Much more than compensating for the harm done to an individual, the harm done to all must be compensated. And this happens by wronging the wrongdoer as an "expiation." He is to experience, as Kant put it, what his deeds are worth. Certainly, in this archaic concept punishment is thought of as restoration, but not as the rehabilitation of the perpetrator. He is *not* the object of the punishment, as he is in Plato where one talks of curing the soul. Curing the soul means more for Plato than resocialization. What is meant is that the soul is not yet cured when it has an insight into the wrong. The order, which has been upset by the person, is also the order of his soul, and that which has to occur for the restoration of this order serves also to restore his own order. He cannot rehabilitate himself by himself. He is dependent upon forgiveness. Punishment is thought of here as the prerequisite necessary for forgiveness.

There is in this thinking a profound insight which can mediate in the discussion which has already gone on for hundreds of years about expiation, reform, and deterrence theories of punishment. There is something mythological in the idea of expiation, the thought of making a sacrifice in order to appease an angry divinity. Kant clearly professes this idea, when he holds that a state which is to dissolve itself still has the duty to execute the remaining murderers, since otherwise the murders would remain unexpiated. What is true in this kind of thinking cannot be examined here. Christianity has, at one and the same time, confirmed and brought to an end its truth by its teaching on the expiatory death of Christ for the sins of all humans. This perfects the myth and ends its practical relevance. In this sense Kant's position is a regression. Thomas Aquinas views state punishment from a strictly social-utilitarian viewpoint.

Nevertheless, it would be fatal to completely eliminate the expiatory aspect. This would have the consequence that at any time even the innocent could be subjected to such social-utilitarian measures. Only by holding fast to the thought of expiation do we guarantee the freedom of citizens who do not incur a penalty. But the thought of expiation has to be completely freed from *jus talionis*, from thought of "retaliation." Its rational sense, which is directed to the rehabilitation of the perpetrator, can only be the following: As a rational being the perpetrator has forfeited his claim to that right which he himself has negated through his act. Otherwise one has to view him as insane. His action is a human action only when it can be interpreted in the medium of language and reason. If the perpetrator were to have gone completely out of this medium and were to act only out the centrality of his organic nature, in which he is the middle point of his world, then he would no longer be recognizable as a human. But in the moment that he reclaims a right, he allows us to recognize that he exists in the medium of rational universality, and his actions have a structure which can be generalized. He has then forfeited for his own person the subjective right which he himself has negated. But this means that from a certain viewpoint he has made himself into a thing, into a part of mere nature. Still, to treat him now simply as this part, as a thing, would mean to capitulate to untruth. For he is still more than what he has made himself to be in the wrongdoing. The expiation consists precisely in his submitting to those measures which are made necessary on account of social utility – that is, made necessary from the viewpoint of restitution or the protection of society or even his own resocialization. There are no measures which are suggested for reasons of expiation. The expiation consists in a partial objectification of the perpetrator. But in that this is demanded of him *as* expiation, he is at the same time respected as a person. For, we are concerned here with those measures which he himself would have to demand, if he himself were not affected and had to make an impartial decision about that which the common good demanded. There is expiation in that his own well-being does not enter on the same level into the definition of the common good, and instead he is the object of actions and the object of social welfare. In that he accepts these, his status as subject is restored.

The one who forgives is not in the position of being obligated to rectify superindividual damage in the interest of many others. He can demand an individual restitution, or he can forego it. There is no boundary set to his magnanimity. What remains primary is that he is not a judge, but rather finds himself continually in the position of being dependent upon forgiveness, which spares him from the negating "That's the way you are." In smaller communities the restitution can easily take forms which make the moment of restoration of the one who as fallen outside the order of the community more conspicuous than is possible in a large system. Lévi-Strauss reports upon an Indian tribe which punishes murderers by destroying their houses and everything which they own. They then receive all of this from the community. They live now "new" from the grace of the others, whose debtor – without the duty of materially paying them back – they have become. In comparison to this the primitiveness of our penal system is deeply disturbing.

IV

By way of conclusion we raise the question of whether there is something like forgiveness of one's own self. As regards a trespass against others this is clearly impossible. But what about things like negligence or failures which only affect one's own existence? The question whether there is something like duties to oneself, in which one can fail, precedes the question of self-forgiveness. We return once again to a question which has already been raised. The fact that contemporary ethics does not generally allow for duties to oneself is a consequence of the decision to do "ethics without metaphysics" and to eliminate the religious element from ethics. "Duties to oneself" seems to be an inappropriate formula. I can dispense another from duties which he has to me, but which he cannot dispense himself. If, however, the one who can dispense is identical with the one who has the duties, then the concept of duty becomes untenable. For a duty is not a duty when it is consistently left to the discretion of the one who has the duty to fulfill it or not. But can someone actually dispense another from all the duties which the latter has to him? Even our civil law recognizes the concept of "immoral contracts," a concept which restricts this freedom of dispensing others from the duties toward oneself. For example, one cannot dispense another from the duty to pay a salary for regular work or from the duty not to mistreat one. But to whom can one have these duties, if not to oneself? And to whom, if not to one's own self, can the other have the duty not to allow himself to be dispensed from certain duties? Still, in order to avoid the paradoxes contained in the concept of a duty to oneself, it is better to speak of responsibility for one's own self. And this is what we feel in certain life situations or when we pose the question of how we should treat ourselves. We have the feeling that we have a responsibility for ourselves and for this life which we have to live. Still, we can only *think* that which is felt if we think of the human as an image and a representative of an unconditioned, that is, if we think of the human as someone who does not belong to him or herself. The thought of belonging to oneself is laden with greater paradoxes than that of duties to oneself. For possession presupposes a possessor. A possessor can only be a subject, a being who relates itself to itself. But if I further interpret self-understanding as self-possession, then I would need an infinite iteration. The alternative is not "Either I belong to myself or I belong to the other," but "Either I am responsible for myself or I am a *res nullius*, whose self anyone else can make what he wants." The thought of responsibility for oneself is a religious thought; it is even a constitutive thought for religion. The addressee, the "to-whom" *(Instanz)* of this responsibility can, of course, be thought of in a variety of different ways. When it is thought of impersonally, when the absolute is not thought of as a subject, then the bearer *(Instanz)* of this responsibility cannot be thought of as the subject of possible forgiveness. But if this is granted, then the human cannot forgive himself his irresponsibility to himself, and then there is no forgiveness for this. But where there is no forgiveness, there, as we have seen, is also no possibility of distancing oneself from one's individual character as the source of guilt. And where this is impossible, the talk of guilt becomes a figurative *façon de parler*, a metaphor for the fateful being-thus-and-not-being-otherwise. The thought of responsibility to oneself can only be consistently held when forgiveness is also a possibility, and this possibly includes a subject of forgiveness.

Afterword

Robert Spaemann's *Philosophische Essays*

Arthur Madigan, S.J.

In 1983 the Stuttgart publishing firm of Philipp Reclam brought out a slim volume containing an introduction and seven essays by Robert Spaemann, then Professor of Philosophy in the University of Munich. Entitled *Philosophische Essays*, it presents and illustrates Spaemann's philosophical project: to understand the phenomenon of modernity, to criticize the deficiencies of modern thought, and to preserve what is good in modernity by rehabilitating the teleological understanding of nature that modernity largely rejected. A second edition in 1994 included three more essays.[1] As little of Spaemann's work has yet appeared in English,[2] the aim of this essay is modest: to present as clearly and accurately as possible his position in the *Philosophische Essays*, in the hope that this may serve as an introduction to his thought.

Robert Spaemann was born in 1927 in Berlin. After training in history,

---

1 Robert Spaemann, *Philosophische Essays*, 2nd. ed. (Stuttgart: Reclam, 1994). All translations from this work are my own. To reduce the number of footnotes I have inserted most references to *Philosophische Essays* in the text. Parentheses inside a sentence document the sentence in which they appear. Parentheses outside of sentences document either the whole preceding paragraph or the sentences following the previous such reference.

2 Spaemann's *Moralische Grundbegriffe* (Munich: Beck, 1982) is available in English as *Basic Moral Concepts*, translated by T. J. Armstrong (London and New York: Routledge, 1989). Four of Spaemann's essays are also available in English: "Remarks on the Problem of Equality," *Ethics* 87 (1976–77): 363–69; "Side-effects as a Moral Problem," translated by Frederick S. Gardiner, in *Contemporary German Philosophy*, vol. 2, ed. Darrel E. Christensen, Manfred Riedel, Robert Spaemann, Reiner Wiehl, Wolfgang Wieland (University Park: Pennsylvania State University Press, 1983), 138Ð51; "Remarks on the Ontology of 'Right' and 'Left'," *Graduate Faculty Philosophy Journal* 10.1 (1984): 89–97; and "Is Every Human Being a Person?" translated by Richard Schenk, O.P., *The Thomist* 60 (1996): 463–74.

philosophy, theology, and Romance literature, he taught in the Technical University in Stuttgart, the University of Heidelberg, and the University of Munich. His first major publication was *Der Ursprung der Soziologie aus dem Geist der Restauration*,[3] a study of the French traditionalist thinker L. G. A. de Bonald. In this work Spaemann found that the period of restoration or reaction against the French Revolution was not opposed to modernity but rather brought modernity to completion in the notion of functionality, i.e., interpreting metaphysics (or religion or anything else) as a means to human self-preservation. This was followed by *Reflexion und Spontaneität*,[4] a study of Fénelon, Bossuet, and the seventeenth-century debate over the pure love of God, i.e., the debate about whether human beings can or should love God to the point of not caring about their own happiness. Here Spaemann found that the inversion of the classical teleological view of things, i.e., the shift from looking on things as having ends in themselves to looking on them as means to the satisfaction of human ends, gave rise to the modern antithesis of self-fulfillment versus self-transcendence. In 1977 Spaemann published a volume of political essays, *Zur Kritik der politischen Utopie*.[5] The thread uniting these political pieces is the critique of the abstract utopia of the rule of pure reason. His next book was *Rousseau – Bürger ohne Vaterland. Von der Polis zur Natur*,[6] in which he argued that Rousseau used a non-teleological conception of nature as a standard by which to criticize modernity. In *Die Frage Wozu? Geschichte und Wiederentdeckung des teleologischen Denkens*, written in cooperation with Reinhard Löw,[7] Spaemann surveyed the history of teleological thinking from the Greeks through the medievals and moderns down to the nineteenth century, offering a rebuttal to these criticisms and arguing for a revival of teleological thinking. In *Moralische Grundbegriffe*,[8] originally a series of talks on Bavarian Radio, he discussed the concepts of ethical relativity, moral development, justice, conscience, and equanimity. Spaemann has also published a volume of philosophical anthropology, *Das Natürliche und das Vernünftige*,[9] as well as *Glück und Wohlwollen*,[10] in which he endeavored to formulate an

---

3   Munich: Kösel, 1959.

4   Stuttgart: Kohlhammer, 1963; expanded edition Stuttgart: Klett-Cotta, 1990.

5   Stuttgart: Klett, 1977.

6   Munich: Piper, 1980.

7   Munich and Zurich: Piper, 1981; expanded edition, 1988.

8   Munich: Beck, 1982.

9   Munich and Zurich: Piper, 1987.

10   Stuttgart: Klett-Cotta, 1989. This now appears in English as *Happiness and*

ethical position that goes beyond the familiar antithesis between eudaimonism and deontology while doing justice to both. In 1996 Spaemann published *Personen: Versuche über den Unterschied zwischen 'etwas' und 'jemand'*,[11] a wide-ranging exploration of the notion of personhood and of its ramifications for ethics.

Spaemann's formidably varied educational background makes it difficult to say who has had the most pronounced influence on his thought. In the Introduction to *Philosophische Essays* Spaemann cites the following as having influenced him: Thomas Aquinas's *Summa Theologica*; the lectures of Joachim Ritter on the topic of past and future[12]; the volume *Dialektik der Aufklärung*, co-authored by Max Horkheimer and Theodor W. Adorno[13]; and C. S. Lewis's volume *The Abolition of Man*.[14] (10–11) It is evident from numerous references throughout *Philosophische Essays* that Spaemann is thoroughly at home with Kant and Hegel, but also – and perhaps more significantly for fixing his own position – he is clearly influenced by a reading of Socrates' conception of philosophical activity, by Plato's ethics, especially as found in *Republic* I, by his theory of pleasure as found in the *Gorgias* and *Philebus*, and by Aristotle, particularly by Aristotle's teleological understanding of nature. His indebtedness to all these thinkers is clear and candidly acknowledged. But Spaemann's thought is also the product of

---

Benevolence, translated by Jeremiah Alberg, S.J. (Notre Dame, Indiana: University of Notre Dame Press, 1999).

11   Stuttgart: Klett-Cotta, 1996.

12   Joachim Ritter (1903–1974) is perhaps best known as the founding general editor of the *Historisches Wörterbuch der Philosophie* (Basel and Stuttgart: Schwabe, 1971–) on which Spaemann was one of the original collaborators. I have not been able to find out whether the lectures that Spaemann cites ever appeared in print. Unfortunately the Festschrift *Collegium Philosophicum: Studien Joachim Ritter zum 60. Geburtstag*, ed. Ernst-Wolfgang Böckenförde (Basel: Schwabe, 1965) does not contain a bibliography of Ritter's publications.

13   *Dialektik der Aufklärung* was first circulated in mimeographed form in 1944, then published as a book in Amsterdam in 1947 (the form in which Spaemann mentions it). A revised edition appeared in 1969; it is currently available as Volume 3 of Theodor W. Adorno, *Gesammelte Schriften* (Frankfurt am Main: Suhrkamp, 1981). The English translation by John Cumming, *Dialectic of Enlightenment* (New York: Continuum, 1987) is based on the revised edition of 1969.

14   London: Geoffrey Bles, 1967. Spaemann remarks that this little book, first published in 1943, says more briefly and less dialectically everything that *Dialektik der Aufklärung* was trying to say (11).

controversy with thinkers whose views he finds in one way or another problematic. Spaemann has invested a great deal of time in the study of early modern theologians such as Fénelon and Bossuet, of Rousseau, and of the traditionalist movement represented by de Bonald. The essays show a familiarity with Descartes and Hobbes, Nietzsche and Weber. Spaemann's philosophical position developed in opposition to the ideology of National Socialism that was dominant in the Germany of his youth. Other adversaries include the sociologists Ralf Dahrendorf[15] and Niklas Luhmann,[16] the behaviorist B. F. Skinner, and the movement of discourse ethics whose most prominent exponent is Jürgen Habermas.

Spaemann's project is, first of all, a venture in intellectual history: to understand modernity. Study of modernity discloses a dialectical progress of opposed abstractions. Modernity has developed in two directions: as a transcendental philosophy or philosophy of consciousness, and as a reductionist naturalism. Modernity has tended to interpret itself as a radical emancipation from what preceded it, and in particular from a teleological view of nature. But a philosophy of consciousness that tries to proceed without

---

15   Ralf Dahrendorf, now Lord Dahrendorf, was director of the London School of Economics and Political Science from 1974 to 1984. Spaemann criticizes his claim that National Socialism brought Germany into modernity, his thesis that there is a "continuum of conflict," i.e., that physical force and verbal argument are basically two ways of bringing about the same ends, and his rejection of the notion of a common good over and above particular interests (8, 61, 183–84). Spaemann cites his *Gesellschaft und Freiheit* (Munich: Piper, 1961), and in particular his essay "Lob des Thrasymachos." This essay can be found in Dahrendorf's *Pfade aus Utopia* (Munich: Piper, 1974), 294–313, and in English translation as "In Praise of Thrasymachus" in Dahrendorf's *Essays in the Theory of Society* (Stanford: Stanford University Press, 1968), 129–50.

16   Niklas Luhmann is a student of Talcott Parsons. A brief account of his thought may be found in the Introduction by the translators Stephen Holmes and Charles Larmore to Luhmann's *The Differentiation of Society* (New York: Columbia University Press, 1982), xiii–xxxviii. According to Holmes and Larmore, Luhmann's project is to develop categories adequate to understand modern society. Luhmann is skeptical about pronouncements that modern society is in crisis, attributing such pronouncements of crisis rather to the fact that older conceptual schemes are inadequate to describe modern society (xiv). Spaemann criticizes Luhmann's dismissal of natural right (70–71). A fuller statement of Spaemann's differences with Luhmann is found in "Niklas Luhmanns Herausforderung der Philosophie," the *laudatio* that he delivered on the occasion of Luhmann's receiving the Stuttgart Hegel Prize. This is published with Luhmann's acceptance speech in Niklas Luhmann, *Paradigm lost: Über die ethische Reflexion der Moral* (Frankfurt am Main: Suhrkamp, 1990), 49–73.

reference to teleology falls prey to the objections of a reductionist naturalism that spells the end of philosophy and the death of reason. The second element in Spaemann's project is, then, to rescue modernity from its own interpretation of itself as a radical emancipation from what has preceded it, and to infuse it with a teleological outlook.[17] Modernity is beset by terrible conflicts that it cannot resolve, but there is no question of returning to a premodern outlook. The task is to take the great positive contributions of modernity – enlightenment, emancipation, human rights, modern natural science with its accompanying mastery of nature – into a kind of protective custody. (10–17)

I. Spaemann's Conception of Philosophy

Spaemann understands philosophy as a continuing unsettleable controversy. The essay "Die kontroverse Natur der Philosophie" ("The Controversial Nature of Philosophy") examines the distinctive character of philosophical controversy, and especially the differences between scientific and philosophical controversy. All science involves controversy, but science normally operates with a degree of consensus on certain basic assumptions. In philosophy, by contrast, everything is controversial, including what counts as philosophy. Spaemann proposes three theses: Philosophy is by its very nature thoroughly controversial; the attempt to resolve philosophical controversy only intensifies it; despite this, philosophy is neither senseless nor superfluous. (106)

Spaemann defines philosophy as a continuing discourse about ultimate questions, such as we face in life-decisions, in crises, in confronting death. As discourse, it is a matter of argument, not to be settled by religious or political authority. Philosophy has always been marked by controversy, but in the modern period the differences go even deeper. (106–11) Modernity has seen three attempts to put an end to these differences: self-evident foundations (Descartes, Fichte, Husserl); drawing of boundaries between theoretical and practical (Kant, Comte); and method (Leibniz, followed by ideal language analysts in the twentieth century). All these moves presuppose that philosophy ought to make cumulative and consensual progress by following the path of mathematical natural science, but Thomas Kuhn has shown that the

---

17   Spaemann evaluates the emancipation brought about by modernity both positively, as a recognition and expansion of freedom, and negatively, as a disregard of norms of good and evil. In the latter sense he speaks of the Marquis de Sade as a figure of naturalistic emancipation (29–30), and of the National Socialist period in Germany as an era of radical emancipation (65).

model of cumulative consensual progress does not apply in science. (111–13) If we can no longer use that model to understand philosophy, can we use the Kuhnian model of paradigm shifts? No, says Spaemann. First, because philosophical shifts are even more radical than paradigm shifts in science. There is no pragmatic control in philosophy. Philosophy is not defined by sets of questions to which there are agreed-on answers; it is always trying to think out and express the unspoken things that make ordinary discourse possible, but can never do so completely. (113–16) Second, because philosophy's ideal of rationality is antidecisionist. To do science, one has to make the decision at some point to stop asking the question "why?" Philosophy, by contrast, never drops that question. Philosophy is always engaged with contingent particularity, but it is always trying to think contingent particulars universally. Third, because philosophy is about itself in a way that science is not (the question "what is physics?" is not a question in physics). Philosophy's situation is in a way tragic, inasmuch as it is bound to raise questions that it cannot solve (120–21). To construe one philosophy as a limit case of a more advanced philosophy is precisely to deny that the first philosophy is an answer to the questions, "what is real?" and "what is good?" The three great historical forms of philosophy are metaphysics, transcendental philosophy, and linguistic analysis. But the later do not simply supersede the earlier, nor do the three come to some sort of peaceful coexistence. Each is still an independent attempt to think the whole. (116–22)

Is the history of philosophy simply a history of ideologies, interpretations of reality that are really covers for particular interests? No, says Spaemann. Philosophy is sometimes enlisted in ideological conflicts, but it has no fixed ideological loyalties. It has longer-term interests or tendencies, such as the Galilean-Kantian-analytic tendency to devise ways to represent nature and so to control it, and the Aristotelian-Hegelian-hermeneutic tendency to experience the world as home, to understand ourselves as part of nature without giving up our status as freely acting beings – interests that may now be heading toward convergence. Not that the philosopher can just jump out of his or her historical particularity; the self that thinks is conditioned by a history of thought. (122–25) There is no impartial, all-powerful judge in philosophy, not even history; it would not be philosophical to accept a philosophical position simply on the ground that it has prevailed, is prevailing, or will prevail (126–28). The controversial nature of philosophy is bound up with human freedom, and the definitive resolution of philosophical controversy would be the end of the free human being. Philosophy is inherently disorderly, even anarchic, for while thought requires rules, the question is, "which rules?" (128–29). "The elimination of this anarchy would be equivalent to man's resigning in favor of his products" (129).

"Philosophie als Lehre vom glücklichen Leben" ("Philosophy as a Study of the Happy Life") points out that in some 2500 years there has never been a consensus about happiness. Happiness (*Glück*) is ambiguous as between fortune or luck (*fortuna*) and felicity or blessedness (*felicitas*). We can begin to reduce the diversity of views about happiness to unity by distinguishing theoretical questions, questions of what is and what it is to be real (questions about similarities, *Ähnlichkeiten*), from practical questions, such as what our interests are, what we really want when we are at one with ourselves (questions of identity, *Identität*). The point of asking the latter kind of question is to bring about a unity in our willing. The question of what we ought to do is bound up with the question of what we want to do. Ethics is an attempt to see our lives as wholes and thus to bring unity into our willing. (80–83)

Western ethics begins with people like Antigone, who take a certain order as given. Then the sophists, in an attempt to provide willing with a principle of unity, contend that the object of willing is pleasure (83–84). But hedonism is either false or trivial. Vulgar or debunking hedonism, which says that all that people pursue is pleasure, is false, for people do act for other motives. And philosophical hedonism, which says that all that people ought to seek is pleasure, is also false, for in some cases at least people would not wish to be able to act otherwise. Hedonism reduces to the triviality that people do what they want because they want to do it. (84–86) The hedonistic principle is self-refuting, insofar as it cannot explain why someone proclaims that hedonism is true. The hedonistic conception of pleasure is out of touch with reality, insofar as it does not differentiate types of pleasure or satisfaction. (86–89) As Scheler pointed out, only bodily pleasures can be pursued directly. Other pleasures "piggy back" on actions and are impeded by the attempt to intend them directly. Happiness involves what Spaemann calls a reference to reality. He explains this with the example of a person on a table, having pleasurable feelings induced electrically. However pleasant the person's condition, we would not change places, and that shows that pleasure as such is not what we want. Thus hedonism fails to bring the desired unity to willing. (89–91)

Can a person be happy at the expense of others? Plato tried to show that an unjust person could not be happy, because he would be at variance with himself. Does Plato see a guaranteed connection between being good and being happy? Not in this life – think of the just man being crucified – but only in a life after death. Still, there is the *polis*, which can, so long as it preserves its own freedom and self-sufficiency, try to guarantee a connection between being good and being happy. But while Aristotle's theory of philosophical happiness influenced Stoicism and Christianity, his theory of civic happiness was not immediately influential, and its two moments or aspects were unfortunately split up: the aspect of life (self-preservation, self-sufficiency, self- assertion), which Spaemann correlates with the later political right, and the aspect of the good life (self-fulfillment), which he correlates with the later political left. (95–99)

The early modern period saw another attempt to treat happiness as something that could be practically achieved: Descartes's combination of the Stoic ideal of contentment with the project of achieving all goods through science. But Kant and Freud dispelled the notion that the progress of civilization brings happiness, and we are left with an antinomy (an alternative or disjunction between two abstractions, 102) between self-sufficiency and self-fulfillment. This antinomy takes three forms. The first is: Should we increase our needs or wants (with the sophists, and with Rousseau's opponents), or lower them (with the Cynics, Stoics, Epicurus, and Rousseau himself)? The way out of the antinomy is to think in terms of nature, understood as specifying upper and lower bounds for our needs or requirements: a *telos* that is both a boundary and a goal. (100–101) The second form is: Should we seek euphoria, or simply (as Schopenhauer counsels) freedom from pain? Here Spaemann speaks in favor of achieving some sense or meaning (*Sinn*) in the present, as opposed to deferring all to the future; if we cannot achieve some sense in the present, it is pointless to work for it in the future. (101–2) The third form is: Is happiness a matter of adjusting to what is (cynicism), or of trying to change what is into something else (fanaticism)? Cynicism pays no attention to the issue of sense or meaning, while fanaticism tries to create sense out of nothing. The way out is to pay attention to the good, understood not as the goal of a productive activity but as itself the immanent norm of conduct. Happiness only results from conduct that is itself grounded in happiness. (102)

Philosophy is concerned with happiness, but it is not a science of happiness. Philosophy works with a conception of good that is constantly guiding and transforming life, but that is nonetheless never actually achieved. Happiness is a concept of reflection (*Reflexionsbegriff*). It is not so much something to be achieved as something already present that we do not notice. Spaemann approves Wittgenstein's remark that only the person who lives not in time but in the present is happy. Recalling Aristotle's thesis that only a whole life can be judged to be happy, and facing the experience that we enjoy only a few happy moments in our lives, Spaemann sees these two claims as consistent: Our moments of happiness are the moments when we see our lives as wholes. We are happy when we notice that we have been happy all along. Life is happiness, and to speak of a happy life is to utter a tautology.[18] (103)

II. Nature, Natural Teleology, and Natural Right

The core of Spaemann's philosophical project is to rehabilitate the concepts of nature, natural teleology, and natural right. This project is represented by the essays "Natur" ("Nature"), "Naturteleologie und Handlung" ("Natural Teleology and Action"), and "Die Aktualität des Naturrechts" ("The Contemporary Relevance of Natural Right").

As Spaemann notes, the term "nature" is highly ambiguous (19). At the risk of making his exposition seem more schematic than it is, we may distinguish five senses in which he uses the terms "nature" and "natural": (1) the nature of a species, and in particular our human nature, with its natural teleology; (2) the natural world, the biosphere or ecosystem; (3) that which is naturally right, as opposed to that which is naturally wrong; (4) merely natural process or natural development (*Naturwüchsigkeit*), that which happens of itself apart from human reason or decision; and (5) the state of nature, a state without effective or moral government. Nature in senses (1), (2), and (3) deserves our respect.[19] Nature in sense (4) is not subject to moral evaluation, nor is it a sufficient basis for moral evaluation. Humans are continually in danger of degenerating into (5).[20]

Spaemann's view of nature is essentially Aristotelian. Nature and human being are complementary concepts, and human nature, that which is true of

---

18   More on Spaemann's conception of philosophy may be found in "Philosophie als institutionalisierte Naivität," *Philosophisches Jahrbuch* 81 (1974): 139–42.

19   Spaemann maintains that attentiveness to natural teleology is essential to ethical thinking, but he also insists that moral justification cannot be teleological in a utilitarian or consequentialist sense, a justification of means by ends. He discusses this point at length in "Über die Unmöglichkeit einer universal-teleologischen Ethik," *Philosophisches Jahrbuch* 88 (1981): 70–89. Spaemann is particularly critical of the tendency of some Roman Catholic moral theologians to give up the classical notion of teleology in favor of a utilitarian approach to moral justification; see "Über die Unmöglichkeit. . . ," 88–89, and *Philosophische Essays*, 253.

20   The key issue for Spaemann is not whether the state of nature was a historical fact or a theoretical construct, but the practical issue of political philosophy: How do we keep from degenerating into a state of nature?

humans precisely not as a result of human positing, is what makes human action possible. Human willing presupposes a natural dynamic of drives (as is recognized in the Augustinian and Thomistic distinction between natural inclination and free will). (19–22) Anaxagoras, Plato, and Aristotle held that the concept of an end or goal, borrowed from the world of human action, enhanced our knowledge of nature. Aristotle thought that the regular generation of beings adapted to a goal could not be explained as the result of natural selection. It is difficult for us moderns even to reconstruct Aristotle's view, in which the *telos* is one moment of a complex causal structure within which causes and goals cannot be understood apart from one another. (41–48)

The most important motive for the modern rejection of the teleological understanding of nature was the Christian theology of creation, which, instead of accepting nature as something ultimate, insisted on looking behind it for its origin. This led to the view that if there is art in nature, it is due not to nature itself but to the intention of God directing nature. Here Spaemann cites Aquinas' Fifth Way, which recognizes teleology but understands it as the direction of things by an intelligent and conscious being. For later thinkers such as Ockham and Buridan, the view that things have orientations intrinsic to themselves seems to conflict with the theological affirmation of the glory of God. Natural teleology comes to be considered a form of idolatry, and the mechanical view of the world is affirmed as a vindication of divine glory. (23–24, 43–44)

A further motive for the rejection of natural teleology is found in the theological antitheses of nature versus grace and natural versus supernatural. These are attempts to adapt the classical distinction of nature (the given) and praxis (what humans do with the given) to the Pauline and Johannine affirmation that humans cannot, in their *de facto* condition, become what it is their tendency to become. (23–24) These attempts lead to alterations in the concept of nature. Once nature is identified with the flesh and blood that cannot inherit the Kingdom of God, then praxis – at least praxis under the influence of grace – has nothing to do with nature. Albert the Great has the idea of nature as curving in on itself, and Aquinas has the quite un-Aristotelian idea of an immanent teleology (the natural desire for beatitude) that is incapable of reaching its end, because that end is infinite. Later scholastics, seeing that the end cannot be reached by the species as a whole, cease to call it a natural end. Sixteenth-century theologians criticize the notion of a natural desire for salvation as making grace something to which we would have a claim, rather than a free gift. To save the gratuity of salvation, they term the orientation to salvation supernatural (24–26). They speak of a system of pure nature, with grace as something added on top. But either nature is oriented toward something, and so has a claim on it, or nature is on its own. With the system of pure nature, human action falls on the side of nature, and the kingdom of grace loses inner necessity. Given the Enlightenment critique of revelation and the supernatural order, nature becomes the totality of what is, human action is, like nature, curved in on itself, and self-preservation becomes the key concept. (27–29)

The denial of natural teleology also has the latent function of legitimating mastery over nature.[21] (22–23) Bacon's claim that natural teleology is useless, and Hobbes's claim that imagining a thing is imagining what we can do with it when we have it, are the reverse of the sympathetic understanding of nature that marked the teleological outlook. Science is no longer *theoria*, it is in the service of praxis. (44–46) If you want to be free to treat a thing as you please, the question of the thing's natural orientation is disturbing, but if there is no such thing as a natural orientation, then nothing you do to a thing is violence against it. (22–23) True, the older view also regarded humans as ruling over nature. But that was in the context of a hierarchical system of nature, in which it made sense, for example, for Socrates to say that the end of the shepherd's art was the good of the sheep – something that makes no sense on the modern view. The older view supposed an objective teleology in which things are ends not simply for themselves but in themselves. The modern view recognizes only ends for themselves, that is, the end of self-preservation. Modern biology and cybernetics recognize a sort of teleology, but they understand the *telos* in a purely functional way, as the self-preservation of a system. (44–46)

Every speculative concept becomes dialectical when it is detached from its correlative. If nature is no longer seen as oriented toward fulfillment and transcendence, there are two ways to understand it. One is as a system of needs and powers that appears when we wipe away the effects of history and tradition. Then nature takes on an emancipatory function, as it did for the Greek sophists. The case of de Sade shows the problems with this naturalistic emancipation. (29–30) The other way is to understand nature as an original condition that precedes history. Then nature is a starting point for freedom, but freedom is a matter of getting beyond nature, as in Hobbes. Nature and humanity are in conflict. Thus Rousseau treats being human and being a citizen as mutually exclusive alternatives. (30–33)

Kant was the first to work out the status of causal and teleological state-

---

21   A latent function of a belief is a consequence of the belief, but a consequence that the person holding the belief does not intend and of which he or she may not even be aware (see 209–13).

ments. In physics, he held, teleological statements were purely regulative. But he took a different view of biology, for without teleology biology would have no specific subject matter – which Kant thought it had, though he could not justify this view. Hegel then showed that the regulative function of principles was constitutive for knowledge in the concrete, but in the progress of the natural sciences people ignored Hegel's point. The vitalists were unable to show that teleology was more than an *ad hoc* hypothesis. The antiteleological view went even further in behaviorism, which tried to understand even human actions as nonteleological natural events. But the attempt to carry out the behaviorist program is itself a case of behavior that cannot be interpreted behavioristically. (46–48) Contemporary systems theory and cybernetics represent a return to Aristotle, in that they recognize directed process, including adaptation to changed circumstances, but they also tend to describe this adaptation as the result of mechanical causal processes. (48)

In the final pages of "Natur" Spaemann offers a series of philosophical theses about nature. Nature is a normative concept. We should speak not only, as modernity has often spoken, of liberation from nature, but also of the liberation of nature. Nature is not just a *terminus a quo*. It is also a standard that we can use to judge this or that development or *terminus ad quem* as natural, unnatural, or counternatural. When progressive domination over nature becomes an end in itself, then we fall back into purely natural process (*Naturwüchsigkeit*). Only the remembering of nature as a standard of conduct makes it possible to get beyond nature. (33) Spaemann invokes the Kantian distinction between nature in a formal sense (the inner principle of a thing) and nature in a material sense (the world of what is experienced). The two are closely allied: The system of what is (nature taken materially) is constituted by the tendencies or principles of the things that are (nature taken formally). But the law of nature taken materially is that nature taken formally constantly suffers violence. That is why emancipation can be understood both as freedom from nature and as freedom of nature. From the standpoint of nature in the material sense, no individual or species has a claim on the system; the question of justification does not arise. (33–34)

If we do not accept the law of material nature as the last word (and Spaemann thinks that we do not), then we place ourselves in contrast with the system of nature (34–35). We face the choice between increasing our mastery over nature and freely remembering nature (35–37). Our consciousness of freedom in action discloses the contrast between ourselves and nature. The laws of nature are not subject to our influence. We rely on them for our ability to deal with the world and for the continuity of our own drives and intentions. But it is a mistake to abandon the viewpoint of action and to regard human action, which presupposes the determinacies of nature, as though it were itself simply part of nature. If human action is simply part of nature, then control of nature includes control of human beings. "Natural science, understood as a science of domination, is indifferent to the distinction between the human being and nature" (35). A human history that is simply a history of domination of nature is a purely natural history. The distinction of natural and unnatural has no place in it. From that point of view, concern for the ecosystem is groundless, because a garbage heap is as natural as a mountain spring, and even the destruction of the biosphere would be just one more natural phenomenon. (34–36) We escape this objectionable understanding of nature only when we remember nature as itself, when we cease to think in terms of progressive domination and start to think in terms of a symbiosis of humans and nature. Our growing domination of nature is now threatening the human race itself. Instead of lessening human domination of humans, it expands both the necessity and the possibilities of such domination. The supposed emancipation from all historical ways of life tends to promote a functional approach to human beings, as in behaviorism. There are attempts to justify manipulation on the ground that humans are not really free and should be rationally directed. But freedom is not something left over from the subjugation of nature. The fundamental act of freedom is to let something be (*Seinlassen*), that is, not to subjugate it precisely when we could subjugate it. Natural beings get beyond nature only by mutual recognition, by mutually letting one another be. (36–37)

In the latter part of "Naturteleologie und Handlung" Spaemann argues for the same basic point, but along somewhat different lines. He pleads for what he terms *oratio obliqua*, indirect discourse, that is, for standing back and considering our first order discourse about ends both linguistic-analytically and pragmatically. If we cannot prove the existence or the nonexistence of final causes, we can at least ask what we mean when we speaks of ends or goals, and we can ask what interests of reason are involved in affirming or denying them. Then we may be able to determine where the burden of the argument lies, which is the crucial consideration in almost all philosophical questions. (49)

We cannot understand our teleological statements so long as we assimilate them to statements of laws, understanding teleology as a sort of inverse causality (pulling instead of pushing). Teleological processes are also causal processes, but speaking of causal processes in teleological terms means understanding them as in some way like the structures of our human action. "Natural teleology is a hermeneutic of nature" (49). Applying this hermeneutic involves a fusion of horizons, at the risk of error and without the possibility of precise testable predictions. When we see someone running through a train station and there is no train, we cannot tell why the person is running simply by looking. We have to interpret the action. Teleological interpretations presuppose the notion of a normal state. When we interpret the movements of fish in a net as attempts to escape, we are presupposing that it is normal for fish to swim freely. Normality is not the same as statistical regularity: The fish are trying to get out of the net even if, statistically, very few do, and pain is not the normal human condition, even if most people are in pain. (49–50)

The notion of natural ends brings us into a gray area between undirected causal processes, which are only interpreted by an external observer as attempts at self-preservation, and conscious intentions informing action. Someone may object that there are goals only when there is conscious action; but conscious action presupposes preconscious goals: our needs, drives, and impulses. (50–51) System theory tries to explain such goals as epiphenomenal enhancements of a system; but to articulate the processes whereby a system reproduces itself, system theory has to use the notion of a goal. A system is first of all a system for us. If we construe it as a system in itself, it is still we who call it something living and interpret it teleologically. Far from being able to reduce our life to nonteleological objectivity, we find that we cannot talk about objectivity without bringing in teleology. To state a causal law, we need the notions of beginning states and end states. To get beyond statistical regularity to genuine causality, we need the notion of someone's intervening in or coming to grips with something (*eingreifende Handlung*). (51–52)

The interest that leads to forgetfulness of teleology is the interest in mastery of nature (22–23, 44–46 discussed above). But there is a contrary interest: the interest in being able to understand ourselves both as natural beings and as acting beings. If we understand humans on the analogy of a nature that has itself not been understood on the analogy of humans, then humans, along with the rest of nature, are objects of manipulation (as in Skinner). Nature in itself leaves the problem of teleology open. "In the end, teleology is a postulate of reason, reason making sense" (53). Spaemann gives the Frankfurt School credit for acknowledging the role of teleology in the human case, but criticizes the school for not extending teleology to nature in general. (52–56) He quotes Leo Strauss with approval: The answer to the question, whether natural right makes any sense, depends on how we interpret the motions of the planets.[22] We cannot really think of motion without the notion of an anticipation of what is to come. We can master motion with the help of calculus, analyzing the motion into an infinite number of discrete states; but calculus brings us back to the thinking subject. Leibniz saw that if we wish to think of something in motion as itself, we have to use the analogy with the subject. (56–57) "One may call this anthropomorphism; but to renounce the anthropomorphic view of nature leads inevitably to the point where the human being itself becomes an anthropomorphism" (57).

"Die Aktualität des Naturrechts" outlines the ethical and political implications of remembering nature and natural teleology.[23] Here Spaemann is writing as a political philosopher and not simply as a historian of ideas. He begins by vindicating the claim that there is such a thing as natural right. People argue about whether it makes any sense to speak of natural right, but that does not change the basic facts: People distinguish good and bad conduct, good and bad laws; they make judgments about cases in which their own interests are not involved; even when their own interests are involved, they try to show that these interests are justified. Some people allege that these disputes count against there being something naturally right and wrong, but the fact of dispute counts the other way. Dispute over right and wrong is different from conflict between adversaries, and it is not the same as a negotiation that seeks compromise. Not that it is necessarily clear what is naturally right; but the persistence of argument over what is naturally right is evidence in favor of there being some such thing. (60–61)

Negatively, natural right is not a set of values in the sense invoked in post-World War II German jurisprudence, a sort of metaconstitution for a judge to use in interpreting positive law. Such an appeal to a judge's values or to society's values is no less relativistic than the appeal to positive law and brings us no closer to what is naturally right. (61–63, 78) In positive terms, the first demand of natural right is that people leave the state of nature. This is affirmed by Hobbes and Kant, and by Aristotle. Aristotle, however, says more: only in something like a *polis* can humans become selves and actualize what they are by nature. Here Spaemann borrows from his mentor, Joachim Ritter, who countered the contemporary suprahistorical notion of natural right, drawn from an abstract picture of human needs, by going back

---

22   *Natural Right and History* (Chicago: University of Chicago Press, 1963), 8. In this English version Strauss cites Aristotle, *Physics* 2.4.196a25 ff., and 2.8.199a3–5.

23   I translate *Naturrecht* as "natural right" rather than "natural law" in order to preserve the connection between *Naturrecht* and *das von Natur Rechte*, "that which is right by nature" or "that which is naturally right" (see 60–61).

to Aristotle and looking to the concrete realities of life, institutions, and judicial practice.[24] But Aristotle's world is not our world. We have to see what divides us from Aristotle, and how the understanding of natural law as a set or table of values became inevitable. (64) As Ritter saw it, Aristotelian natural right reconciles the rupture (*Entzweiung*, a Hegelian term with roots in Rousseau) between the social dimension and the personal ethical dimension, the dimension of "private" freedom. Aristotelian natural right is a hermeneutic of existing law with a view to reconciling these two. Spaemann basically accepts Ritter's interpretation, but thinks that its validity is limited to a phase of modernity that is now passing, a phase in which the "emancipatory" tendencies of modernity and a more traditional outlook were fairly evenly balanced. Now the "emancipatory" tendencies are gaining in strength.[25] Contemporary society tends to judge everything in terms of whether it meets some need or want (*Bedürfnis*), but this system based on needs or wants is not really natural. Needs and wants provide no criterion to judge among forms of life (Spaemann points to the Marquis de Sade). And if Rousseau is right that culture or civilization means stepping away from nature, then nothing in culture or civilization can provide a criterion to distinguish natural from unnatural needs or wants. (64–66)

Modern science rejects teleology in order to seek control over nature. Of course the phenomena, the facts, resist this rejection of teleology, and so, to save the phenomena, we have a series of substitutes to do the work of teleology: the two-world theories, which distinguish between a realm of causes and a realm of ends, between is and ought, between facts and values. These theories are residues of the preceding Aristotelian notion of entelechy, of a thing's having a *telos* within it. (66–67) The powerful interest in mastery over nature is the source of the humans versus nature antithesis, which opposes the traditional symbiosis. Renewal of the teleological conception of nature today involves recognizing that taking mastery over nature as an end is itself a merely natural (*naturwüchsig*) phenomenon. The formula "more power over nature, no power over human beings" is terribly naive, for so

---

24   Ritter's interpretation of Aristotelian natural right may be found in the essay "'Naturrecht' bei Aristoteles," in his *Metaphysik und Politik. Studien zu Aristoteles und Hegel* (Frankfurt am Main: Suhrkamp, 1969), 133–79.

25   Spaemann understands the period of German National Socialism as a period in which a movement of "radical emancipation" was dominant, and the fifteen years after World War II as merely a breathing space before the current (the essay first appeared in 1973) renewal of the tendency toward radical emancipation.

long as mastery over nature is not guided by respect for teleology, it is bound to be mastery of humans as well. (67–69)

At this point Spaemann turns to the Old Stoa. This may seem to be a detour, but Spaemann's aim is to argue for a concept of natural right that is more than logical consistency. The Stoic conception of natural right was circular: The rational will is supposed to want what is naturally right, but what is naturally right is the rule of reason.[26] Is living consistently with nature the same thing as living consistently, period? Can the reference to nature be eliminated without loss? Rousseau seems to have thought so: Whether one chooses to be a natural human being or to be a denatured citizen is a matter of indifference; the essential point is that one not try to be both at the same time; the important thing is inner unity or consistency. If this is the correct view of natural right, if there is no reference back to nature, then the only norm we have is internal consistency within a sociopolitical system that is trying to maintain itself (as in Niklas Luhmann). But then we are just talking about the interests we may have in such and such a system. Normative talk about nature makes sense only with reference to a freely acting being. It cannot be reduced to talk about goals or systems of action; it has to do rather with presuppositions of action. (69–72)

Rousseau and Kant believed in a preestablished harmony between the workings of nature and what is naturally right. This presupposes that whatever goes against natural right also works against the preservation of the system in question, and suggests that we could without loss eliminate talk about what is naturally right and wrong and confine ourselves to talk about what contributes to or detracts from the preservation of the system. But that is an error, for it presupposes that the system can be described without reference to its members' convictions about what is right. (72–73) Natural right transcends systems, not as a metatheory over against positive law and individual consciousness, but insofar as human action is more than simply a function within a system. Agents have a natural identity that is more than a product of sociopsychological processes. Living consistently, then, has to mean living consistently with nature.

But how can nature be a norm of action? Having argued for the necessity of a reference to nature, Spaemann then argues against the view that this reference can be unmediated, that it is a simple matter to look to nature and read off what is right. That view prescinds from human freedom and subjectivity.

---

26   Spaemann says that this circularity is also found in the Christian conception of natural right, and that it is the source of the current (1973) crisis in Catholic circles over natural right (69).

To say that nature simply gives, without mediation, a teleological conception of the human, telling us what makes a human being happy, would mean giving up the whole modern notion of a subject, as well as the whole linkage between happiness and freedom that has been constitutive of our conception of the subject since the start of Christianity. Imposed happiness is not happiness. A political eudaimonism that prescinded from freedom would be just a tyranny of the intellectuals who defined what happiness was – a parody of Plato's *Republic*. (73–74) But if we cannot simply inspect human nature and read off the norm of what is naturally right, what sense does it make to speak of such a norm? It seems impossible in modernity to take nature as a norm without violating the claims of autonomy and subjectivity. And the being that acts still has to recognize the presuppositions of action before they can really count as presuppositions. Natural right is not something unmediated. "Even natural right is right only if it is willed" (74–75). But if we do not presuppose natural right, the alternative is to fall back into nature. "Freedom has reality only as remembered nature, just as it only makes sense to talk about nature given the presupposition of freedom" (75).

There are two moments to natural right: the right to freedom, and natural right in the strict sense. The right to freedom is "the set of a priori conditions for mutual recognition and justification on the part of agents, that is, the conditions required, from the very nature of the case, for the formation of any kind of consensus" (75). Natural right in the strict sense is "concerned with those conditions of action that are presupposed in all formation of consensus and that can be violated only at the cost of self-destruction" (75). The distinction between the two is not so clearly explained as it might be, but this much at least is clear, that for Spaemann natural right in the strict sense introduces a reference to nature and the natural conditions of human existence that goes beyond the right to freedom. He criticizes the attempt to separate the right to freedom from its natural conditions, on the ground that this leads to the utopian conception of "masterless communication" (*herrschaftsfreie Kommunikation*), which ignores the conditions that enable some people to dominate others, such as skill in speaking, stamina, possession of information, being on the scene, and the fact that decisions have to be made within limits of time. The utopian conception results from the attempt to have the right to freedom without accepting natural right in the strict sense. (74–75) This is a criticism of Jürgen Habermas's discourse ethics.[27]

Natural right is not a catalogue of norms or a metaconstitution. It is a mode of thought that tests legitimations of action. Its basic premise is that the notion of a total freedom in opposition to nature is illusory. Our only choice is whether to remember nature, bearing it in mind as we act, or to forget it and to fall back into it. (78)

III. Some Specifics

Given Spaemann's view of natural teleology as a hermeneutic, and his view of natural right as a mode of thought rather than as a table of values, it would be a mistake to construe his positions on practical questions as strict logical deductions from his views on nature, natural teleology, and natural right. Nonetheless his appeal to pragmatics invites the question, where does "remembering nature" lead us?

At the close of the essay on natural right Spaemann sketches three practical applications of natural-right thinking. The first is respect for the environment. In opposition to the utopian view that all damage to the environment can be remedied by further technical measures, natural right requires that human freedom respect its natural conditions, including the environment. Natural-law thinking does not yield a list of prescriptions and prohibitions, but it enjoins a certain style or procedure for thinking about environmental issues, namely, to shift the burden of the argument to the side of those who favor expansionist measures. (75–76) A second application goes against genetic manipulation. We cannot legitimately make the biological form of future human beings the object of our own willing, for we lack legitimate criteria to do so. (76) Again the burden of the argument falls on those who would manipulate nature, and in this case Spaemann finds that the burden cannot be met.

A third application concerns the moral implications of biological humanity. We might conceivably determine who is a subject of rights and duties on the basis of someone's contribution to society. But then the Indians of the Amazon Basin would have no claim to recognition, and the citizens of Brazil would be free to exterminate them, for they make no contribution to the Brazilian system. Or we might accord recognition on the basis of possession of reason and freedom, excluding the unborn, the very young, and the mentally ill. But it is difficult if not impossible to specify the criterion or criteria of freedom; and it is circular to use freedom as a criterion of recognition be-

---

27   More on this point can be found in Spaemann's essay "Die Utopie der Herrschaftsfreiheit," *Merkur* 26 (1972): 735–52, in Habermas's reply "Die Utopie des guten Herrschers," *Merkur* 26 (1972): 1266–73, and in Spaemann's rejoinder, 1273–78. All three pieces are reprinted in Spaemann's *Zur Kritik der politischen Utopie* (Stuttgart: Klett, 1977), 104–41. For an account of Habermas's discourse ethics, see David M. Rasmussen, *Reading Habermas* (Cambridge, Mass.: Blackwell, 1990), 56–74.

cause freedom is not a bare fact independent of recognition, but something that arises within a context of recognition.[28] The third possibility is to take membership in the human biological species as the criterion for recognition as a subject of rights and duties. Spaemann does not try to validate this third approach directly, but argues that it is at least not open to the objections that lie against the first and the second.[29] (76–78)

The issue in "Moral und Gewalt" ("Morality and Force"), first delivered in 1970, is whether individuals are ever justified in using violent means to resist the power of government and to bring about political change. Spaemann begins with Kant's arguments against revolution. Kant distinguishes between a state's being *rechtlich*, a system in which there are laws and they are enforced, and its being *rechtsmässig*, a system in which the laws are just. The former represents, independently of the latter, both the departure from the state of nature and the condition of possibility for any deliberate progress toward the latter. Violent revolution cannot be justified because it does away with the legal order – the subject that the revolution was supposed to have improved and the necessary context for moral justification. (159–65) The attempt to legitimate force morally amounts to justification of means by ends; but moral justification cannot be teleological, even if the end in question is a moral one. Illegal force amounts to return to the state of nature. (169–73)

In the main Spaemann follows Kant, but he recognizes three cases in which an authority has itself caused a return to the state of nature and the victims may be justified in using force: the state's suppression of free criticism (174–75), the denial of peacetime emigration (175–76), and the legal or constitutional impossibility of improving the laws in the direction of reducing discrimination (176–78). He then argues that morality in warfare is not a matter of refusing to defend oneself but of how one defends oneself. The first rule is not to use right and wrong as weapons of war. The enterprise of moral justification presupposes the distinction between discourse and force, and

---

28   For an elaboration of this point, see Paul W. McNellis, S.J., "The Family and the Analogy of Gratitude: The Role of the Family in Johannes Messner's Thought" (Ph.D. Dissertation, Boston College, 1993), especially Chapter 4. McNellis argues that gratitude, specifically gratitude for all that we receive in the context of family, is the way to what Spaemann terms remembering nature.

29   Does Spaemann have to argue directly for the third approach? He might well answer No. He says that certain things, such as that good is one thing and evil another, are simply given. People know these things even as children. They do not really have to be taught them. What they have to do is not let themselves be talked out of them. (8)

resort to force means abandoning that enterprise.[30] People who exert revolutionary force against society should not make moral claims on society. (178–80) Of its very nature force is something mechanistic. Resort to force means the right of the stronger and represents the failure of reason. One may look on force as the midwife of a new age, but all that really means is that the new age will be one more variation on the old. (180–81)

One might question the relevance of "Moral und Gewalt" to the American context, which has been marked less by revolutionary violence than by non-violent civil disobedience, in which those who violate the law do so in a way that underlines their fundamental allegiance to the legal system. The relevance of the essay "Unter welchen Umständen kann man noch von Fortschritt sprechen?" ("Under What Conditions Can We Still Talk about Progress?") is more obvious. Spaemann distinguishes two types of progress: A-progress, in which a given development is only justified as a step on the way to a goal, and B-progress, an actual improvement in the life of an organism, a human being, a society. A-progress presupposes a fairly clear distinction between means and ends, whereas in B-progress means and ends tend to blend together. The model of A-progress is the manufacture of a product. The model of B-progress is the development of a living thing. For human life to make sense, A-progress has to be subordinated to B-progress; or at least A-progress ought not to occur at the expense of B-regression. (130–34)

Since the eighteenth century there has been a tendency to speak of "progress" in the singular, with the human race as its subject, but we should not be taken in by talk of "progress" in the singular. True, history has seen a development in the stock of available information and the possibilities of mastering nature, first through writing, then through printing, now through data processing. But as the ecological crisis suggests, this is not progress without qualification. (135–37) First, there is a disproportion between the scientific subsystem and the social system taken as a whole. The case of Marx illustrates this point. Marx looked forward to a period of A-progress leading to the classless society. Once that goal was reached a new period of B-progress would begin, in which increasing mastery of nature by science would bring about substantive improvements in human life. Marx was assuming that scarcity could be overcome, but now we know that scarcity cannot be overcome. We have no prospect of an A-progress leading to the overcoming of

---

30   In this context Spaemann attacks Ralf Dahrendorf's thesis of a "continuum of conflict," in which parliamentary debate and civil war are just two points on a continuous scale of conflict, on the ground that this thesis not only leaves the philosophy of right without any object to study but also conflicts with the presuppositions of human discourse about practical matters (183–84, n. 36).

scarcity, only of B-progress. Science cannot provide a standard by which to measure progress. Insofar as science prescinds from teleology, it cannot tell what anything is good for. Advances in science and technology are not the same thing as progress *tout court*. (138–41)

Second, the whole idea of scientific progress is in crisis. Modern science, guided by interests in mastery of nature and in emancipation from nature, has tended to wipe out mind, life, feeling, willing – anything anthropomorphic – and to reconstruct living things, even human beings, on the model of a dead nature, so as to objectify and control them. From this point of view, the goal of progress would be computerized euphoria (cf. 90). If we reject that outcome, then we have to take the term "progress" in a more modest sense. We have to stop talking about universal A-progress toward a goal (A-progress in the singular), and talk about B-progress, that is, improvement(s) in the lives of human beings who are already goals in being. (142–45)

Third, the concept of emancipation has broken down. There is a tendency, especially in biology, to suppose that evolution is a process of increasing complexity, and that the human race is one stage in this progress, a stage destined to be superseded as humans become superfluous. But that would not be progress because there would be no conscious subject of the supposed progress. Such a future situation has no claim on us, as though we ought to work to bring it about. And if we are told that we ought to abandon such notions as "better" and "worse" as archaic, it is not clear why we ought to do anything. (145–46)

Fourth, scientific knowledge has become so vast and differentiated that it cannot be mastered by a single conscious subject. This is not progress. (Neither is the acceleration of the tempo of life to the point where people in the second half of their lives cannot understand their world.) This so-called progress of science is really the advance of particular interests, and it is better to recognize these interests than to suppose that some entity called "science" demands great expenditures to learn this or that. (147–48)

There is a kind of knowledge that gives its possessors the power to control other humans. It is not enough for this knowledge to be under democratic control. That just means that whoever democratically controls the knowledge can use it. An increase of technological control means a decrease in the concrete freedom of coming generations. Nature is turning out not to be an inexhaustible reservoir of resources. The only genuinely "progressive" approach is to let nature be. The notion of progress in the singular has become an instrument of human self-alienation, standing in the way of progresses in the plural. We have to give it up. (148–50)

"Sein und Gewordensein. Was erklärt die Evolutionstheorie?" ("Being and Having Come to Be: What does Evolutionary Theory Explain?" discusses the implications of evolutionary theory for human self-understanding. Evolutionary theory acknowledges human subjectivity but construes it functionally, as an evolutionary adaptation or means of survival. This is circular: the person who claims that subjectivity is a means of survival is making a truth claim, not just employing a means of survival. Still, when people today speak about subjectivity, they tend to presuppose that our ordinary language is only preliminary to a scientific language that can do without talk of subjectivity. But this scientific language is not an adequate translation of our ordinary language. For example, "good" as we use it cannot really be translated into the functional "good for. . . ." Evolutionary theory can reconstruct the basic contents of human ethics in functional terms, but it cannot derive the form of ethics, its unconditional character, or the non-relational sense of "good." (191–95) Human subjectivity and moral awareness have indeed developed under certain evolutionary conditions, but they are themselves unconditioned. We have at least three kinds of awareness that cannot be explained as adaptations for survival: the experience of pain as something that ought not to be the case, the awareness of the other as other, and the conception of the absolute. (196–200)

Evolutionary theory does not regard evolution as moving in a predetermined direction, and some people think that the thesis of directionless evolution undermines human awareness of the self as an end. Spaemann disagrees. Our awareness of the self as an end in itself is not awareness of the human species as an end in itself, and it does not depend on whether the human species is the end of a teleological process oriented to produce it. Human dignity is rooted in what Spaemann calls acosmism, namely, the human ability to reflect, to distance itself from natural ends, to accept or reject them. (200–202) The scientific paradigm of evolution is essentially neutral as regards human self-understanding. The ideology of evolutionism is another matter. This Spaemann explains by contrasting "evolution" and the older term "descent." To speak of descent supposes that ancestor and descendant are distinct. To speak of evolution suggests that some one thing is evolving, taking on different forms. Evolutionism understands everything as a state of an underlying substrate, and that conflicts with our self-understanding, for we cannot understand ourselves as properties of something else. (203–4)

The essay "Funktionale Religionsbegründung und Religion" ("The Functional Explanation of Religion and Religion Itself") criticizes the attempts of social-scientific functionalism to understand religion. Functionalism tries to understand forms of behavior not by treating human motives or intentions as irrelevant, but by situating them within a further horizon that abstracts from them. It tends to construe actions and practices as having the latent function of preserving a group or a situation (for example, a rain dance as strengthening the unity of a group). Developed to interpret behavior in foreign cultures, functionalism becomes a problem when applied to its own culture, because articulating the functionalist interpretation undoes the latency of the function. (209–13) That does not make much difference for elementary cases like eating and having sex, but it does affect social contexts such as meals and love relations. In the cases of passion, artistic and aesthetic experience, and scientific activity, the functional interpretation is just incommensurable with the subject's self-interpretation, not necessarily incompatible with it. But in philosophy, moral experience, and religion, functional interpretation is incompatible with self-understanding. A functional interpretation of philosophy is the end of philosophy. A functional interpretation of ethics, an interpretation of ethics in non-moral terms, is equivalent to the destruction of ethics. (213–18) A functional interpretation of religion is a relativization of the absolute, and that is equivalent to its disappearance. One may try to interpret religion as a way of preserving society, but for a religious person society itself is not something ultimate. One may try to interpret religion as a way of mastering contingency, but that is too general and too external to be an adequate interpretation of religion; and religions of creation, at least, even heighten the problem of contingency by taking the world as a whole to be a contingent fact. There is a sense in which religion is concerned with self-preservation, but thematizing this function is not the core of religion. (218–24)

Spaemann thinks that religion does have a function: It gives human dignity content. It "keeps things open," in opposition to liberalism, collectivism, and perfectionisms without a conception of the good. (224–25) But religion can perform this function only if it is understood in categories compatible with its own self-understanding. The Christian religion can only be interpreted in ontological categories; functional categories are not an adequate replacement. We can ask, for instance, about the function of belief in eternal life for human conduct, without being committed to this belief; but religion is a matter of taking eternal life as real. The presupposition of modern science ("even if there were no God") has been fruitful for science, but when applied to religion it tends to destroy its object, for religion looks at the world precisely under the aspect of divinity. A scientific understanding of religion apart from belief in God is like a solipsistic theory of love. If philosophy of religion is not to misconstrue its object, it has to be religious philosophy, a "theory of the absolute." (225–29)

IV. The End of Modernity?

The essay "Ende der Modernität?" ("An End to Modernity?") pulls together many of the themes of *Philosophische Essays*. The term "modern" often conveys the notion of superseding what went before, of emancipating humankind from its previous condition. If we take modernity in this sense, then the end of modernity seems to mean the failure of this project and regression to what was before. But not if we grant two assumptions: that modernity has achievements that deserve to be protected, and that the end of modernity does not mean giving up these achievements. Spaemann grants these assumptions, and hopes to protect these achievements against the self-destructive tendencies of modernity itself. (232–34)

Modernity has seven characteristics. (1) It understands freedom as emancipation from something rather than as the ability to move toward something. (234–35) (2) It believes in the myth of necessary and unending progress toward an optimal point. (235–37) (3) Its paradigm of progress is natural science, understood as an instrument for progressive domination of nature. (237–38) (4) It posits a sharp distinction between subject and object. It does not recognize ends as immanent in objects, but regards objects simply as means to human ends. When humans themselves become objects of science, they too are objectified, and humanity is reduced to a mere anthropomorphism. (238–40) (5) Modernity takes scientific experiment as the paradigm of experience in general. It does not recognize what does not fit into this type of experience, for example, substantial change or miracles. (240–42) (6) It treats everything as hypothetical, and so is disinclined to make definite truth claims. (242–44) (7) It believes in the unity of humanity, but this universalism is naturalistic. The only arguments it recognizes are arguments from human needs, so that religion, for example, is only justified insofar as it meets human needs. This kind of thinking rules out any unconditioned reality. (244–47)

Modernity has always been accompanied by a critique of modernity. There were always doubts about the domination of nature, criticisms of reductionism, of deformation of the human reality, and so on. What is new in our day is that ecological awareness has thrown into question the very possibility of objectifying and mastering nature. The Marxist utopia of overcoming scarcity was emblematic of modernity. Now that utopia is dead, and with it the concept of unitary world progress. These are signs that the kind of consciousness that is typical of modernity is coming to an end. (247–49) Ecological awareness knows that mastery of nature takes place in a context that binds subject and object together. This throws modernity into crisis, but the crisis is ambiguous. It may mean a revival of respect and letting be (*Seinlassen*) in the face of what is. But it may also lead to a universal utilitarian program of optimization, an attempt to solve all the problems of the world through central planning. (249–53)

The reduction of experience to planned experiment is over. The experimental type of experience has been relativized. The popular interest in all sorts of other forms of experience is a symptom of the crisis of modernity. But again the crisis is ambiguous. These other forms of experience may be assigned their own niches, commercialized, or whatever. The experience that cannot be homogenized, however, is the experience of the world as a limited totality, of persons, things, situations, as unique and unrepeatable. That does not contradict experimental reason, but the two are incommensurable. An integral view of experience has to include the unconditioned: the religious, moral, and artistic. That is the only way to protect the achievements of modernity. (253–55)

Science may be hypothetical, but the ecological consequences of our actions are not hypothetical. Religion and ethics have always recognized that there was something irreversible about our actions, but now it is clear, at the ecological level, that we cannot count on "mother" nature to reverse the effects of our actions. Instead of modern probabilism, with its doctrine that in doubtful cases we should stand for freedom, we need a new tutiorism that is risk averse on the large issues, though open to risk on lesser social and political issues, precisely in order to avert larger risks. But once again there is ambiguity. Even in the ecological movement there are functionalist tendencies, tendencies to treat the patrimony of the earth, nonhuman life, even human life in the womb, as means to satisfy the needs or wants of the current generation. (255–57)

Naturalistic universalism is also in crisis. Consensus is not an adequate standard to tell us what is right by nature. Naturalistic universalism tried to neutralize particularity in the name of universality. It tried to do away with particular normative convictions, in favor of a common minimum based on the requirements of abstract human nature. These attempts have failed. (257–59) Spaemann closes with a fanciful illustration based on Mozart's *The Magic Flute*. The Queen of the Night does not go along with enlightenment, and Sarastro, the incarnation of totalitarian modernity, orders her liquidation. But the Queen survives, only unreconciled. Modern rationality had pretensions to reconcile the other, but it has not reconciled the other, nor has it recognized that the magic flute itself is a gift of the Queen of the Night. If only the Queen and Sarastro would come to an understanding and get married! This is not a prediction. As Spaemann admits, he has given an improbable tale an even more improbable ending. (259–60)

V. Evaluation

An adequate evaluation of Spaemann's thought must be based on the full range of his work.[31] The evaluation offered here, based as it is on the *Philosophische Essays*, is preliminary and tentative.

Spaemann is not an easy thinker to categorize. (1) He is an assiduous student of modernity, but (to borrow a distinction from Charles Taylor's *The Ethics of Authenticity*) he does not fit easily either among the "boosters" or among the "knockers" of modernity. He thinks that we can, indeed must, pick and choose among the many elements that go to make up modernity, rejecting or revising some precisely to protect others. (2) One might have expected Spaemann to elaborate an ethical system, but his conception of philosophy precludes system building. He sees philosophy as an ongoing conversation. His ethics is dialectical and *ad hominem*. He aims to expose error, to foster certain attitudes and habits of thought (the hermeneutic of nature, the remembering of nature, the alertness to teleology, the denial of teleological justification, the critique of hedonism, the insistence on present sense, mindfulness of the distinction between A-progress and B-progress, and so on), rather than to posit first principles and to deduce conclusions.

Spaemann's thinking is suggestive and full of promise. (1) Theorists of natural law in the Anglo-Saxon world have in recent years been divided by the controversy over the so-called new natural law theory of Germain Grisez, John Finnis, and Joseph Boyle. At its root this is a controversy about the meaning or meanings of nature, the meaning or meanings of reason, and the relations between nature and reason. With his nuanced understanding of nature and of the workings of practical moral reason, Spaemann has something to contribute to this debate.[32] (2) If Spaemann's style of ethical reflection (the hermeneutic of nature, and so on) can take us beyond the all too familiar dichotomies of deontological ethics versus consequentialist ethics,

---

31   A bibliography of Spaemann's published work to 1987 is found in *Oikeiosis: Festschrift für Robert Spaemann*, ed. Reinhard Löw (Weinheim: Acta Humaniora, 1987), 321–39.

32   Ulrich Steinvorth sees Finnis and Spaemann as representing two species of what he calls "classical ethics," with Finnis standing for a plurality of basic values and Spaemann standing for a single basic value: the life of reason and freedom. See his *Klassische und moderne Ethik. Grundlinien einer materialen Moraltheorie* (Reinbek bei Hamburg: Rowohlt, 1990), 122–33.

of Kantian versus utilitarian ethics, that would be a gust of fresh air both for metaethics and for applied ethics. Of course the question whether Spaemann's ethical reflection fulfills these conditions can be answered only after an examination of his other works, especially *Happiness and Benevolence* and *Personen*. (3) In North America today, discussion of human responsibility for the natural environment and discussion of human life issues such as genetic engineering, abortion, euthanasia, and assisted suicide tend to proceed in separation from one another. Many people hold fairly strict views of our obligations in one of these areas but fairly permissive views in the other. Spaemann maintains that our stance toward the biosphere and our stance toward the members of our own species are two sides of the same coin. This claim needs more argument, but the linkage between respect for the environment and respect for even the weakest members of the human species deserves attention.

Philosophische Essays leaves some unfinished business. (1) For Spaemann, merely natural processes do not ground moral claims, but as we act we have to be mindful of our nature; natural right is not a list of duties but a way of reading nature; we have a duty not to fall back into the state of nature; we ought to treat the natural world with reverence; and so on. The relations among these different senses of nature and the natural need to be worked out in a more systematic way than takes place in the *Philosophische Essays*. (2) Spaemann asserts that we have knowledge of right and wrong, but also that philosophy does not yield final definitive truths. The relation between these two claims needs to be clarified. The same is true for the claims that ethical thinking has to bear natural teleology in mind but that moral justification cannot be teleological. The distinction between the right to freedom and natural right in the strict sense could also stand clarification. (3) The thesis of a worldwide and possibly terminal ecological crisis is an important element in Spaemann's case that modernity is over and that humanity needs an outlook that is more respectful of nature, but nowhere in *Philosophische Essays* does he attempt to substantiate it. Perhaps this thesis is taken for granted in European philosophical circles, but I am not sure that the same is true in North America. This side of Spaemann's argument needs more work.

Spaemann often combines historical narrative and philosophical argument. Yet none of his books or essays gives his reading of Western philosophy as a whole, or even of modernity, in the way that *The Closing of the American Mind* presents Allan Bloom's reading, or that *Sources of the Self* presents Charles Taylor's reading, or that *A Short History of Ethics, After Virtue, Whose Justice? Which Rationality?* and *Three Rival Versions of*

Moral Enquiry allow us to trace the development of Alasdair MacIntyre's reading. If Spaemann himself, or someone thoroughly familiar with his work, were to weave from his many studies a single connected narrative, its wealth of detail and persuasive power might win for Spaemann's insights and arguments the wider attention and closer scrutiny that they certainly deserve.[33]

---

33   Prof. Spaemann received an honorary doctorate at the Catholic University of America on 7 October 1995. The address that Richard Schenk, O.P., delivered on that occasion is an excellent introduction to Spaemann's work as a whole. It deserves prompt publication and wide readership. This article has been much improved by the comments and suggestions of Jeremiah Alberg, S.J., Andrew Krivak, S.J., Alasdair MacIntyre, J. Patrick Mohr, S.J., James Swindal, and especially Paul McNellis, S.J.